Palgrave Macmillan Memory Studies

Series Editors: **Andrew Hoskins** and **John Sutton**

The nascent field of Memory Studies emerges from contemporary trends that include a shift from concern with historical knowledge of events to that of memory, from "what we know" to "how we remember it"; changes in generational memory; the rapid advance of technologies of memory; panics over declining powers of memory , which mirror our fascination with the possibilities of memory enhancement; and the development of trauma narratives in reshaping the past.

These factors have contributed to an intensification of public discourses on our past over the last 30 years. Technological, political, interpersonal, social and cultural shifts affect what, how and why people and societies remember and forget. This groundbreaking series tackles questions such as: What is "memory" under these conditions? What are its prospects, and also the prospects for its interdisciplinary and systematic study? What are the conceptual, theoretical and methodological tools for its investigation and illumination?

Aleida Assmann and Sebastian Conrad (*editors*)
MEMORY IN A GLOBAL AGE
Discourses, Practices and Trajectories

Brian Conway
COMMEMORATION AND BLOODY SUNDAY
Pathways of Memory

Richard Crownshaw
THE AFTERLIFE OF HOLOCAUST MEMORY IN CONTEMPORARY LITERATURE AND CULTURE

Yifat Gutman, Adam D. Brown and Amy Sodaro (*editors*)
MEMORY AND THE FUTURE
Transnational Politics, Ethics and Society

Mikyoung Kim and Barry Schwartz (*editors*)
NORTHEAST ASIA'S DIFFICULT PAST
Essays in Collective Memory

Erica Lehrer, Cynthia E. Milton and Monica Eileen Patterson (*editors*)
CURATING DIFFICULT KNOWLEDGE
Violent Pasts in Public Places

Motti Neiger, Oren Meyers and Eyal Zandberg (*editors*)
ON MEDIA MEMORY
Collective Memory in a New Media Age

Evelyn B. Tribble and Nicholas Keene
COGNITIVE ECOLOGIES AND THE HISTORY OF REMEMBERING
Religion, Education and Memory in Early Modern England

Forthcoming titles:

Anne Fuchs
ICON DRESDEN
A Cultural Impact Study from 1945 to the Present

Joanne Garde-Hansen and Owain Jones (*editors*)
GEOGRAPHY AND MEMORY
Exploring Identity, Place and Becoming

Amy Holdsworth
TELEVISION, MEMORY AND NOSTALGIA
Experience and the Mnemonic Imagination

Curating Difficult Knowledge

Violent Pasts in Public Places

Edited by

Erica Lehrer

Cynthia E. Milton

Monica Eileen Patterson

palgrave
macmillan

First published 2011 by
PALGRAVE MACMILLAN

Palgrave Macmillan in the UK is an imprint of Macmillan Publishers Limited, registered in England, company number 785998, of Houndmills, Basingstoke, Hampshire RG21 6XS.

Palgrave Macmillan in the US is a division of St Martin's Press LLC, 175 Fifth Avenue, New York, NY 10010.

Palgrave Macmillan is the global academic imprint of the above companies and has companies and representatives throughout the world.

Palgrave® and Macmillan® are registered trademarks in the United States, the United Kingdom, Europe and other countries.

ISBN 978–0–230–29672–5

This book is printed on paper suitable for recycling and made from fully managed and sustained forest sources. Logging, pulping and manufacturing processes are expected to conform to the environmental regulations of the country of origin.

A catalogue record for this book is available from the British Library.

Library of Congress Cataloging-in-Publication Data
Curating difficult knowledge : violent pasts in public places / edited by Erica Lehrer, Cynthia E. Milton, Monica Eileen Partterson.
p. cm.
ISBN 978–0–230–29672–5 (hardback)
1. Political atrocities—Exhibitions. 2. Crimes against humanity—Exhibitions. 3. Museums—Curatorship. 4. Museum exhibits. I. Lehrer, Erica T. II. Milton, Cynthia E. III. Patterson, Monica.
JC571.C79 2011
303.605—dc2 2011013810

10 9 8 7 6 5 4 3 2 1
20 19 18 17 16 15 14 13 12 11

Transferred to Digital Printing in 2014

Contents

List of Figures

List of Plates

List of Maps

Acknowledgments

This volume grows out of the international conference *Curating Difficult Knowledge* held at Concordia University and co-sponsored by the Université de Montréal on April 16–18, 2009. We gratefully acknowledge the support for this event and the subsequent volume from the Social Science and Humanities Research Council of Canada, the Canada Research Chairs program, the Université de Montréal Faculty of Arts and Science, and the Concordia University Vice President for Research and Graduate Studies. We also thank all the conference participants for their enthusiasm and thoughtful contributions to the discussion out of which this volume developed. We are especially indebted to Shelley Butler, Anna Sheftel, the CEREV Post-conflict Studies reading group, and Palgrave Macmillan's anonymous reviewer for thoughtful comments on earlier drafts. Thanks as well to Mark Beauchamp, Felicity Plester, and Catherine Mitchell for helping us with the finer details necessary to bring this volume to print. As the chapters provide fine-grained discussion of curatorial practices, an art section displays the works of many artists and institutions, whom we wish to acknowledge for their gracious permission to include reproductions of their work: Jane Alexander, Mirosław Bieniecki, Igor Grubić, James Mader, Dalibor Martinis, Judith Mason, Lika Mutal, Sam Nhlengethwa, Yael Rojas, Sue Williamson, Jim Crow Museum of Racist Memorabilia, District Six Museum, Kliptown Museum, Iziko Museums, Wits Art Museum, Legacy of Hope Foundation, Museum of Contemporary Art in Zagreb, Migration Museum of Southern Australia, and Sarajevo Center for Contemporary Art.

Notes on Contributors

Andrew Herscher teaches at the University of Michigan in the Taubman College of Architecture and Urban Planning and the Departments of Slavic Languages and Literatures and Art History. He is author of *Violence Taking Place: The Architecture of the Kosovo Conflict* (Stanford University Press, 2010).

Heather Igloliorte is an Inuk curator and art historian from the Nunatsiavut Territory of Labrador currently completing doctoral studies at Carleton University. Her research examines the exhibition of Inuit and other global indigenous arts and cultures in relation to mid-twentieth-century modernist primitivism and contemporary critical museology. She is the curator of the Legacy of Hope Foundation exhibition featured in her chapter in this volume.

Erica Lehrer is an assistant professor in History and Anthropology-Sociology at Concordia University in Montreal, where she also holds the Canada Research Chair in Post-Conflict Studies. She is author of the forthcoming *Revisiting Jewish Poland: Tourism, Memory, Reconciliation* (Indiana University Press, 2012), and has undertaken experimental curatorial work on Jewish heritage and memory in contemporary Poland.

Cynthia E. Milton holds the Canada Research Chair in Latin American history and is Associate Professor in the Département d'histoire at the Université de Montréal. She is author of *The Many Meanings of Poverty: Colonialism, Social Compacts, and Assistance in Eighteenth-Century Ecuador* (Stanford: Stanford University Press, 2007), co-editor of *The Art of Truth-Telling about Authoritarian Rule* (Madison: University of Wisconsin Press, 2005), and is presently working on the edited volume *The Art(s) of Truth-telling in Post-Shining Path Peru.*

Erin Mosely is a PhD candidate in African Studies and History at Harvard University. Her research explores the political and social roles of artists in the wake of prolonged conflict and war. Particular interests include transitional justice, truth commissions, collective memory and memorialization practices, and post-conflict visual culture.

Darren Newbury is a professor of photography at Birmingham City University. He has published widely on photography and photographic education. His book *Defiant Images: Photography and Apartheid South Africa* (UNISA, 2009) is a study of photography during the apartheid period and its role in commemoration and historical representation in post-apartheid South Africa.

Sławomir Kapralski is a faculty member at the Warsaw School of Social Sciences and Humanities. He has published on the subjects of social and cultural theory; nationalism, ethnicity, and identity; time, space, and collective memory; anti-Semitism; representations of the Holocaust and Polish-Jewish relations; and Roma communities of Central and Eastern Europe.

Tamar Katriel is a professor in the Department of Communications at Haifa University. She has published extensively on a range of topics related to contemporary Israeli culture and patterns of communication. Her present research looks at counter-discourses produced and circulated by dissident groups of feminists and former IDF soldiers in campaigns protesting their government's policies and practices in the Occupied Palestinian Territories.

Monica Eileen Patterson is a postdoctoral fellow in the History Departments at Concordia University and the Université de Montréal. Her teaching and research interests include colonial and postcolonial southern Africa, anthropology and history, childhood, violence, memory, and public scholarship. She is co-editor of *Anthrohistory: Unsettling Knowledge, Questioning Discipline* (University of Michigan, 2011).

Roger Simon is Professor Emeritus at the University of Toronto. His research has addressed the pedagogical and ethical dimensions of practices of cultural memory particularly as this applies to the remembrance of mass systemic violence. His work has explored the intersections of social and political theory, cultural practice, and pedagogy.

Amy Sodaro is a PhD candidate in sociology at the New School for Social Research. Her research focuses on the use of memorials and museums as mechanisms for coming to terms with past conflict, violence, and atrocity. She is co-editor of *Memory and the Future: Transnational Politics, Ethics and Society* (Palgrave Macmillan, 2010).

Viv Szekeres holds an Honours degree in History, a BA in Education, and a diploma in Montessori Teaching. She has worked at the South Australian Migration Museum for more than twenty years and was Director from 1987 to 2009. She has published several articles on issues of diversity and representation in Australian Museums.

Introduction: Witnesses to Witnessing

Erica Lehrer and Cynthia E. Milton

What happens when the invisible is made visible, when knowledge relegated to society's margins or swept under its carpet is suddenly inserted into the public domain? The iconic images of German civilians forced to view the newly liberated Nazi camps, standing at the edges of hastily dug trenches full of emaciated bodies are emblematic of an era in which we have faced not only previously unimaginable episodes of mass violence, but have been consternated by how we might engage with these pasts: who should look, at what, how, and to what end? There is an enduring sense that reluctant publics must be forced to confront horrific realities with which we may be somehow complicit—if only in our desire not to really know.

Yet in an age saturated with media images of human suffering and ever-democratizing technologies for their dissemination, simply making people face the horrors humans are capable of perpetrating seems to have lost some of its galvanizing force. The much-repeated mantra "Never Again" has transmuted into a resigned recognition of the potential for "ever again." In this context, a shift of focus can be discerned among memory-workers, away from the inevitably stymieing preoccupation with the graphic, the incomprehensible, the unrepresentable. It has been made depressingly clear that depictions of humanity's vilest deeds do not diminish our capacity for future crimes. If knowledge of the facts of atrocity is no longer seen as a panacea, neither is confrontation the sole communicative posture of endeavours to leverage the past in the present. Memory-workers have begun to explore other modes, including attempts to kindle social aspirations like empathy, identification, cross-cultural dialogue, to recognize multiple perspectives, or to catalyze action.

In the early 1990s in newly post-communist Eastern Europe, the power of public deployment of historical images to re-shape public consciousness was brought home through simple yet compelling initiatives. In May 1990 in Prague, a row of kiosks lined Wenceslas Square, plastered with images and documents about World War II, the 1952 Slánský show trial, and the 1968 Prague Spring. Any "difficult knowledge" of these devastating, generation-defining events (in this case meaning any knowledge beyond "the party line") had been removed from public circulation for decades. As Praguers awoke and wandered toward the kiosks in the pale morning light, they clustered in excitement, discussing their feelings and the implications of these new public revelations. Thus, a silenced history resurfaced.[1]

In 1996 the Polish exhibit *And I Still See Their Faces: Images of Polish Jews* was a tour-de-force of memory curation and activation, a photography exhibit whose participatory process of creation was as powerful and provocative as the final product.[2] Compiled from a nationwide call for "photographs of Jews," the resulting 9000 pre-Holocaust images evoked a lost world. But its greater power lay in the countless moments of discovery and witnessing that must have occurred as thousands of Poles opened dusty boxes, unsealed yellowed envelopes, paged through old albums with a fresh eye, phoned aged relatives to ask after unknown names or faces—and the dinner-table conversations and late-evening soul-searching that one can only imagine ensued. The notes mailed in by participants along with the outpouring of photographs offer a glimpse of the textures of remembering: *When the Germans came and the Jews had to go into hiding, Lejzer's son came a few times for hot tea. We would cry to think how cold they were. / Throughout the occupation, I worked in the Zawiercie steel-works. To clean the machines, we used clothing from the liquidated ghetto. This photo was among the remains.*[3]

Halfway across the world in Latin America another wave of difficult transitions was taking place. Southern Cone countries experimented with truth commissions of various sorts as a means of excavating their authoritarian pasts, accompanied by creative public pathways to consider and debate these histories (Bilbija et al., 2005). In 2003, Peruvians were invited to a dilapidated home on the outskirts of Lima to view photographs—made by photojournalists, members of a social photography workshop, families, and others—of "the faces of suffering, the visible proof of the injustices committed" during the previous two decades of internal conflict (Lerner Febres, 2004: 136–7). The exhibit, called "Yuyanapaq," the Quechua term for "to remember/remembering/to wake up/waking up," was a multi-sensory experience: the derelict structure housing the exhibit embodied the ruined nation; the need for reconstruction from the ground up spoke wordlessly through its physical fissures. The photos, ranging from small, intimate frames to larger than life, were set off by diaphanous drapes conveying both transparency and healing gauze. The curators made their objective clear: "To look, to understand, to process by way of images and testimonies implies a concern of Peruvian society to know the history of what happened. In this sense, the decision to walk through this house requires a decision to remember."[4]

As scholars working in post-Holocaust, post-communist Eastern Europe and post-authoritarian Latin America respectively, our own encounters with these potent attempts to re-frame and activate the past anew led us to the present project: a wide-ranging consideration of the goals and challenges, the possibility and the pitfalls, of "curating difficult knowledge."

Curating difficult knowledge

Unique challenges arise in attempts to frame memories and documents of violence for public display, and these have inspired innovations in exhibition, museology, public cultural interventions and the activation of memorial sites. And new knowledge emerges when we consider memory—in its spatial, material, public dimensions—not simply as latent in the social fabric, nor only in top-down efforts by the state to encode preferred memory, but also as it is mindfully deployed by individuals and groups in attempts to provoke, enable, and transform. We call, then, for an understanding of museums, monuments, and heritage sites not only as texts that visitors read, but also as sites of practice that are social, embodied, and generative. Such sites spur dialogues in familiar forms like contemplation and discussion, but memory and meaning are also made and contested through commodification, graffiti, and vandalism.

Accordingly, this volume attempts to open a space at the intersection of multiple discussions. We are convinced that some of the most interesting perspectives on memory work are emerging on the borders where academic and other spheres of cultural practice meet: the museum, the memorial site, the heritage tour. We draw on academic literature and public discussion of critical museology, heritage management, collective memory, public scholarship, and transitional justice, as common themes swirl beneath these domains and the disciplines that engage them. We ask where we are—as scholars, curators, artists, activists—in our imperfect attempts to "bear witness" to conflicts that have passed, even as their echoes, or in some cases the structures that gave rise to them, persist.

Questioning curation

Taking the word "curate" in its root meaning of "caring for" allows us to expand our discussion outward from museums and exhibitions to encompass heritage sites, memorials, and other (including virtual) locations along the increasingly interlinked spectrum of spaces dedicated to connecting publics with difficult histories—anywhere that attempts are made to "[present] combinations of images, objects, text, and sound within a particular *mise-en-scene*," as Roger Simon puts it (this volume). This is to say that to "care for" the past is to make something of it, to place and order it in a meaningful way in the present rather than to abandon it. But how does one "care for" the past? What custodial or curatorial practices and decisions are involved? How do we—as scholars, curators, artists, activists, survivors, descendents, and other stakeholders—attempt to bear witness, to give space and shape to absent people, objects and cultures, to present violent conflict without perpetuating its logic? These are among the challenges confronting those who wish to invoke the difficult past in order to quell—or do justice to—its hauntings.

Thinking about curation not only as selection, design, and interpretation, but as care-taking—as a kind of intimate, intersubjective, interrelational obligation—raises key ethical questions relevant in an age of "truth-telling": What is our responsibility to stories of suffering that we inherit? When do they need to be protected and nurtured, and when might the new truths they give rise to themselves become ossified, calling for "tough love" to re-activate their ethical potential? Is the goal of curation to settle, or rather to unsettle established meanings of past events? Is it to create social space for a shared experience of looking, listening, and talking, creating alternative relationships and publics, for constructive meaning making and action taking? How can we manage the tensions among these impulses? And shadowing all of these questions is the ever-present need to ask which "we" is inquiring, deciding, acting—and on whose behalf.

The notion of curation as "care" is meant neither prescriptively nor timidly. Rather, we use it expansively to draw attention to the profound senses of obligation the authors in this volume express to *deal with* the past where it impinges painfully on the present. Such a "custodial" understanding of curatorial practice simultaneously avoids some of the presumptions embedded in discourses of heritage management that refer to "dark tourism" destined for sites of "difficulty," "pain," or "shame." While suggestive, such frames can be limiting as they risk presuming affective states and meanings a priori, as if these flowed predetermined from landscapes or displays, rather than being borne, projected, and negotiated by visitors individually and socially, in terms of culture, ethics, and politics. Often swept up willy-nilly in such negative rubrics are memory practices that, if one scratches their surfaces, may be revealed as neither "dark" nor "tourism." While visits to sites of former atrocity raise concerns about voyeurism and crass commercialism, they may just as often draw people earnestly seeking to meditate on peace, imagine common futures, and even forge these through dialogue or political action. Our interest is thus less in charting a historical moment of fascination with atrocity than in examining the conceptual strides and challenges presented by this moment's accompanying innovations in curatorial practice. We are concerned with approaches, ethics, and intentions—in short, with cultural projects—that animate attempts to draw attention to painful pasts.

"New museology" is now a few decades old, and in the throes of further transformation as it meets still newer critical curatorial voices (Macdonald, 2006; Karp et al., 2007). The present museological moment is one of democratization not just of access, but also of authority. There are ever more rationales for—and an expanding corpus of experiments around—breaking down the mono-vocal, authoritative, objectivist, material-centric framework of exhibiting culture that has defined museology since its consolidation as a branch of science and a tool for refining the citizenry a century ago. Classically styled museums are still decidedly celebratory, affirming national triumphs and distinct group identities. But museums are increasingly turning to face our communities' "never agains," and discussions of difficult subjects have been key drivers of innovative curatorial theory and practice. Barbara Kirshenblatt-Gimblett proposes the category of "museums of conscience," which reflect the intersection of the current museological moment with a shift in commemorative practice to include scrutiny of both the ignominious sides of national histories and the museum's own previous practices in relation to these (Kirshenblatt-Gimblett, 2002).[5] Paul Williams notes that it is the high stakes associated with the topics and content of memorial museums, and the drama these can produce, that places them at the forefront of today's "performative" museological paradigm (Williams, 2007: 96).

We can no longer assume that historians, anthropologists, or curators are, or should be, the sole authoritative producers of narratives about the past. If some in these positions still struggle with the idea of giving up responsibility or expertise, they are nonetheless faced with newly visible, active categories of stakeholders influencing how curatorial work is shaped, including community groups, the state, and funding agencies. Complicated compromises must be reached vis-à-vis the display and interpretation of artifacts and experiences. Further, the goal of curatorial work is no longer simply to *represent* but to *make things happen.* Audiences are being transformed into participants in ever more dialogic curatorial experiments. Comment books are no longer the sole trace of visitor opinion; indeed, their inscriptions may end up on the exhibition wall as objects in their own right. In the original Peruvian photography exhibit *Yuyanapaq,* a son wrote that his mother was not mentioned among the victims of the internal war. If he were to return to the exhibit today, he would see her name (and his whole comment) prominently displayed on the wall. Visitors are even being called upon to register their responses by re-curating the very objects on display, moving them, sorting them, recording their stories about them. A truck in Sweden brought the exhibit *Difficult Matters: Objects and Narratives that Disturb and Affect* to small towns, where local people were invited to select objects and debate their very appropriateness for display (Kirshenblatt-Gimblett, 2002). In the Manchester Museum's (UK) project "Collective Conversations," invitations went out to members of immigrant groups to be filmed as they discuss the meanings of museum objects to them, in an attempt to make visible and enhance the "contact zone" that exhibitions create.[6] Heather Igloliorte (this volume) describes how a traveling exhibit is both a catalyst for, and evolves with, input from the Inuit people in Canada's far North who are its subjects and key audiences. So if curators today are no longer simply experts, but increasingly brokers, negotiators, facilitators, and sharers of authority, how—if at all—may evidence of evil be used to create positive change?

This question brings curation into conversation with directed political transformation. Attempts to curate difficult knowledge often take place in the context of transitional justice, as part of the symbolic aspect of efforts at national reconciliation. It is clear that public spaces can become de facto venues for encounter, truth telling, and dialogue, organic means for aggrieved groups to cope with, communicate, or work through the difficult past. But what happens when such spaces are *crafted* in strategic attempts by state, international, or community institutions to engineer (or simply proclaim) a desired social outcome? We may legitimately ask how much—and what kind—of debate and contention we want, recognizing that the curation of difficult knowledge can exacerbate conflict, or keep wounds traumatically open when they might otherwise heal. Yet curating "reconciliation" risks other erasures, neglects, and negations, potentially inflicting further harm by silencing those living with scars, still-open wounds, or ongoing injustice. There is a need for curatorial work that can both reveal and contain such tensions, highlighting the ways that aggrieved parties live in "contentious coexistence" in the aftermath of violence, while also creating spaces for more robust "dissensual community" to emerge.[7]

Disambiguating "difficulty"

Such discussions of curation link to the second half of this volume's title: "difficult knowledge." What kinds of knowledge are difficult? Or rather, what is it that is *difficult* about difficult knowledge? On the most basic level, we might agree that what unites the papers in this volume is the nature of their common historical subject matter: violent, tragic, gruesome, horrific, and painful. Certainly experiences of war, genocide, and human rights violations can be difficult to confront for this reason.

But more difficult, perhaps, are questions of what such knowledge does to us—or what we do with it. Both the lived experience and the politics of such common and seemingly innocuous notions like empathy, identification, comparison, and bearing witness become deeply fraught in the context of the public depiction, transmission, and reception of the suffering inflicted on distinct groups of people. More difficult than regarding other people's suffering may be scrutinizing our own habituated responses to it (Sontag, 2003).

It is troubling, for example, to consider what Edward Linenthal has called "comfortable horrible" memory, or the ways that official narratives of tragedy may not do much beyond confirming what "we," as a pre-determined collectivity, already know, think, or feel (Linenthal, 1995: 267). Still more disturbing may be the recognition that legitimate processes of mourning and community-building in the aftermath of massive injustice and violence can simultaneously create further exclusions, or retrench old divisions and prejudices of the sort that helped precipitate the original tragedies. Finally, perhaps most difficult is to acknowledge that suffering does not necessarily ennoble, but may more often embitter, isolate, and agitate. In Derrida's words, "What is most painful is that the painful is not painful for others" (1994: 56).

The notion of "difficult knowledge"—a category capacious enough to accommodate these various aspects, and one that inspired the present volume—can be traced to educational theorist Deborah Britzman, who distinguishes it from "lovely knowledge" (Britzman, 1998; Pitt and

Britzman, 2003). "Lovely knowledge" is easily assimilable, the kind of knowledge that reinforces what we already know and gives us what we are accustomed to wanting from new information we encounter. Lovely knowledge allows us to think of ourselves—due to our identifications with particular groups—as, for example, timelessly noble, or long-suffering victims, and to reject any kind of information about ourselves or others that might contradict or complicate the story. The North American pioneer myth of hardy settlers courageously conquering bare wilderness free for the taking, or immigrant narrative of foreigners who were welcomed and succeeded in pulling themselves up by nothing more than their bootstraps (Vukov, 2002) are examples of such lovely tales. The exhibitions described here by Igloliorte and Patterson in North America and Szekeres in Australia disrupt these narratives with more complex, difficult realities.

"Difficult knowledge," conversely, is knowledge that does not fit. It therefore induces a breakdown in experience, forcing us to confront the possibility that the conditions of our lives and the boundaries of our collective selves may be quite different from how we normally, reassuringly think of them. Such knowledge points to more challenging, nuanced aspects of history and identity, potentially leading us to re-conceive our relationships with those traditionally defined as "other." Acknowledging that as North Americans we continue to benefit from the colonial projects that created our nations is one kind of difficult knowledge.

In this vein, Roger Simon suggests a productive relationship with "difficulty" based on a "process of confronting and dismantling [of] expectations" upon encountering such unfamiliar knowledge (Bonnell and Simon, 2007: 67). While Simon theorizes this deep, pedagogical approach to curating difficult knowledge in his epilogue to this volume, here we draw attention to some of the concrete, practical challenges and questions that arise in the process of both designing and analyzing such curatorial work. How might one usefully intervene in public sites that function as significant nodes in practices of identity formation? How might we—as scholars, artists, curators—"activate," "re-activate," or perhaps "de-activate" public sites of memory in ways that repair severed cultural continuities, enhance inter-group understanding, and destabilize problematic boundaries, especially when such sites have more often been employed in the reproduction of divisive notions of self and other? How might theoretical critiques of the "traumatic repetition" of history in collective identity be translated and enacted as public interventions?

The various disciplinary approaches represented in this volume share some suggestive categories of concern that call for fuller articulation. For example, there are a variety of *analytical approaches* to sites, objects, and images: Are they texts to be read, representations to deconstruct, screens onto which myriad readings are projected, or agents in their own right, and therefore active players in the social arenas that their presence helps to delineate? There are also questions of *experiential and communicative modes*: What is the relationship between affective and cognitive states, and where might "action" fit in? In trying to curate suffering, is our responsibility to determine and convey—as far as possible—that suffering's precise ontology? Or is it to turn this suffering into something productive, either to redeem it, or to redeem ourselves?

There are a range of possible *curatorial poetics, and postures* in which heritage, memory, and history can be presented. Truth telling can be confrontational, suggestive, a "call to action" or a documentation of present and past injustices for future memory, as Tamar Katriel illustrates (this volume). Curatorial work can be self-reflexive, highlighting underacknowledged challenges and suggesting its own limitations. It can be partial or encyclopedic, authoritative or dialogic, creating spaces for healing or dialogue. The danger is that attention to one form of "difficult knowledge" may simultaneously obscure, or do violence to, others.[8] So much is deemed "too difficult" to be viewed in public at all. Is this perspective patronizing? Should curators push back a bit, and audiences simply "toughen up"?[9] Or are certain displays of violence gratuitous, an added injustice for victims of the original assault, while simultaneously numbing viewers to others' future suffering, as critic Susan Sontag herself experienced (Sontag, 2003)?

It is primarily the *audience* that defines the success or failure of a curatorial project. Demands are being made for processes of curation to involve local stakeholders, survivors, community members of different generations, funders, collection donors, and in some cases former perpetrators. Given partisan agendas, can the diverse needs of these different constituencies be integrated in still-divided societies? Local, national, and international contexts are often at play, as are differences between elite and vernacular interests.

The emotional as well as the material stakes of a given display may vary widely for different audiences, as visitors inhabit a wide range of subject positions vis-à-vis the content of exhibits. Further, these change over time, as communities engage unevenly in processes of "working through" in relation to their communal tragedies. These differences need to be identified and negotiated. Perhaps a successful curation is one that, at least provisionally, "kindles a sense of ownership" on the part of multiple communities (Brown, 2009).

Finally, what are our *goals*? What do we hope public curation of difficult knowledge can do? Is preserving the past a kind of gift? Photographs, for example, may help "stop the flow of time" in ways that open a space for critical reflection, as Newbury suggests (this volume). But there has been an overwhelming bias in the practice of curation (extending to the discussions in this volume) privileging a Western museological framework, in which preserving the past—at times via technologically heroic measures—is taken as an unquestioned good. Similarly, heritage sites and monuments—including avant-garde "counter-memorials"—still imply strong mandates for remembering, even if remembering is pursued via multiple forms of unsettledness.[10] It is worth considering other notions of the life cycles of objects and the qualities of time, memory, and history that propose different relationships to the past. These may have underappreciated benefits in relation to "difficult knowledge," especially when communities become trapped in enduring legacies or traumatic cycles. If liberation from the traumatic force of memory is one of the goals, how can curation serve this end? Is it ever acceptable to bury the past, let it go, or put it to rest? While preservation is powerful, there are other gifts.

And life, of course, goes on. In curation and narration, the temporal frames continue to shift, and with them priorities and interests. As Erin Mosely (this volume) illustrates, artists in post-apartheid South Africa felt the ground move under them as they adapted a robust tradition of "protest art" to an emerging era of "truth and reconciliation," reflecting upon the past and posing hard questions of the "truths" that were emerging, with an ethical voice and aesthetic eye. As messengers who both curate and are curated, artists may bring us "emotionally" closer to discerning the ongoing unknown (Maclear, 1999: 24).

As researchers, curators, and educators, we need to consider these choices carefully. What are we, as spectators, to do in the face of past (and indeed, present) violence? Is Dori Laub's call, in the context of Holocaust testimonies, "to bear witness to our witnessing," sufficient (Laub, 1992)? Yet we surely cannot know, understand, or convey all pasts, and in a dogged attempt to do so, we may bind ourselves in a "claustrophobic relationship between ethics, critical analysis and loss" (Salverson, 2009). Tensions exist between the kind of broad public attention to difficult knowledge that we hope for, and the trivializing that often accompanies mass consumption.[11] Yet amidst our fears of ignorance, trespassing, appropriation, or even of our own emotions, what roles—or what necessity—might there be for humor, failure, forgetting, and love? It is the fundamental tension spanning the two domains embedded in this volume's title that fascinates and troubles us: between *curating/caring for* and the *difficult knowledge* of violence and oppression. There is an uneasy relationship between praise and critique, between deconstruction and reconstruction, that scholarship on the aftermath of violence has yet to fully plumb.

The "difficult knowledge" addressed in each chapter of this volume is difficult in different ways. In its most mundane form, difficult might simply refer to logistical matters: how to arrange a display, how to distinguish this museum or memorial site from others. But these problems quickly become implicated in a range of deeper concerns. Sometimes the key issue is how knowledge is packaged and instrumentalized—politically, commercially, or otherwise. In curating contested histories, whose knowledge should be privileged and whose interests served? Those of curious publics? Of victim communities? Of a transitional government? In other cases the problem may be that the past is presented as a period that is *over*, and our knowledge of it complete; how often are we shown the ways in which some wounds remain open, bleeding into the present? Do we agree on the oft-invoked "lessons of the past" and how we want them enacted? Or what a "successful" memorial act might look like or do? And in the end, our curatorial vision and best efforts notwithstanding, what is the audience's response? Despite different geographical and disciplinary approaches, the scholars and practitioners in this volume are united in an attempt to be critical, responsible witnesses to projects of "witnessing."

Organization of the book

The chapters that follow present a rich array of overlapping engagements with the problems of curating difficult knowledge. The prefaces to each section are intended to further enhance the conversations among and within the chapters. While we have arranged the chapters in thematic groups to highlight what we found to be particularly generative constellations, we hope readers will make their own connections between and across categories.

Part I: Bearing Witness between Museums and Communities

This section addresses the difficult negotiations that confront curators and communities who share a sense of ownership of or implication in a historical episode or cultural problematic, but whose goals, attitudes, or methods may be fundamentally or periodically at odds—either with each other, or with engrained exhibitionary traditions. These authors raise novel concerns and illuminate the potential for expanding curatorial vision.

Heather Igloliorte asks what strategies of curation are appropriate for an exhibition aimed primarily at an audience of local survivors, "intended to supplement, assist, and encourage" a range of healing initiatives? In "'We were so far away': Exhibiting Inuit Oral Histories of Residential Schools," she recounts, from the position of exhibition curator, the challenges in developing an exhibit with and for a traumatized community still actively struggling with the privations of the past and their reverberations in the present. Curation of Inuit survivor voices is a process of working to undo multiple silences—those in the Canadian education system, and those among reticent survivors themselves—without doing further damage. The logistical problems in reaching remote Arctic communities that lack traditional exhibition sites and contain a diversity of linguistic proficiencies also present opportunities to develop original modes of communication and help enlarge the "space" available to tell a still largely unarticulated story. Great care has been taken to develop modes of presentation that are culturally appropriate to communities in which the oral tradition is central and that allow the participants to retain ownership of the self-representations they co-created with the curator. Igloliorte suggests further that attentive curation that leaves room for audience dialogue can facilitate the re-claiming of indigenous meaning from problematic colonial imagery, while contributing these hidden meanings back into an evolving historical archive. Amassing these unheard histories provides an additional tool in the ongoing fight for inclusion in government policies of recognition.

In "The Past is a Dangerous Place: the Museum as a Safe Haven," Vivienne Szekeres illustrates the role a museum can play in bringing social issues to public discussion by helping communities to represent themselves and some of their more difficult stories. Mindful of the inherent fractures and competing agendas within every community, the Migration Museum in Adelaide, Australia works to tell immigration's "other" stories, stories that are not all about gratitude and easy assimilation. In doing so, the institution has had to navigate a pressurized relationship between national politics and its own projects and possibilities, using the cultural capital associated with museums to create a safe haven for democratic participation. As a responsive, participatory institution, the Migration Museum had long been a barometer of broader public opinion. But the museum was catalyzed to become more explicitly a tool to influence such opinion, using careful strategies to take big political risks. At the same time, below the power politics, the museum quietly grew into a unique ritual space shared by many local communities—a keeper of their stories and a place to make their voices heard.

In her chapter, "Teaching Tolerance through Objects of Hatred: The Jim Crow Museum of Racist Memorabilia as 'Counter-Museum,'" Monica Eileen Patterson engages the museum as a technology for confronting painful subject matter and delivering scholarship about it to broader publics. She illustrates how the Jim Crow Museum of Racist Memorabilia employs a multifaceted approach to curation that rejects conventional museum categories. Framing an open-ended assemblage of everyday objects, the museum works to highlight links between past and present around a deep-seated and deeply troubling manifestation of racism. The museum's founder has developed a methodology that strives to confront without provoking, to invite and listen while also educating and enlightening, and to illuminate the "fraught nature of racism as experienced by everyday people in real life" by drawing visitors into dialogue about their own experience through material culture.

Finally, Amy Sodaro's chapter, "Politics of the Past: Remembering the Rwandan Genocide at the Kigali Memorial Centre," addresses tensions inherent in an increasingly widespread international model for state regimes dealing with difficult national heritage: the memorial museum. Intended locally as democratic spaces where a citizenry can face and work through the traumatic past (by using diverse media, giving and hearing testimony, and undertaking historical research), these institutions are also political tools in the international arena. A paradigm developed for Holocaust museums, this model may not translate well into a volatile social context like Kigali, where genocidal ideology still bubbles just beneath the officially peaceful surface, justice has in no definitive way been served, and organic local memorials languish for lack of funding. In such a context, commemoration runs the risk of prematurely foreclosing precisely the process of attaining justice (of which it is intended to form a key part) by univocally declaring reconciliation where none has been achieved. Politically expedient on an international stage, where aid is delivered based on perceptions of stability, commemoration by a fragile state can function as a tool of authoritarianism. The lack of blame for the genocide ascribed in the museum exhibit to anything more proximate than the legacy of colonial forces is telling.

Part II: Visualizing the Past

The authors in this section offer fresh viewpoints for considering visual representations of violence and its aftermaths. Their discussions illustrate the value of melding artistic, representational, historical, and ethnographic approaches to apprehend the various levels on which images make meaning, and offer a glimpse of the social lives of these complex objects. We are shown how gallery spaces, due to both their relative independence and to their particular spatial and temporal qualities, can serve uniquely as public memory sites in ways unavailable to other forms of mass media like television, radio, or the Internet.

Darren Newbury's "Living Historically through Photographs in Post-Apartheid South Africa: Reflections on Kliptown Museum, Soweto" offers a close reading of this mode of representation in a post-apartheid site of memory. Despite controversies around the domination of national memory over local memory or the failure of the larger curated environment to serve the needs of the local traders and residents (due to the privileging of abstract ideas and tourist attention), Newbury presents Kliptown's photographically-based museum as a worthy representational attempt to reinvest the site of a historic subaltern declaration of human rights with the memory of these key political events. He suggests that the Kliptown display may package potentially difficult knowledge too redemptively, by presenting those who suffered apartheid not as victims but as historical agents who opposed it and by making injustice seem like a dark past that has been entirely overcome by the democratic present. Nevertheless, he argues, the Kliptown museum's approach to curating photographs along with information about the ethical conditions of their production offers both "an invitation to live historically" in the present, and a site at which to consider the politics of representation itself. In relation to the latter, he contends that the photographs are staged in such a way as to highlight for the public the danger of turning history into spectacle, and the "incompatibility of looking and acting." Newbury admits that his somewhat optimistic "reading" represents imaginative potential, and not local social actuality.

In "Showing and Telling: Photography Exhibitions in Israeli Discourses of Dissent," Tamar Katriel addresses witnessing in a direct sense, in the context of two projects of dissident activist documentary in Israel today. Both photography exhibitions take a challenging stance vis-à-vis their target audiences in an attempt to "condemn social silences and denials" about the daily reality of military occupation, and to break these silences by inserting harsh hidden realities into the blinkered center of Israeli existence. Viewing exhibitions both as sites of visual representation/communication and as interactive social arenas for performance and interpersonal exchange, Katriel's discussion troubles assumptions about the relationship between commemoration and activism, illustrating the "particular blend of present-oriented activism and future oriented memory" in the life cycle of each project. She points out how these two modes may pull in different directions, reiterating the potential incompatibility between looking and acting noted by Darren Newbury. Her chapter also raises the uncomfortable question of just who is served by making difficult knowledge public. Are such displays in the interest of those currently *suffering* injustice, or only those struggling with their *knowledge* of it?

In "Visualizing Apartheid: Re-framing Truth and Reconciliation through Contemporary South African Art," Erin Mosely argues for viewing artists as "conspicuous agents of change" in the transition from violent authoritarianism, who through their unique roles and creative media are positioned to challenge selective, hegemonic narratives of the past. Art's inherently partial and free-flowing mandate makes it a privileged site for working through challenges and layers of subjective complexity not amenable to more neutral or regimented official venues of truth telling. Yet Mosely suggests that many artists have nonetheless shouldered a mandate of nation building through healing, empathy, community reconstitution, and solidarity with many of the voices left unheard and experiences unacknowledged in the country's celebrated Truth and Reconciliation Commission.

Part III: Materiality and Memorial Challenges

The chapters in this final section reveal the sometimes uncanny ways that places can have a voice in debates about the past, acting as stubborn irritants to attempts at closure, or posing difficult questions that certain groups would wish away.

In "Points of No Return: Cultural Heritage and Counter-Memory in Post-Yugoslavia," Andrew Herscher offers a sustained theoretical reflection on state-sponsored efforts to curate a multi-ethnic heritage in postwar Kosovo. He shows how these projects of creating appropriately stable, reconciled national subjects meet with popular resistance that both reveals heritage as ideology and refuses state assertions of appropriate memory in favor of a wider range of engaged responses to the past. Herscher critiques the widespread valorization in recent memory studies of "unsettledness" as a fundamentally ethical memorial posture. Indeed, in examining resistance to historic preservation in former-Yugoslavia—from modernist interventions to postmodernist substitutions—he questions the celebration of "memory" as the ultimate outcome of memorials. To this end he offers examples of memory's displacement, distortion, parody, exaggeration, and other forms of transformation that reach beyond memorialization to "political discourse and action."

Cynthia Milton parses opposing currents in Peru's collective memory of their bloody internal war (1980–95) through an analysis of acts of vandalism perpetrated against one of the country's few sites of memory, the Eye that Cries (Ojo que llora), in Lima. Originally intended as a space for remembering and paying homage to the victims of the armed conflict, in "Defacing memory: (Un)tying Peru's Memory Knots" Milton illustrates how the site has become a space for contesting disputed memories. While the memorial site is entirely a creation of artistic imagination, repeated attacks on the site have endowed it more directly with socially accrued meaning. The stained and broken stones of the memorial site telegraph the desire on the part of certain groups to stifle the emerging memory of the victims of the war years. Ironically, this potential re-victimization has amplified public discourse and inspired communities of remembering that might never have emerged had the relatively obscure site been left untouched. Yet the ongoing conflicts over the past made visible at this site (over how, what, and whom to remember) point to the limits of memory work in Peru, and the perils of such symbolic endeavours for present-day reconciliation efforts.

Sławomir Kapralski's "(Mis)representations of the Jewish Past in Poland's Memoryscapes: Nationalism, Religion and Political Economies of Commemoration" delineates various modes with which the material traces of Poland's Jewish past are managed in the country's shifting post-war memorial economy. Employing the notion of "memoryscapes," he illustrates how different periods in Poland's recent past (post-Shoah, communism, and democracy) have given rise to different approaches to remembering and representing Jewish Poland: oblivion, erasure, and preservation. He reveals how mono-ethnic, intra-Polish memorial struggles—such as communism vs. ethno-nationalism—have at times overpowered, silenced, and eliminated the space for local reckonings with the Jewish past.

While considering the complexities of difficult knowledge, we ask readers to let themselves be affected by the striking images contained in these chapters, which suggest the unique power of curatorial work:

> *The small boxes holding Cambodian immigrants' few possessions for their new lives. The U.S. postcard depicting four naked black children on the bank of a river with a caption reading, "Alligator Bait." The stained and broken memorial stones of Peru's "Crying Eye." The color family snapshots of murdered Rwandans free for the taking at a local memorial. The insistence of the Jewish past in Poland in the form of ghostly lettering that brightens and fades with changing regimes of memory. The collection of car*

keys confiscated from Palestinian drivers at Israeli checkpoints. The immigrant story told by way of a cell containing only a single naked lightbulb, a chair, and a bucket. Inuit residential school survivor Carolyn Weetaltuk recognizing her mother in an unlabeled photograph of school children during the preparation of an exhibit. Jane Alexander's sculpture "Butcher Boys," half-men, half-beasts whose scars and disfigurements make visible and visceral apartheid's psychic wounds—dark, dormant creatures loitering in everyday places, ominously poised to re-awaken.

We are witnesses as these images and objects, emerging from hateful contexts, are transformed into the visible, material touchstones of new experiences and narratives. We hope their curation may evoke empathy, understanding, self-scrutiny, and a productive struggle with too much difficult knowledge.

Notes

1. The outdoor kiosks led into an indoor exhibit called *Kde Domov Můj?* [Where is My Home?]. Named after the Czechoslovak national anthem and sponsored by the political party *Civic Forum* (Občansky Forum), it was part of the larger movement to return knowledge of national history to the Czechoslovak citizenry.
2. The exhibit, in Polish *I ciągle widzę ich twarze: Fotografia Żydów polskich*, was conceived and created by Golda Tencer, director of Warsaw's Shalom Foundation.
3. The first quote is from photograph contributor Zofia Sobel, Urzedów, Poland. Available at http://motlc.wiesenthat.com/site/pp.asp?c=jmKYJeNVJrF&b=478594 [Accessed November 10, 2010]. The second one is from Jan Kochanski, Zawiercie, Poland. Available at http://motlc.wiesenthat.com/site/pp.asp?c=jmKYJeNVJrF&b=478613 [Accessed November 10, 2010]. Emphasis mine.
4. "Yuyanapaq: Para Recordar," exhibition pamphlet, 2003. See also Milton and Ulfe, 2011.
5. See also Sevcenko, 2004.
6. Available at http://www.museum.manchester.ac.uk/community/collective-conversations/ [Accessed November 10, 2010]. For a discussion of the limits of such attempts at democratic co-production of museum knowledge, see Lynch and Alberti, 2009.
7. Leigh Payne coins the expression of "contentious coexistence" as a potential political model in societies where perpetrators and survivors must live together (Payne, 2008). John Borneman (2002) develops the concept of "dissensual community."
8. Dominick LaCapra asks, "What modes of narrative are most suited for rendering traumatic events, especially in ways that do not harmonize, stylize, or even airbrush them and thus border on repression or denial? What non-narrative forms complement, supplement, and contest narrative

representations?" (LaCapra, 2001: 205). Michael Rothberg adds that certain esthetics or strategies may be more or less "adequate to the task of representing and recalling history's *overlapping* forms of violence" (Rothberg, 2009: 35)

9. This stance was encouraged by one of our conference participants. The call to "toughen up" is complicated by the fact that many public spaces are open to children. The Holocaust Museum in Washington protects children from difficult images by placing them in recessed display cases, out of their reach.
10. The notion of the "counter-memorial" is from Young, 1992.
11. As Andreas Huyssen has argued, the commodification of past events does not necessarily diminish their historical importance. All depends on "strategies of representation and commodification pursued and on the context in which they are staged" (Huyssen, 2003: 18–19).

Works cited

Bilbija, Ksenija, Jo Ellen Fair, Cynthia E. Milton, and Leigh A. Payne (eds) (2005). *The Art of Truth-telling about Authoritarian Rule*. Madison: University of Wisconsin Press.

Brown, Kris (2009). "Cultural and Curatorial Struggles: Recording and Remembering the Conflict in and about Northern Ireland." Unpublished paper presented at *Curating Difficult Knowledge* conference, Montreal, April 16–18.

Bonnell, Jennifer and Roger Simon (2007). "'Difficult' Exhibitions and Intimate Encounters." *Museum and Society* 5(2): 65–85.

Borneman, John (2002). "Reconciliation after Ethnic Cleansing: Listening, Retribution, Affiliation." *Public Culture* 14(2): 281–304.

Britzman, Deborah (1998). *Lost Subjects, Contested Objects: Toward a Psychoanalytic Inquiry of Learning*. Albany: State University of New York Press.

Derrida, Jacques (1994). *Spectres of Marx: The State of the Debt, the Work of Mourning, and the New International*, Trans. Peggy Kamuf. London: Routledge.

Huyssen, Andreas (2003). *Present Pasts: Urban Palimpsests and the Politics of Memory*. Stanford: Stanford University Press.

Karp, Ivan, Cory Kratz, and Lynn Szwaja (2007). *Museum Frictions: Public Cultures/Global Transformations*. Durham: Duke University Press.

Kirshenblatt-Gimblett, Barbara (2002). "The Museum as Catalyst." In Per-Uno Ågren (ed.). *Museum 2000: Confirmation or Challenge?* Stockholm: Riksutställningar [Swedish Traveling Exhibitions], Svenska museiföreningen [Swedish Museum Association].

Laub, Dori (1992). "Bearing Witness or the Vicissitudes of Listening." In Shoshana Felman and Dori Laub (eds). *Testimony: Crises of Witnessing in Literature, Psychoanalysis, and History*. New York: Routledge, 57–74.

Lerner Febres, Salomon (2004). *La rebelión de la memoria: selección de discursos 2001–2003*. Lima: IDEHPUCP, CEP, CNDDHH.

LaCapra, Dominick (2001). *Writing History, Writing Trauma*. Baltimore: Johns Hopkins University Press.

Linenthal, Edward (1995). *Preserving Memory: The Struggle to Create America's Holocaust Museum*. New York: Viking USA.

Lynch, Bernadette T. and Samuel J. M. M. Alberti (2009). "Legacies of Prejudice: Racism, Co-production and Radical Trust in the Museum." *Museum Management and Curatorship* 25(1): 13–35.

Macdonald, Sharon (2006). "Introduction." In Sharon Macdonald (ed.). *A Companion to Museum Studies*. Malden, Mass. and Oxford: Wiley-Blackwell, 1–13.

Maclear, Kyo (1999). *Beclouded Visions: Hiroshima-Nagasaki and the Art of Witness*. Albany: State University of New York Press.

Milton, Cynthia E. and María Eugenia Ulfe (2011). "Promoting Peru: National Memory, Identity, and Tourism." In Ksenija Bilbija and Leigh A. Payne (eds). *Accounting for Violence: The Memory Market in Latin America*. Durham: Duke University Press, 207–33.

Payne, Leigh A. (2008). *Unsettling Accounts: Neither Truth nor Reconciliation in Confessions of State Violence*. Durham: Duke University Press.

Pitt, Alice J. and Britzman, Deborah P. (2003). "Speculations on Qualities of Difficult Knowledge in Teaching and Learning: An Experiment in Psychoanalytic Research." *International Journal of Qualitative Studies in Education* 16(6): 755–76.

Rothberg, Michael (2009). *Multidirectional Memory: Remembering the Holocaust in the Age of Decolonization*. Stanford: Stanford University Press.

Salverson, Julie (2009). "Bearing Foolish Witness." Unpublished paper presented at *Curating Difficult Knowledge* conference, Montreal, April 16–18.

Sevcenko, Liz (2004). *The Power of Place: How Historic Sites Can Engage Citizens in Human Rights Issues*. Minneapolis: The Center for Victims of Torture New Tactics in Human Rights Project.

Sontag, Susan (2003). *Regarding the Pain of Others*. New York: Picador.

Vukov, Tamara (2002). "Performing the Immigrant Nation at Pier 21: Politics and Counterpolitics in the Memorialization of Canadian Immigration." *International Journal of Canadian Studies/Revue internationale d'etudes canadiennes* 26: 17–40.

Williams, Paul (2007). *Memorial Museums: The Global Rush to Commemorate Atrocities*. Oxford: Berg Press.

Young, James (1992). "The Counter-Monument: Memory against Itself in Germany Today." *Critical Inquiry* 18(2): 267–96.

Part I
Bearing Witness between Museums and Communities

Introduction

Monica Eileen Patterson

In the aftermath of violence, survivors and affected community members need attention, support, acceptance, and care—as well as condemnation and rejection of the acts that caused their suffering. Violence not only shatters, it also embeds itself in the landscapes of the human heart in ways that can never be completely understood. Opening up spaces for empathy, respect, and inclusion without shocking, numbing, inciting, or repelling presents great challenges.

Stepping into this fray, curatorial practice offers a paradox: on the one hand, a productive space for engagement, understanding, and interaction; on the other, the inescapable partiality of all attempts to redeem and "reconcile," often in contexts that knew no prior conciliation. In such settings, as the authors in this section discuss, the implied call for a "return" to an earlier, healthier state of coexistence risks not only distorting history, but potentially obscures the real work required to bring opposed sides together. Curating difficult knowledge takes place within fraught fields of temporal overlay and embedding: we look back at the past for the sake of moving forward to a safe, secure future, often from unsettled, unstable presents. The work of engaging with violence by bringing it to light, putting it on display, and addressing its impact can blur divisions between us and them, then and now, how things have been and how they could, or should be. As many scholars have argued, and as the chapters in this section illustrate, memory debates are always as much about the present and future as they are about the past.

With diverse diasporas scattered across an increasingly globalized world and normative national institutions straining to remain relevant to diversifying populations, we see museums taking tentative steps toward becoming supportive spaces for communities that have been victims of violence and oppression. Working within that fragile, shifting space of possibility that exists, mirage-like, between atrocities of the past and aspirations for the future, museums can serve as powerful platforms for education, dialog, and expression that create more inclusive, tolerant publics.

1

"We were so far away": Exhibiting Inuit Oral Histories of Residential Schools

Heather Igloliorte

In the spring of 2008, two Inuit residential school Survivors[1] from each of the four Inuit geographic territories of Canada—the Inuvialuit settlement region, Nunavut, Nunavik, and Nunatsiavut—traveled to Ottawa, Ontario to share their stories for the creation of a national exhibition about the Inuit experience of the residential school system. During the sensitive filmed interviews, the Survivors recounted the impact that residential schools had had on their lives before, during, and after their time as students. Individually, their stories described a range of distinct circumstances, as they attended schools in different times, in different parts of the country, and experienced varying degrees of abuse, trauma, and long-term negative impact. Yet read together, themes emerged that resonated across the stories of all eight of the Survivors, providing invaluable source material around which to build the exhibition.

As curator of *"We were so far away": The Inuit Experience of Residential Schools*, it was my great honor to conduct these interviews with the eight participants and bear witness to their personal testimonies. It was my responsibility to take care of these stories and the people who shared them with me. Doing so depended on the development of a unique curatorial approach to representing this sensitive knowledge to a particular hierarchy of audiences: residential school Survivors, Inuit communities across the Arctic and Subarctic where the exhibition would tour, and the broader Canadian public. While these eight testimonies became the foundation of the exhibition, we also included historical images from archives across Canada, along with the Survivors' personal photographs and objects that they felt were important to their memory of residential schools. We hoped that these personal stories, combined with their intimate childhood images, would help make this difficult history more tangible to the general public, and more relatable to other Survivors in the North. A year later, at the first opening of the exhibition at Library and Archives Canada, one of those eight Survivors, Carolyn Weetaltuk of Kuujjuarapik, Nunavik, recognized her mother in one of the unlabeled archival photographs of "anonymous" school children, thereby reclaiming a piece of this history for herself. It was a remarkable moment—and it reinforced our conviction that the primary audience for this exhibition was first and foremost Inuit Survivors and their families and communities. For Inuit, none of the archival images were "anonymous," and every archival photograph held the potential to be personal.

The nationally-touring exhibition *"We were so far away": The Inuit Experience of Residential Schools* is thus the culmination of a collaborative effort between myself, the Legacy of Hope Foundation (LHF), and the eight courageous Inuit Survivors who shared their stories. The exhibition is intended to supplement, assist, and encourage the many healing initiatives that are already being undertaken in communities across the Canadian North. This chapter explores some of the challenges that arose and the strategies we developed in creating an exhibition with a motive to heal, and a mandate to tour the Arctic.

1.1 The residential school system in Canada, from the 1830s to the 1970s

The exhibition was conceived at a significant moment in the history of Canada's settler/indigenous relations. While the Aboriginal Healing Foundation was formed in 1998 to encourage and support community-based, Aboriginal-directed healing initiatives to address the legacy of residential schools, the history of the residential school system had only very recently come to the attention of Canada's national media, reaching its greatest exposure in June of 2008 when the Canadian government made its first public apology to First Nations, Métis, and Inuit peoples.[2] Yet still today there is a lack of public comprehension around the federally funded, church-run boarding schools that operated in Canada for more than a century, and this lack of public knowledge and understanding is exacerbated by the exclusion of this history from our educational system, and the unwillingness or inability (until very recently) of Survivors to speak about their experiences in the schools.

Simply put, the purpose of residential schools was to assimilate the Aboriginal population into the dominant colonial culture by removing children from the care of their parents and communities and placing them into institutions far from their homes, where they could be taught the Western way of life and corresponding "values." Based upon the fundamental belief that the colonial culture was superior to that of Aboriginal peoples, the Canadian government and churches adopted the paternalistic goal of "saving" the Aboriginal population from their so-called savage, heathen ways through assimilation and conversion. As John Milloy describes in *A National Crime: The Canadian Government and the Residential School System, 1879–1986*, it was believed that this transformation could best be accomplished by removing Aboriginal children to off-reserve boarding institutions that would "civilize" the Native population and prepare them to participate in the Euro-Canadian economy as industrial laborers or domestic workers, while isolating the children from the interfering influence of Aboriginal parents or communities (Milloy, 1999: 26).

In contrast to these idealistic goals, however, and tragically so, the disastrous legacy of the residential school system is most often a story about loss and neglect, abuse and mistreatment. Conditions in the off-reserve boarding schools were usually deplorable as chronic underfunding and gross mismanagement of resources and staff compounded the problems of substandard living conditions, over-crowding, and disease. Aboriginal languages and practices were considered unfit for civilized society, and children were prohibited from speaking their language or practicing their culture, frequently resulting in harsh punishments for minor "offences." This widespread forced adaptation to English threatened to wipe out the dozens of Aboriginal languages spoken by First Nations, Métis, and Inuit. Many children suffered physical, mental, and sexual abuses, and the legacy of that trauma has been passed on through generations from parent to child.[3] As Prime Minister Harper noted in his now famous apology on behalf of Canada to former students of residential schools:

> For more than a century, Indian Residential Schools separated over 150,000 Aboriginal children from their families and communities. In the 1870s, the federal government, partly in order to meet its obligation to educate Aboriginal children, began to play a role in the development and administration of these schools. Two primary objectives of the Residential Schools system were to remove and isolate children from the influence of their homes, families, traditions and cultures, and to assimilate them into the dominant culture. These objectives were based on the assumption [*sic*] Aboriginal cultures and spiritual beliefs were inferior and unequal. Indeed, some sought, as it was infamously said, "to kill the Indian in the child." Today, we recognize

> that this policy of assimilation was wrong, has caused great harm, and has no place in our country.
>
> (Younging et al., 2009: 357)

The LHF, a charitable organization formed in 2000 by the Aboriginal Healing Foundation, was created to educate, raise awareness, and foster understanding about this history of residential schools in Canada. For this exhibition, we hoped to raise that level of awareness to include an appreciation for the Inuit-specific residential school experiences and the legacies that still resonate in Inuit communities today.

1.2 The Inuit-specific experience of residential schools

One of our main motivations for highlighting the Inuit experience of residential schools as unique within the broader history of the Canadian residential school system is that for Inuit, the residential school system was but one facet of massive and rapid cultural changes taking place in the first half of the twentieth century. In the few short decades preceding the introduction of the residential school system across the Canadian Arctic and Subarctic, Northern cultural practices had been significantly eroded by the incursion of European culture. While Aboriginal communities in southern Canada had undergone several centuries of intensifying Western European colonization and missionary involvement since the arrival of Columbus in 1492, Inuit communities, isolated by the harsh Arctic climate and the difficulty of traveling in the North, were relatively unaffected by outside contact until the early twentieth century. Within the span of only a few short decades, however, the pre-contact way of life underwent dramatic changes.

One of the first of these tremendous changes was the settlement of Inuit in communities around trading posts for the purpose of becoming fur trappers, which often led to the over-hunting of wildlife in the immediate area and an increasing dependence upon preserved food and packaged goods imported from the South. This was soon coupled with a decreasing animal population and an economic downturn brought on by the depression years between World War I and World War II, which strained the formerly good relations between the Inuit trappers and the European traders (Innis, 1927: 49). These new settlements also became breeding grounds for highly infectious diseases, including smallpox and tuberculosis, which spread quickly throughout the settled Inuit population (Mitchell, 1993: 336). In "The Colonization of the Arctic," artist and author Alootook Ipellie indicates that "between 1956 and

1961, one in seven Inuit were in various southern sanatoriums receiving treatment for tuberculosis. The incidence of otitis and meningitis in Iqaluit were above the national average" (1992: 51). In Nunavik and Nunatsiavut, several Inuit communities were entirely relocated, with devastating consequences since the relocated populations often lived in overcrowded and infelicitous conditions (Tester and Kulchyski, 1994; Dussault and Erasmus, 1994; Brice-Bennett, 2000). It has also been recently alleged that Royal Canadian Mounted Police officers orchestrated the slaughter of thousands of sled dogs across the Arctic to force Inuit to stay in their new communities, a tragic story recently investigation by the Qikiqtani Truth Commission. The loss of sled dogs had immense impact on Inuit life and was arguably a strategic act to limit their movement and facilitate forced assimilation of Inuit people to Western settler-colonial ways. Meanwhile, the widespread and rapid proselytizing in the Arctic led to the near total conversion of Inuit to Christianity in the span of just a few short decades. Christian missionaries had been dispatched across the Arctic and Subarctic in the late nineteenth century—and much earlier in Nunatsiavut—but it was not until the 1910s and 1920s that a great number of Inuit were converted to Catholic or Anglican faiths, a transformation sometimes even overseen by other Inuit.[4] As Jose Kusugak explained in his article "On the Side of Angels," "many Inuit became Christians because the churches had what Inuit wanted: biscuits, beans, prunes, hope, and gifts of clothing from other Christians from the south" (2009: 15). The missionaries prohibited Inuit converts from practicing Inuit spiritual customs and cultural traditions, believing themselves to be saving Inuit souls from heathen and savage practices (Norget, 2008: 222). As Ipellie summarized in "The Colonization of the Arctic,"

> Seen through the eyes of "civilization," the good that these purveyors of trade and religion did is incalculable. But the exploited Inuit saw their once-strong traditional culture left to disintegrate and flounder. For countless generations the Inuit had had an iron grip on their culture, it took less than one generation for it to be put through the government's "cultural mill," never to be melded back to its original form.
>
> (1992: 46)

In the midst of this cultural turmoil residential schools were introduced across the North with the rationale that they would be "the most effective way of giving children from primitive environments experience in education along the lines of civilization leading to vocational training to fit them for occupations in the White man's economy" (National Archives of Canada, 1954). Numerous Inuit children were taken to schools far from their homes and introduced to a completely foreign way of life. Although federally-funded, church-run schools had been operating in southern Canada since the 1830s, in the North, for the most part, the residential school system was not fully established until around 1955 when Minister of the Department of Northern Affairs and National Resources, Jean Lesage, announced a new federal education system for the Northwest Territories and Northern Quebec (Milloy, 1999: 243). Until the federal government was compelled to do so, the Department of Indian Affairs had little interest in providing formal education to Inuit; the government policy until that point had been "keeping the Native Native" (Diubaldo, 1985: 49). Prior to 1955, less than 15 percent of school-aged Inuit children were enrolled in residential schools; within a decade, this number would climb to over 75 percent (King, 2006: 10). After assuming responsibility for Northern education, the Department's jurisdiction encompassed all of the Northwest Territories, the Yukon Territory north of the Peel River, the Ungava area of Northern Quebec and along the east coast of the Hudson Bay in Quebec (see Map 1.1).[5]

The government residential school system for Inuit was an educational experiment: while so-called Federal Day Schools were built within communities, most students were still forcibly removed from their families who lived elsewhere in the Arctic and housed in dormitories, hostels, or tent camps adjacent to the schools; some Inuit children were boarded with local families.[6] While this system differed from the off-reserve boarding school system for First Nations students, the philosophy behind it was much the same as in the southern Indian Residential School System. In a 1952 report mentioned in the Report of the Royal Commission on Aboriginal Peoples titled "The Future of the Canadian Eskimo," an unnamed federal administrator said of the Inuit, "their civilization, because it is without hope of advancement, should be ruthlessly discouraged."[7] As John Amagoalik argued in "Reconciliation or Conciliation? An Inuit Perspective," it was this attitude toward Inuit that spurred the implementation of brutal assimilative practices across the North (Amagoalik, 2008).

Like their southern First Nations and Métis counterparts, Inuit children suffered terrible physical, psychological, and sexual abuses as well as a devastating loss of language, culture, and parenting. Indeed, their isolation in the North further compounded this impoverishment, as communication lines were nearly nonexistent, and returning home

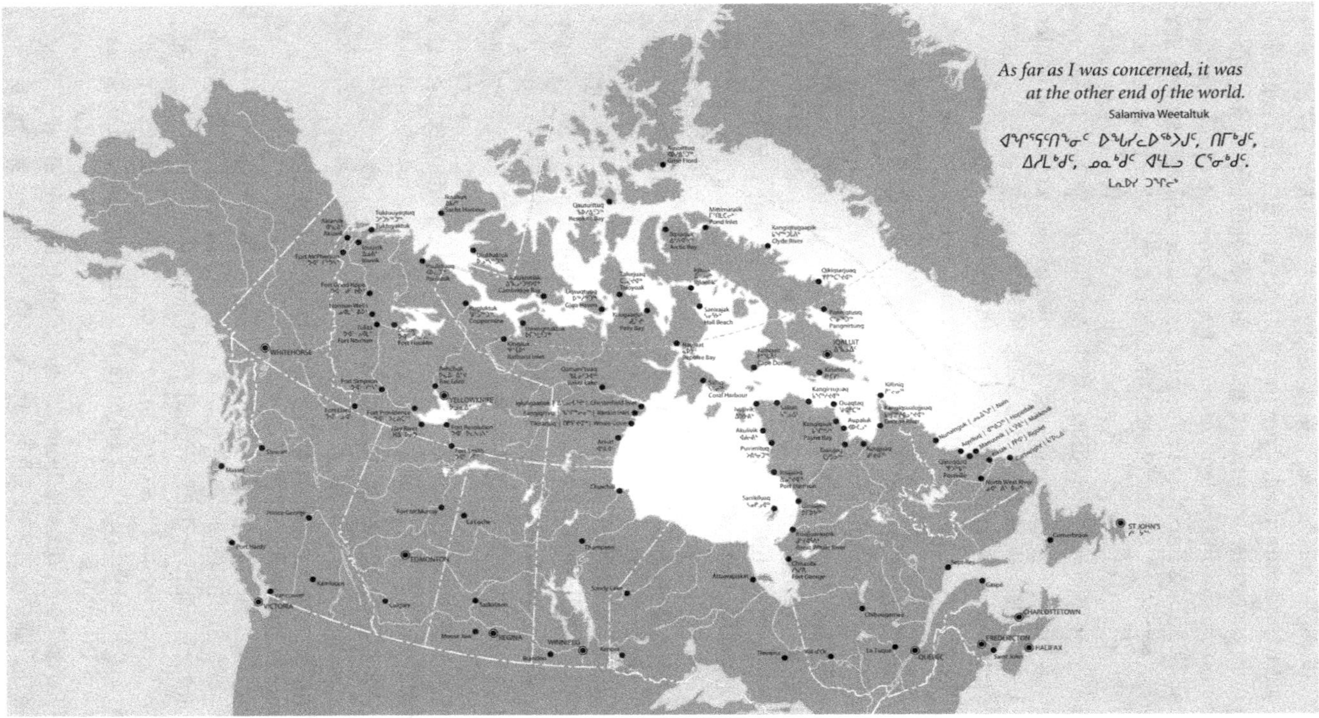

Map 1.1 Inuit communities map, "'We were so far away': The Inuit Experience of Residential Schools". (Image courtesy of the Legacy of Hope Foundation.)

was only possible once a year for most students, while some students did not get to go home at all. Even today 90 percent of Inuit communities are only accessible by air, and many households lack basic means of communication like telephones and the Internet (Inuit Tapiriit Kanatami, 2006). As Survivor Peter Irniq explained in his interview for *"We were so far away"*, contact with family was rare. "We weren't able to communicate with our parents for the entire nine months that we were in Chesterfield Inlet. We just didn't have communication facilities; no telephones. I remember I got two letters from my mother that particular year in 1958 and 1959" (Igloliorte, 2010: 103).

While many Survivors are grateful for the education they received, they paid a very high price for it. The deleterious effects of the residential school system on the health and well-being of Survivors and their families were evident everywhere in the communities, compounded by the converging impacts of colonialism in the North (Stout and Kipling, 2003: iv–v). As we now know, many students grew up to be traumatized adults whose lives still resound with the echoes of this early trauma. Furthermore, Inuit children were made to feel ashamed of their traditional way of life, and many acquired disdain for their parents, their culture, their centuries-old practices and beliefs, and even for the food their parents provided. Labradorimiut Survivor Shirley Flowers explains, "When I went to the dorm I lost my taste for wild food. I couldn't eat seal for years after that" (Igloliorte, 2010: 89). Several of the Survivors interviewed remembered feeling superior to their parents when they returned home after years in the residential school system, having been made to believe that their parent's way of life was "primitive" and "filthy."

Yet despite being taught never to speak of their experiences, over the last decades Inuit have begun to speak out, taking an active role in reasserting Inuit culture and healing their communities.

1.3 The development of the exhibition: obstacles and opportunities

The brave Inuit Survivors who shared their stories for the creation of the exhibition—Shirley Flowers and Marjorie Flowers of Nunatsiavut; Salamiva Weetaltuk and Carolyn Niviaxie of Nunavik; Marius Tungilik and Peter Irniq of Nunavut; and Abraham Anghik Ruben and Lillian Elias of the Inuvialuit region—all agreed that their goal was to educate the public and support the healing efforts of Inuit within their communities (Igloliorte, 2010). It is for this purpose that the exhibition was created, with the hope that it would tour across the Canadian Arctic and Subarctic to reach as many Inuit as possible. However, the sensitive nature of the subject matter and the disturbing, often-explicit content of the stories presented a series of obstacles to the curatorial process that demanded careful consideration. Perhaps the greatest challenge was how to represent Survivors' recollections without precipitating trauma or distress among visitors, many of whom would be residential school Survivors themselves. This risk was intensified by a lack of access to professional counseling services to deal with the impacts of the abuses they endured, and a lack of resources or expertise to deal with the intergenerational impacts that today affect up to three living generations of Inuit in the North.[8]

The exhibition planning was also complicated by a number of design and communication issues. The difficulty and expense of transportation in the North demanded lightweight, durable, and compact exhibition materials and crating. And the dearth of "real" exhibition spaces such as galleries or cultural centers and the small scale of alternative venues such as classrooms and community halls required that the exhibition be flexible, make maximum use of available wall space, and employ freestanding elements where walls were not possible. Finally, the huge geographical and linguistic range of primary audiences meant accommodating not only the officially-mandated French and English languages in all texts, signage, and publications, but also making the exhibition accessible in the different Inuit languages of the four northern regions, of which one—the Inuvialuit region—has three official dialects.

We resolved the language issue by employing both a regional and national perspective. Most of the contemporary Inuit population lives in the eastern Arctic, in Nunavut and Nunavik; there the most commonly read version of Inuktitut uses syllabics. All general texts were printed in English, Inuktitut Syllabics, and French, assuming that all visitors would be literate in one of the languages; that this is a safe assumption is a direct consequence of residential school education. Whenever the text was about an individual or specific region, however, we additionally translated it into the most commonly written form for the region. For example, rather than syllabics Inuvialuktun participant Abraham Anghik Ruben has the appropriate western Arctic roman orthography on his banner, in the transcription of his story in the exhibition catalog, and in all of his photo captions. In this way, we respect and highlight the diversity of Inuit cultures from across the Canadian Arctic. By translating this knowledge into Inuktitut and the regional dialects, we both honor the perseverance of the language and aid in the development of a lexicon around residential schools and healing. These linguistic strategies were adopted to foster understanding about a difficult topic throughout both the North and South.

For the physical exhibition, we abandoned all rigid materials—frames, glass, fiberboard—and instead constructed the entire exhibit out of large fabric banners (one for each participant). We conducted tests to assess which type of canvas would best resist crinkling, tearing, and fading so that the banners, curatorial text, map, and additional images could be easily rolled up and shipped. We contacted the airlines serving northern Canada to determine the maximum allowable dimensions for packaging, and opted to crate the exhibition in thick cardboard tubes and custom nylon packages that would make the cost of shipping much lower than a typical touring exhibition, enabling us to bring it to many smaller communities across the North. We also designed the exhibition for easy assembly with little more than a drill and some hooks. As a result, the materials can hang on the walls or be displayed via simple, lightweight "pop-up" structures and frames that reduce the need for wall space. These creative curatorial techniques have allowed us to bring *"We were so far away"* into several small venues that could not have otherwise accommodated an exhibition of this scale, reaching audiences usually excluded from such publicly touring exhibits.

But beyond these practical innovations, there were a number of conceptual and methodological concerns that necessitated the development of specific Indigenous curatorial strategies for the presentation of Inuit history. The most prominent of these issues arose during the first planning sessions following my designation as exhibition curator. Before I came on to the project in January of 2008, the LHF had collected approximately 75 archival photographs directly linked to the history of Inuit residential schools from church, private, and government archives across the country. It was thought at the time that these would be the basis of the exhibition, and that the Inuit exhibition would closely resemble its predecessor *Where are the Children? Healing the Legacy of Residential Schools*, the still touring LHF exhibition from 2002. *Where are the Children?* had employed a vast archive of enlarged, framed historical photographs from Library and Archives Canada and other sources, which curator Jeff Thomas brilliantly tied to the colonial history of ethnographic photography and to research he had uncovered on the hidden history of residential schools. Thomas's exhibition was an act of reclamation, taking back these photographs for community purposes. Although this idea resonated deeply with First Nations peoples, who were intimately familiar with the process of being objectified through images and photographic practices—those of Edward S. Curtis, as well as other anthropological surveys and the like,[9] this strategy would not have made as great an impact on the Inuit, who had experienced colonialism differently than their southern peers. Furthermore, as the Inuit exhibition was meant to tour throughout the north on tiny planes and in subzero temperatures, glass frames would have been a potential disaster, and mounting text on typical exhibition panels would have been too heavy and costly to ship across the North.

The solution to both of these problems was found by exploring what might be culturally appropriate in representing the Inuit specific experience, and by placing primary importance on the integration of Inuit philosophies and epistemologies into the exhibition. We decided to foreground the cornerstone of our Inuit culture for thousands of years: oral tradition. We gave prominence to first person oral testimonies by participants, an approach that also helped emphasize that these stories were a part of a *living* history. Each of the fabric banners, which appear at the beginning of the installation and are carried through the exhibition, contains a large, close-up portrait photo of a Survivor's face, as well as personal photographs and items that each particular Survivor considered significant to his or her experience in residential school, and—most importantly—key excerpts from his or her interview. Each banner also presents a particular theme emphasized by the Survivor during the interview, such as loss of language, or the impacts of assimilation. (See Plate 1.1.)

Our focus on oral history in the exhibition manifested in several levels of the exhibition. While visitors can read contextual information before entering the main exhibit, and view a map of the residential schools attended by Inuit near the entrance, the bulk of the exhibition is made up by the eight Survivors' stories, experienced in a variety of media. Playing on a loop near the rear of the exhibition, yet loud enough to hear from its entrance, is a DVD recording assembled from the interviews; in this way the visitor not only reads, but also receives the stories aurally, having an opportunity to experience and bear witness in a way reading alone cannot provide. While the transcribed quotes and the recording provide only a brief snapshot of these stories, the exhibition catalog, produced in 2010, is novel in that it contains the full transcripts of each interview, providing an invaluable resource on a scale rarely seen in exhibition materials. The nearly 200-page, full-color catalog will be provided free of charge at exhibition openings in the North and South, and there are plans to create a complimentary education kit to accompany the exhibition to schools and libraries across the country.

The full, unedited recorded video interviews have also been deposited, at the Survivors' request, in the LHF's archive of stories from residential school Survivors, a collection of hundreds of hours of footage from over 500 Survivors across the country (Legacy of Hope Foundation, 2006). By using only selections of the testimonies on the banners and panels, we were able to control content that might be too graphic for children or Survivors to confront while touring the exhibition. It is important to note here that the transcripts of the interviews, the quotations on the banners and in the curatorial text, the use of personal images, and even the quotations in the present chapter have been approved by the Survivor participants, who retain ownership over their stories and the way they are represented, as laid out in their release forms. This practice ensures that Survivors retain control over the presentation and dissemination of their own stories and demonstrates to participants our commitment to honoring their experiences.

Beyond the seating area in the exhibition for viewing the DVD, we set up a three-projector slide show of the original 75 archival photographs. We felt that the historical images should still be included because they provided an important historical counterpoint to the contemporary viewpoint expressed in the main exhibition. But we physically de-centered the arrangement of slide projectors and rows of chairs so that it would come at the end of the exhibition, in order to ensure that visitors understand that the primary focus is on the living histories of the Inuit participants. Archival photographs of residential school children from this period inevitably present a one-sided view of the event. The pasts inscribed in these photographs speak to the official government and church narratives of the schools as well as to the events surrounding the creation of the photographs, but not always the lived experiences of the children pictured. Some of the images in the slide show, for example, depict visits from the bishop or other religious dignitaries, and in those images the children are relatively well clothed, lined up together in front of the bishop with a group of nuns, perhaps with a row of flags flying in the background, or a meal laid out for the guest. Survivors have described these events as highly deceptive and staged; children would be better clothed, better fed, and better treated during such visits, just as they were at the end of the school year when their imminent return home often prompted teachers to be kinder and gentler as well. Historically, photography was often used as a tool to depict the residential school system as a positive force for converting Aboriginal people from "savage" to "civilized" through staged photographs depicting Native children washing up or brushing their teeth, saying their prayers, or learning in classrooms.[10]

Despite the problematic history of colonial photography vis-à-vis Indigenous peoples, productive work can be done by bringing the images back to the communities in which they were made, as in the aforementioned *Where are the Children? Healing the Legacy of Residential Schools*. Having communities view the photographs can shift the focus from the original intent of the images (anthropological, colonial, imperial, etc.) to the familial and collective. In return, archival collections may gain not only lost factual materials, but fresh meanings and new ways of understanding and seeing when they are viewed through the eyes of source community members.[11] At a private exhibition opening for Survivors at the Prince of Wales Northern Heritage Centre in Yellowknife, NWT, in November of 2009, many of the former students who gathered to watch the slideshow at the end of the exhibition tried to guess the locations of the images shown, or name the people in the photographs as the carousel rolled through the archival collection, thereby reclaiming them for Inuit communities. At that particular opening, the slide show also acted as a catalyst for conversation and reminiscing, and most of the former students present, many of whom had traveled from neighboring communities to attend, stayed at the Prince of Wales Northern Heritage Centre to catch up with each other over tea and bannock bread long after they finished touring the exhibition.

Despite the convivial atmosphere that permeated the Yellowknife opening, it has been our policy to approach openings as potential sites for the re-inscription of trauma and to take therefore a number of precautions to create a safe space for exhibition visitors, many of whom we expect will be residential school Survivors or their relatives. For that reason, a warning in all five languages is placed outside the entrance to the exhibition, and in the beginning of the catalog text. The LHF has also arranged for both clinical and community-based health care workers to be on location at all exhibition openings throughout the North. Health care teams provided by Health Canada are comprised of Native and non-Native staff, who are experienced working with Survivors (and who are often Survivors or intergenerational Survivors themselves). Furthermore, for the duration of the exhibition Health Canada postcards, with regional and national numbers for confidential counseling, are kept stocked in a "quiet room" (where possible) or seating area with other resource material on residential schools. While such cautionary steps go far beyond the norm in Western exhibitionary practice, our primary mandate for this exhibit is to protect and respect the Survivors and their stories, and to be conscientious regarding the dignity and safety of all visitors who come to engage with this difficult knowledge. In this sense, the guiding principle of the exhibition has been *protecting*, a stance characterized in Linda Tuhiwai Smith's seminal text *Decolonizing Methodologies* as a part of the ongoing effort by Indigenous peoples and their allies around the globe to safeguard, protect, and heal the legacies of colonization and imperialism (1999: 158).

As the exhibition begins its tour of Arctic Quebec, having already visited the western Canadian arctic and some international venues, it remains extremely important to the LHF and to me that we continue to foster and maintain a relationship of trust, respect, and dignity with the participants, based on transparency as an organization, and personal responsibility and accountability to the Survivors who have so generously shared their stories with us. We have learned so much from the Survivors and this collaborative project, and the LHF and I continue to benefit from local knowledge and expertise. The knowledge we are gathering with each installation helps us develop and expand the exhibition as it travels, based on the input of former students, other community members, and the contributions of local scholars and historians. Following the launch of the northern tour in Yellowknife, it became apparent that as projects such as this exhibition raise awareness, more Survivors come forward, which leads to the generation and sharing of more knowledge about Inuit experiences in residential schools. Based on discussions with former students, we have decided to produce an interactive map of residential schools with additional place names and bodies of water, so that a greater number of people can locate the schools they attended, creating the most complete record of the Inuit experience that exists in any other single current record. We are exploring new ways for people to leave their marks on this map, so that as the exhibition moves across from West to East we can continue to document and expand what we know about this complex and sensitive part of Canadian and Native history.

Mapping this project may prove to be significant for another reason as well: it may serve to promote the inclusion of Labrador and other Eastern provinces in the Indian Residential Schools Truth and Reconciliation Commission. In 2008 when the Prime Minister made his apology to Canadian Aboriginal people, he deliberately stated that students had come from every province except Newfoundland and Labrador, New Brunswick, and Prince Edward Island. In Labrador, my father and some of my other family friends and relations attended the Yale School living in a dormitory indirectly funded by the federal government through the International Grenfell Association. A consequence of being left out of the settlement agreement has been that these former students will not be given the opportunity to give their testimony to the Truth and Reconciliation Commission, and will not be recognized by the government as having shared a common experience with all other Aboriginal peoples who attended residential schools. But when walking through the exhibition, listening to the stories, and reading the accounts by these eight people from the furthest reaches of our country, it is clear that the experiences are much the same across the broad geographic expanse. By marking Labradorimiut schools on our map, and including them in the exhibition as legitimate expressions of common experience, we may be assisting those unacknowledged Survivors to gain an extra foothold in their fight for recognition.

At this early stage in the exhibition tour, I can only conclude that curating this difficult exhibition has been among the most challenging and gratifying experiences of my career. We had hoped starting out that we would to get to know the participants well enough to anticipate what elements of their stories might make them uncomfortable, or which aspects of their experiences they would want to highlight, so we could accommodate their needs. We could not have known that we would be rewarded with the development of personal relationships that extend far beyond the professional ones. And I believe that in the end our extensive efforts to meet the particular challenges presented in developing this exhibition with a commitment to *care for* and *protect*, rather than seeing them as obstacles to overcome, became the fundamental strength of the exhibition.

Notes

1. Following the definition set by the Aboriginal Healing Foundation, the term "Survivor" specifically refers to "an Aboriginal person who attended and survived the residential school system" (Reimer et al., 2010: xi).
2. For a complete transcript of Prime Minister Stephen Harper's Apology and all the Federal Government apologies made on June 11, 2008, see Appendix Two: Canada's Statements of Apology (Younging et al., 2009).
3. The Aboriginal Healing Foundation has defined intergenerational trauma thusly: "Intergenerational or multi-generational trauma happens when the effects of trauma are not resolved in one generation. When trauma is ignored and there is no support for dealing with it, the trauma will be passed from one generation to the next. What we learn to see as 'normal' when we are children, we pass on to our own children. Children who learn that . . . sexual abuse is 'normal,' and who have never dealt with the feelings that come from this, may inflict physical and sexual abuse on their own children. The unhealthy ways of behaving that people use to protect themselves can be

passed on to children, without them even knowing they are doing so. This is the legacy of physical and sexual abuse in residential schools" (Aboriginal Healing Foundation, 1999: A5). For a rigorously researched account of the scope and extremity of abuses that took place in residential schools, see Miller, 1996.

4. For Inuit perspectives on the transition to Christianity in the eastern Canadian Arctic, see Tungilik and Uyarasuk, 1999.
5. David King has created a listing of all the Federal Day Schools within these regions from the available public records, including the numbers of students recorded enrolled at each institution and the types of accommodations where students were housed (King, 2006: 2–10).
6. The dormitories held anywhere from 8 to 250 students at a time (King, 2006: 1–2). Some parents relocated in order to be near their children, forcing more Inuit into permanent settlement.
7. Quoted from document titled "The Future of the Canadian Eskimo," dated May 15, 1952 (NAC RG22, volume 254, file 40-8-1, volume 2 (1949–52) (Royal Commission on Aboriginal Peoples, 1996: 458).
8. For a detailed overview of the extent of this lack, see Health Canada, 2006.
9. For a history of Edward S. Curtis and colonial uses of photography, see Maxwell, 1999.
10. On the use of colonial photography in residential schools see the catalogue for *Where are the Children? Healing the Legacy of Residential Schools* (Thomas, 2003).
11. This process has been analyzed and explored in the collaborative study by Peers et al., 2006.

Works cited

Aboriginal Healing Foundation (1999). *Aboriginal Healing Foundation Program Handbook, 2nd Edition*. Ottawa: Aboriginal Healing Foundation.

Amagoalik, John (2008). "Reconciliation or Conciliation? An Inuit Perspective." In Marlene Brant Castellano, Linda Archibald and Mike Degagné (eds). *From Truth to Reconciliation: Transforming the Legacy of Residential Schools*. Ottawa: Aboriginal Healing Foundation, 91–100.

Brice-Bennett, Carol (2000). *Reconciling with Memories: A Record of the Reunion at Hebron 40 Years after Relocation/ Ikkaumajânnik Piusivinnik: Titigattausimajut Katiutusumaningit Hebronimi 40 Jâret Kingungani Nottitausimalidlutik*. Nain: Labrador Inuit Association.

Diubaldo, Richard (1985). *The Government of Canada and the Inuit: 1900–1967*. Ottawa: Research Branch, Corporate Policy, Indian and Northern Affairs Canada.

Dussault, René and George Erasmus (1994). *The High Arctic Relocation: A Report on the 1953–55 Relocation*. Ottawa: Royal Commission on Aboriginal Peoples, Canadian Government Publishing.

Health Canada (2006). "Brighter Futures and Building Healthy Community Initiatives: Evaluation Summary." In *First Nations, Inuit and Aboriginal Health: Mental Health and Wellness*, Ottawa: Health Canada 2006. Available at http://www.hc-sc.gc.ca/fniah-spnia/pubs/promotion/_mental/2006-sum-rpt/index-eng.php#bhc [Accessed May 10, 2010].

Igloliorte, Heather (ed.) (2010). *"We were so far away": The Inuit Experience of Residential Schools*. Ottawa: Legacy of Hope Foundation.

Innis, Harold (1927). *The Fur-Trade of Canada*. Toronto: Oxford University Press.

Inuit Tapiriit Kanatami (2006). *Inuit Approaches to Suicide Prevention*. Ottawa: Inuit Tapiriit Kanatami. Available at: http://www.itk.ca/Inuit-Approaches-to-Suicide-Prevention [Accessed June 15, 2010].

Ipellie, Alootook (1992). "The Colonization of the Arctic." In Gerald McMaster and Lee-Ann Martin (eds). *Indigena: Contemporary Native Perspectives*. Gatineau: Canadian Museum of Civilization, 39–57.

King, David (2006). *A Brief Report of the Federal Government of Canada's Residential School System for Inuit*. Ottawa: Aboriginal Healing Foundation.

Kusugak, Jose Amaujaq (2009). "On the Side of Angels." In Gregory Younging, Jonathan Dewar, and Mike Degagné (eds). *Response, Responsibility, and Renewal: Canada's Truth and Reconciliation Journey*. Ottawa: Aboriginal Healing Foundation, 13–28.

Legacy of Hope Foundation (2006). *Our Stories, Our Strength*. Ottawa: Legacy of Hope Foundation. Available at http://www.legacyofhope.ca/OurStories.aspx [Accessed June, 30 2010].

Maxwell, Anne (1999). *Colonial Photography and Exhibitions*. London: Leicester University Press.

Miller, John (1996). *Shingwauk's Vision: A History of Native Residential Schools*. Toronto: University of Toronto Press.

Milloy, John S. (1999). *A National Crime: The Canadian Government and the Residential School System, 1879–1986*. Winnipeg: University of Manitoba Press.

Mitchell, Marybelle (1993). "Social, Economic, and Political Transformation among Canadian Inuit from 1950 to 1988." In *In the Shadow of the Sun: Perspectives on Contemporary Native Art*. Gatineau: Canadian Museum of Civilization, 333–56.

Norget, Kristen (2008). "The Hunt for Inuit Souls: Religion, Colonization, and the Politics of Memory." In Robinson, Gillian (ed.). *The Journals of Knud Rasmussen: A Sense of Memory and High-Definition Storytelling*. Montreal: Isuma Productions, 217–36.

Peers, Laura, Allison K. Brown, and members of the Kainai Nation (2006). *Pictures Bring us Messages: Photographs and Histories from the Kanai Nation*. Toronto: University Press.

Reimer, Gwen, Amy Bombay, Lena Ellsworth, Sara Fryer, and Tricia Logan (2010). *The Indian Residential Schools Settlement Agreement's Common Experience Payment and Healing: A Qualitative Study Exploring Impacts on Recipients*. Ottawa: Aboriginal Healing Foundation.

Royal Commission on Aboriginal Peoples (1996). *Report on the Royal Commission on Aboriginal Peoples, Volume 1: Looking Forward, Looking Back*. Ottawa: Minister of Supply and Services Canada.

Smith, Linda Tuhiwai (1999). *Decolonizing Methodologies: Research and Indigenous Peoples*. London: Zed Books.

Stout, Madeleine Dion and Gregory Kipling (2003). *Aboriginal People, Resilience and the Residential School Legacy*. Ottawa: Aboriginal Healing Foundation.

Tester, Frank J. and Peter Kulchyski (1994). *Tammarniit (Mistakes): Inuit Relocation in the Eastern Arctic 1939–63*. Vancouver: UBC Press.

Thomas, Jeff (2003). *Where are the Children? Healing the Legacy of Residential Schools*. Ottawa: Legacy of Hope Foundation.

Tungilik, Victor and Rachel Uyarasuk (1999). "The Transition to Christianity." In Jarich Oosten and Frederic Laugrand (eds) *Inuit Perspectives on the 20th Century, Volume 1,* Iqaluit: Nunavut Arctic College.

Younging, Gregory, Jonathan Dewar, and Mike Degagné (eds) (2009). "Appendix II: Canada's Statements of Apology." In *Response, Responsibility, and Renewal: Canada's Truth and Reconciliation Journey.* Ottawa: Aboriginal Healing Foundation, 357–71.

2
The Past is a Dangerous Place: The Museum as a Safe Haven

Vivienne Szekeres

The city of Adelaide is the capital of South Australia and home of the Migration Museum, an institution dedicated to the history and experience of migrants to Australia. The location for this museum reflects the region's history of non-conformism and enlightened and radical ideas. South Australia was not a convict settlement but a planned colony for free settlers who were attracted by the promise of religious freedom. Lutherans fleeing persecution in East Prussia, and Quakers and Jews from England were among the earliest immigrants. In 1894, South Australian women fought for and won the right to vote in parliamentary elections, the first women, along with New Zealand, in the world to gain their democratic freedom. Thus, Adelaide and the Migration Museum are unique in the Australian landscape, for they both push the frontiers of what is possible to do and express about social injustices, tensions and conflict. For the Museum, this means navigating the difficult waters of Australia's diverse peoples who share the same lands and the legacy of colonialism and racism.

The Migration Museum, where I have worked as Curator/Director for 25 years, is housed in buildings that were formerly part of a Destitute Asylum built by the Colonial South Australian Government in the nineteenth century, to house early migrants who had fallen on hard times. Violent fluctuations in the economy altered early plans for settling the new colony—a process that had begun in 1836—because the newly arrived immigrants, who mainly came from England, Scotland, Wales, and Ireland, faced high unemployment. When gold was discovered in the neighboring colony of Victoria in the 1850s, a great many young men decamped with hopes of making their fortunes. They left behind their women and children. Colonial authorities built the Destitute Asylum to address the ensuing social crisis of managing large numbers of poor and homeless children and women (many of whom were pregnant at the time of abandonment). Their history is reflected today in the names of the Museum's buildings, such as the Lying in Hospital and the Mother's Wards.

After World War II, Australia began to accept immigrants and refugees from Eastern and Southern Europe. The demographic changes that followed this mass migration changed Australia from a predominantly Anglo-Celtic society to one that could more accurately be described as multicultural. But it was not until the early 1980s, following Canada's lead, that the Australian Federal Government made the political decision officially to adopt multiculturalism as a policy.

It was the recognition of the multicultural nature of our society that prompted the State Government of South Australia to establish the Migration Museum in 1983, as a Division of History South Australia. The Museum is funded by the State Government of South Australia and has continued to receive bipartisan support. The Museum opened to the public in 1986 as the first museum of immigration history in Australia. Its mandate was to research, document, collect, conserve and interpret the history of immigration and settlement. I was fortunate to be hired as the first curator in 1984 and became director in 1987, a position from which I have very recently retired. What follows is an analysis of my involvement in the key exhibitions and decisions made in collaboration with my Museum colleagues and a variety of community groups who work with the Museum, referred to in this chapter as "constituents." I use the term "constituents" (elsewhere often called "stakeholders") to reflect the political agency of community groups in debates about the design of the Museum's exhibitions, and also to reflect the spirit of our museum's common curatorial practice of working in dialog with communities and on their behalf.

In the history and cultural sector, the term 'community' is used so often and in so many ways that it has become virtually meaningless. Nevertheless, at the Migration Museum we use the term too. It has become shorthand to refer to groups of people who come from the same place of origin, or have shared belief systems, similar social backgrounds, or political affiliations. Many identify themselves by belonging to a club or society. Some groups form because of shared feelings of alienation as outsiders to mainstream society. Sometimes individuals are united by the experience of grief and trauma that caused them to leave their countries of origin. Although 'community' may sound straightforward, at the Museum it is multi-layered and complex. Embedded within it are competing agendas, differing points of view, and ancient antagonisms. These can be between different communities or from within the same group.

In spite of these complexities it has been crucial to the Museum's development and success to work very closely with the owners of the stories that we want to tell. One of the reasons is found in the early history of the Museum. When we began the historical research that underpinned the exhibits we found a dearth of secondary sources. With very few exceptions, Australian universities were not interested in immigration history. The Museum curators had to go out in search of these stories. Along with the creation of unique archives of historical knowledge, another positive outcome of this practice was that the process of engaging with individuals and community groups brought people into the Museum to participate and take ownership of the way their story would be told. So, from the outset, community involvement was fundamental to the way we would work.

This involved more than just collaboration. No two projects ever followed the same process. At times the Museum responded to information brought to us by individuals or groups with a story to tell. At other times we went out in search of the stories or the material culture. This could take us from a consulate office to a kitchen or living room in someone's home. It could take us to churches, mosques, or synagogues; to schools, universities or community centers, sports fields, shops, or factories: all of the places where people lived, prayed, played, and worked. Every step along the way we received the permissions to make public the information that was being shared with us.

There is another significant factor that has influenced which stories we might tell and how we tell them. It also defines what we collect and how the Museum functions. It is the fact that we are consciously—maybe even *self* consciously—a social history museum. I have argued elsewhere that the arrival of the discipline of social history in museums democratized the industry in terms of the way curators engage with the public. Perhaps more importantly, social history—with its emphasis on history from below and its focus on the lives of "ordinary" people—set a new agenda for museums. It ensured that the history of the poor, the dispossessed and the marginalized would be included.[1]

Public spaces are used to shape memories of systematic mass violence in many ways. Thus, one of our central questions has been: How can the Museum include the Indigenous histories of Australia in stories that are essentially about European migrants and refugees from Asia, South America and Africa? Like Canada, Australia was a comparatively late acquisition in the history of colonization. Unlike Canada, it was "discovered" and claimed solely for the British Empire by Captain Cook in 1788. It was described at the time as *terra-nullius*, land that belonged to no one. It has been said that history is mostly written by the winners, so it is not surprising that the categories used to describe those who peopled Australia over the next century consisted of "colonists, pioneers, settlers and immigrants." But for Aboriginal people who lived on the land that was defined as belonging to no one, the word "invaders" is more appropriate. The words we use shape the stories we tell and reflect much about the storytellers.[2]

Over the last 24 years, we at the Museum have changed the way we present this history of immigration. These shifts and changes have taken place within a broader political context. For example, in 1992 Prime Minister Paul Keating of the Labor Party committed Australia to seeking reconciliation with Aboriginal Australians. This was a watershed moment in government policy that had a major impact on public attitudes about Indigenous Australians. It sent out a strong message to Australia's cultural institutions that it was time to examine the ways—largely tokenistic or non-existent—in which Aboriginal history and culture had been presented. In response, the Museum embarked on a series of major changes.

2.1 Aboriginal origins, colonialism, and the migration museum

The first project began with a visit from Kaurna elder, Lewis O'Brien. The Kaurna people are the custodians of the Adelaide Plains. Lewis raised the issue of acknowledging the Kaurna presence on the Museum's site. He suggested we mount an illustrated plaque in the Museum's courtyard next to the entrance. Two of the Museum's staff had already undertaken substantial research into Aboriginal associations with the site and were able to source images and draft text. The final design, text, and location were approved by Lewis and other Kaurna elders.

The plaque was significant in several ways. Firstly, it was one of the first public acknowledgments of Aboriginal history in the city. Secondly, the plaque was placed next to a wall that still stands from the first Aboriginal School, which was built in 1848. The school can be seen as a symbol of colonial policy and nineteenth-century attitudes of social Darwinism. Put crudely and simply, the European, colonial administrators believed that Aboriginal people would either be "civilized" and assimilate, or die out.

In addition to the plaque and after considerable consultation, the Museum made the decision to extend the brief of South Australian immigration history by setting it in the wider context of global colonization. Up until this moment the Museum's main exhibit presented immigration to and settlement in South Australia. It charted the arrival of the many different groups from Europe, Asia, the Americas, and Africa since 1836. While it did make reference to the invasion of Europeans, Aboriginal history tended to get subsumed by the grand narrative of the success of European settlement. Extending the theme from immigration to colonization enables visitors to see where Australia's history fits into the global history of colonization, making the real impact of European settlement on Aboriginal people more obvious. This move enabled us to present Aboriginal history as fundamental to any understanding of Australian culture rather than as a side issue. As you enter the Museum today, the first exhibit you will see is the work of Aboriginal artist Darryl Pfitzner Milika who makes a powerful visual statement about the experience of his own people that is understood by visitors of all ages.[3]

The Museum now exhibits the impact that European settlement had on Aboriginal Australians, which threads its way through the chronological story of immigration and settlement. At times the sheer brutality of government policies and bureaucratic practices is breathtaking in its level of prejudice and ignorance of Aboriginal issues. For example, Ngarringjeri man Geoff Cooper (known as Coops) and Kankunjatjara elder Lowitja O'Donoghue recall being taken as small children from their parents and put into state care from which many repeatedly tried to run away. Coops and Lowitja represent the voices of thousands of Aboriginal children known these days as "the Stolen Generation," a history that parallels that of Canada's residential school program discussed in Heather Igloliorte's chapter here. In another part of this program, the voice of Pitnantjutjara elder, Eileen Kampukutu Brown describes the aftermath of atomic testing by the British at Maralinga when hundreds of desert people were covered by nuclear fallout and many suffered burns and blindness. These people are still seeking justice for their suffering and displacement.

This is difficult knowledge. Even when the owners of the stories want to make their experiences public, it is hard for them. Even when they have a long history of working with the Museum and solid relationships of trust exist, it is difficult. It makes no difference that this process of engagement is not new to the Museum; we have been here many times before, ushering in stories where there had been silence, yet it always feels like uncharted territory. In this regard, the curator, Christine Finnimore, is very experienced and understands this history intellectually as well as emotionally. But as she told me when the project on global colonialism was finished, she had felt at times the unbearable weight of these individual and collective tragedies, feelings common to all of us working at the Museum. We could overcome these feelings because our work enabled these stories to be made public, and amplify the voices of those who had not been heard outside their own communities, as part of the national story. As well, all participants seemed pleased with the final exhibition.

One of the challenges in presenting Australia's colonial history up to the present day is to do so without merely producing a litany of atrocities. Much of the history of the last centuries is brutal in the extreme. While the Museum does not habitually dwell on the difficult, the former Minister of Foreign Affairs in the conservative Liberal/Howard government criticized us for being a "museum of misery" and berated me for not foregrounding the "happy migrant story."[4] This is the myth that all migrants succeed, that they find assimilation both necessary and easy, and that it is somehow "un-Australian" or ungrateful not to be "happy" in "God's own country." As I said at the time, even the success stories often start with pain and struggle and all our exhibitions are based in very thorough historical research. It is also important to note that we have developed many exhibitions that have represented and celebrated diversity. In a way, these "happier" exhibitions are simpler to develop and they also play a part in raising awareness about differences. But we have always believed that it is unethical and dishonest to only highlight the positive aspects of cultural history. It is an issue that demonstrates the implicitly political nature of our work.

2.2 Telling migration history in difficult times

The context for recounting diversity altered dramatically in 1996 when Federal elections swept a Conservative Coalition government (Liberal and Country parties) into power. Reconciliation with Indigenous Australians was taken off the political agenda and refugees faced new hostility. The newly elected Howard Government tightened the laws relating to asylum-seekers for those who were arriving informally—especially by boat. This political shift was reflected in populist attitudes about migrants. At the Museum we noticed that racist comments and negative attitudes about refugees began to appear on the visitor comments boards in the exhibition galleries.[5] It seemed that compassion and tolerance were on the decline. Visitors made comments that echoed populist, often hysterical media headlines without an understanding of Australia's international human rights obligations or any historical perspective. This was particularly ironic given that Australia was one of the driving forces behind the drafting of the United Nations Declaration of Human Rights in 1948.

For many years, the Museum has presented stories of refugee experience as part of the overarching story of immigration, but we had never developed an exhibition to attempt consciously to mediate or counteract the misinformation in the media. Given the political climate of the mid-1990s, we changed our mind. The Museum began to develop an exhibition that would show as graphically as possible how anyone, from anywhere, at any time could become a refugee: it only takes a twist of fate. This became the name of the exhibition.

A Twist of Fate: The Story of War, Torture, Pain and Survival opened in February 1998. It took the visitor physically on a short journey through three refugee stories. It was a visually confronting exhibition, which led visitors through a reconstructed bombsite with current statistics about international refugee crises and a list of factors that could cause a person to become a refugee. The main part of the exhibition was a makeshift refugee camp through which three separate stories were accessed by a key. Each story was told through sound, graphics, and reconstructed scenes (see Figure 2.1). These stories located the visitor in terms of time and place, for example a Polish family in 1940, an unaccompanied minor in Vietnam in the 1970s, and a young mother searching for her disappeared husband in Chile in 1980. One of the most emotionally impacting aspects for viewers was that each story moved through a reconstructed padded cell with a single light globe, metal chair, and a bucket. This prison cell was oppressive. It represented the threat of torture, incarceration, aloneness, and alienation. The exhibition ended with eight stories of survival and settlement in Australia.

A Twist of Fate was not for the faint-hearted or for those museum visitors who preferred and expected comforting nostalgia. And it was definitely not for those who had been refugees and experienced torture or trauma, as a warning sign told visitors at the beginning of the exhibition. In the museum industry the exhibition was seen as provocative in that it had virtually no artifacts and the three stories were composite stories that did not belong to any individual person. This created a fair bit of philosophical debate among museum colleagues. But as the curator of this exhibition, and based on my past experience, I felt that it would be too harrowing for former refugees to talk about their experiences in the first person. Thus, to build the three composite stories, I relied on secondary sources that I knew I could trust. We also conducted eight interviews with survivor-migrants that were presented at the exhibition's end. We signed written agreements with the interviewees that we would not ask them for details about how they escaped nor about the circumstances that prompted their departure and arrival in Australia.[6]

In retrospect, I believe *A Twist of Fate* was ahead of its time. It received little media attention and those people it did reach were those who

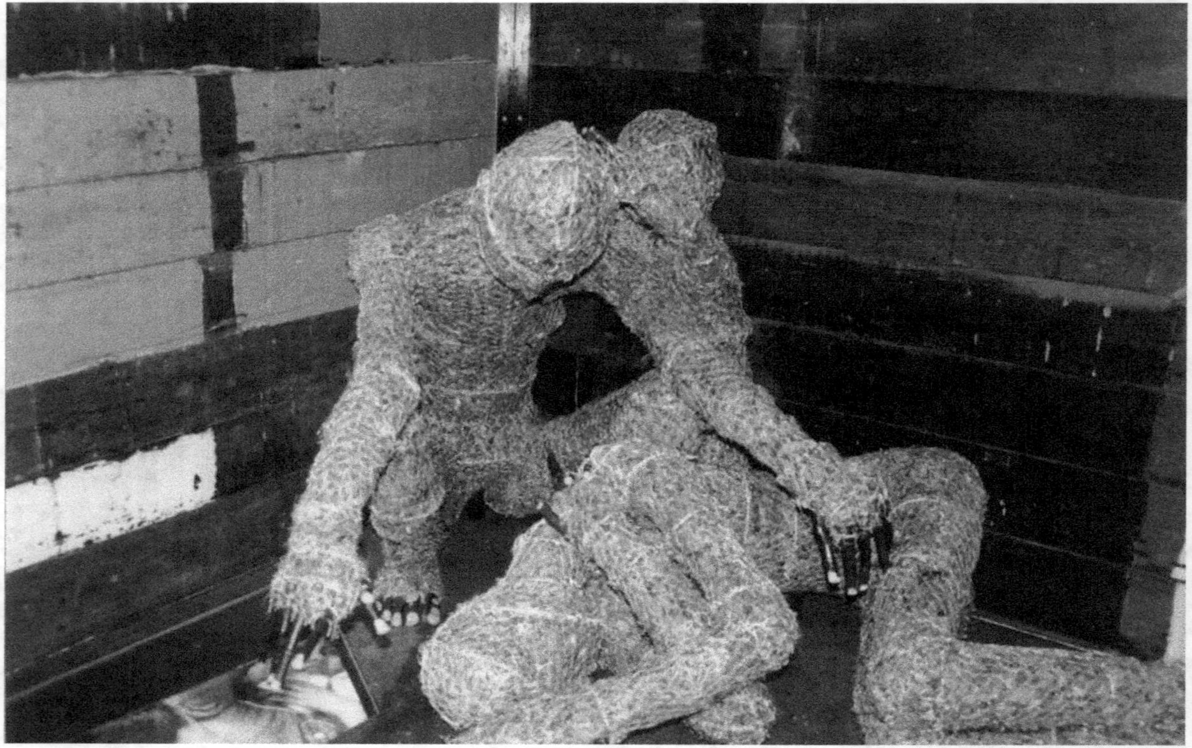

Figure 2.1 Sculptural figures of refugees made by Fay Poole for the exhibition "A Twist of Fate: The Story of War, Torture, Pain and Survival" displayed at the Migration Museum, Adelaide, Australia, 1998.

already felt similarly worried about the direction Australia was taking in terms of human rights. One of my enduring memories was finding an American tourist sobbing in the last part of the exhibition. He was a Vietnam Veteran. "I was there," he kept saying. "I was there in Vietnam. We must never forget. It must never happen again."

The political climate for refugees continued to worsen, despite our efforts to educate a larger public. *A Twist of Fate* was still traveling around Australia a year later when the Australian Government began a policy of detaining refugees. This policy led to the opening of the Woomera Detention Centre on the site of a former missile base in outback South Australia where temperatures regularly reach over 40 degrees centigrade. Woomera was just one of a number of detention centers for the incarceration of all non-citizens arriving by boat without a valid visa.

By mid-2000 there were a number of protests from the detainees in Woomera. There were complaints that conditions were harsh and that it took too long to process claims for refugee status. There were hunger strikes, break outs, riots, fires, and inmates swallowing poison. Some detainees even sewed their lips shut to draw attention to the fact that no one was listening to them. It was only in 2000—following three days of rioting during which water canons, tear gas, and batons were used against the detainees—that a number of human rights lawyers and health professionals were allowed into Woomera to meet with the asylum seekers and their severely traumatized children.

Shortly thereafter the Museum's Education Officer, Rosa Garcia, learned about the existence of about 20 drawings that the children in Woomera had made after the riots. The drawings were brought out of Woomera by one of the lawyers who acted on behalf of the refugees. The Museum worked with this lawyer, the Justice for Refugees organization, and the Otherway Centre, an Aboriginal center that had become involved in helping young unaccompanied minors from Afghanistan and Iraq. We decided to put the drawings on display at the Museum. Serafina Maiorano curated the exhibition in which the original A4-sized drawings were enlarged and mounted on plain white card hung without any interpretive text. The drawings were made by children ranging in age from 8 to 14 years old. They depicted the children's responses to incarceration, the riots, and the use of water cannon and batons by the guards. (See Plate 2.1.) There were drawings of birds and flowers and scenes which they could not have seen, given they were living in the bleakest of environments. The birds and flowers drawn were always caged. The exhibition opened in 2003 and later traveled around Australia for several years during which time the Woomera Detention Centre closed.

2.3 Decentering curators: constituents building exhibitions

Not all of our exhibits have originated with Museum staff. In 2003, a group of Cambodian teachers and health professionals approached us. "It is time," they said, "to tell our story." This group had arrived in the 1980s but it had taken them over twenty years to feel ready to tell their story. The Cambodian group booked the Museum's community access gallery, a space known as "The Forum" that is designated for use by community groups without any cost or intervention from the Museum's curators. They named their exhibition "Stories in Cardboard Boxes: The Survival of Cambodian refugees in South Australia."

Members of the Cambodian community wanted to recount their stories, but they struggled as to how. They knew they wanted to move beyond the traumatic time of the Khmer Rouge and tell their stories of escape and settlement in Australia to demonstrate their community's successes. On their own initiative, the Cambodians met with former Museum curator Marie Boland. Working closely with Boland, they made collective decisions about which of the plentiful ideas generated by the group to include in the exhibit. For example, they identified objects to display that reminded them of happier times and the places they loved and lost. The mainstay of the exhibit, reflected in its title, were boxes covered in plastic to protect an individual's few possessions from the elements, as many traveled in open boats from refugee camps in Indonesia and Thailand to Australia. (See Plate 2.2.)

At a certain point, the group found itself silent. It had reached the point of the unspeakable: the reason why its members now lived in Australia. The first wave of arrivals consisted of refugees escaping from the genocidal regime of Pol Pot. Many had been tortured. All had been dispossessed of their homes. Most had worked as slave laborers in rice paddies or on building sites. Many had been starved and beaten. How was the Cambodian group going to broach this painful past? It decided on a simple black curtain hung alone in a case with only the words printed in white: Pol Pot, 1975–1979.

At the launch of the exhibition the group spoke for the first time about their experiences during Pol Pot's regime. Some of the audience wept openly at the bravery that we were witnessing.

The launch of this exhibition was one of the most moving experiences from my time at the Museum. It led to a series of collaborations between the Museum and the Cambodian community, built on mutual trust. After their display opened, some of the group members struggled with haunting memories. They decided they wanted to go on working with the Museum on several other projects. For instance, they contributed a section about their histories to the Museum's main exhibit. They also made a banner that reclaimed the Krama, the traditional checked/checkered scarf that was worn and used for centuries by Cambodian people, but had been banned by Pol Pot for use only by his Khmer Rouge followers to denote rank. For years this group of refugees could not bear to look at it. The symbolic value of the banner may seem a small victory, but it has the utmost significance for them. It marked a moment of closure.

2.4 Making space for remembering, mourning and ritual

The Cambodian experience, while unique, is one of many stories of escape from persecution and violence. In 1992, community groups began to mount brass plaques on the outside wall of the Museum next to the entrance. This initiative was started by the Baltic Communities Council, a group that wanted to tell the public how they had been forced to flee Latvia, Lithuania, and Estonia in 1941 when the Soviet Union invaded. The Museum established this first project and it grew from there. In 2006, Christine Finnimore gave a very moving conference paper called "Grief, Protest and Public History: The Memorial Wall in The Migration Museum." Of the plaques she said,

> The wording of the inscriptions is stark. Together, the plaques form a chorus of mourning. The experiences they represent are shared, remembered and ritualized within each community . . . The plaques are public memorials of individual and collective grief and trauma that convey political and historical meanings. Their political meaning is overt. They are explicit protests about ideologies that have wreaked havoc and destruction in their lives: Nazism, fascism, communism, racism.

Rituals have grown in the space of the Museum. In the gathering gloom of a cold winter evening, a tall, white-haired, soft-spoken man stands in front of one of the plaques. His head is bowed so that you cannot see the unbearable sadness in his eyes. Behind him stands a silent group of about 60 men, women, and children. He lays flowers and lights a candle on a small table in front of the plaque. He and his community are here to remember July 1995 when 8000 of their countrymen were massacred at Srebenica. This group of survivors came from Bosnia Herzogovina; they are like several others whose histories are recorded on the Memorial Wall. They make an annual pilgrimage to the Museum. Some make speeches, others lay wreaths, all come to remember their history and honor and mourn their dead.

Some years ago, a colleague made the point that the Museum had become a sacred site for many groups. Even though the histories may have happened long ago and in faraway places, their owners have decided to relocate them and place them in the Museum. Furthermore many people we met nearly 25 years ago are still connected to the Museum. They continue to participate in programs, come to launches, bring their friends and family, call in and check on the latest programs, and invite staff to their celebrations and events. When I think about how strong these bonds of friendship remain it is not so surprising. They often begin with disclosures charged with intense emotion. Our constituents have trusted us with their moments of gut-wrenching fear, unimaginable pain, unexpected rescue or escape to safety, and experiences of new lives that they never imagined could happen. Most tell us they feel affirmed and empowered that their story is now in the public arena. They no longer see themselves as victims but as survivors.

2.5 Conclusion

What role can—and should—museums play in interpreting and mediating these difficult pasts? And how do museums navigate the minefields of competing expectations and different versions of history? As with most museums, the Migration Museum is seen as a neutral meeting place for people from many different backgrounds. To encourage their public participation, as well as to foster encounters among diverse groups, the museum's ethic is centrally about accommodating multiple interpretations of history.[7] It is part of the process of moving away from the model of the museum/curator as the definitive authorial voice. For many years we experimented with ways of drawing the visitor's attention to the idea that what they see at the Migration Museum is not the "whole truth" but always our version of it. The comment boards that are throughout the Museum are to encourage dialog and debate about the ideas that we present. When we first introduced some of these ideas in the 1980s they were seen as edgy and innovative, as was the idea of borrowing objects from community members rather than the Museum needing to own them. While the Museum was interested in presenting multiple interpretations of the past, community groups were not. All the exhibitions mounted by community groups in the Forum focus on the positive aspects of cultural history and rarely, if ever, take a critical position of their community's role in past events. Perhaps this is because their histories are recent and still too raw to analyze.

The landscape of the twentieth and twenty-first centuries is littered with the most appalling atrocities. In today's Australia there are many who survived these terrible events. People arrive everyday from Sudan, Iraq, Lebanon, Afghanistan, Tibet, Burma, and Zimbabwe. Many come as part of Australia's official refugee intake, while others risk their lives in leaky boats and end up in detention centers. As the exhibitions at the Museum attest, the past can be a dangerous place. But for those who are ready to tell their stories and trust us with them, the Migration Museum is a safe haven for themselves and their histories.

Notes

1. "The Importance of Museums in the Development of Changes in Social Thinking"; Vivienne Szekeres, Australia-Israel Hawke Lecture. March 9, 2005. www.unisa.edu.au/hawkecentre
2. The terms "Aboriginal" and "Indigenous" are both used to describe Australia's first peoples. But strictly speaking Indigenous is used when Torres Strait Islanders and other Islander peoples are included. Because the vast majority of Aboriginal and Islander peoples were removed from their homelands and sent to missions, both terms are often used interchangeably. "Aboriginal" is used when applied to first peoples who live on the mainland.
3. Darryl Pfitzner Milika is a Kokatha man from the West coast of South Australia. He was introduced to the Museum by Kaurna Elder Lewis O'Brien. Darryl is a well-known local contemporary artist and had previously worked on a significant exhibition with Marie Boland, a former member of the Migration Museum's staff. Together they developed "Same Story, Different Places: An Urban Dreaming. In search of Australia's Black History." His work is pictorial but highly political.
4. The comment was included in a letter from the Minister to the State Premier. The Minister also repeated the statement to me personally in a conversation that occurred in 1996.
5. Examples include, "As a white female, I have experienced little racism—however I have noticed that the most virulent racists are immigrants! Especially Italians and English Immigrants" (2002), "speaking as an Englishman, I would hate to see Australia suffer as we have with the population level and culture completely changed and areas (particularly London) devoid of traditional English" (2003), "there are to [*sic*] many curry munchers in Australia, they should not be in Australia and there are to [*sic*] many black people."
6. This section was called "Rebuilding Lives" and featured Henry who was expelled from Egypt because he was Jewish; Lay who fled Pol Pot, Cambodia; Flora from Albania; Ene-Mai who left Estonia in 1944 and who arrived in

Australia as a Displaced Person in 1949; Dalica from Eritrea who arrived in Australia in 1992; Danny who fled Czechoslovakia in 1969 after the Soviet invasion; and Paul who fled Cyprus after the Turkish invasion.

7. Vivienne Szekeres, "Own Your Own Bias: Subjective Interpretation in Museums," National Conference of Museums Association of Australia Incorporated, October 1989, Melbourne.

3

Teaching Tolerance through Objects of Hatred: The Jim Crow Museum of Racist Memorabilia as "Counter-Museum"

Monica Eileen Patterson

In the last two decades, scholars and practitioners of what has come to be known as the "New Museology" have questioned and challenged many of the traditions upon which museum practice has been based. The exclusion of underrepresented groups in museum collections, exhibits, and staffrooms has come under increasing scrutiny, as have curatorial authority, classificatory and exhibitionary practices, and the relationship between museums and the publics they serve. Within a competitive economy of potential visitors' time, money, and interest, contemporary museums have found themselves forced to democratize their institutions and enliven exclusive and stuffy atmospheres as a means of appealing to broader publics. Despite the rigorous dialog that has been generated in academic, practitioner, and public circles, too often a separation remains between museum theory and practice. Should they wish to survive, today's museums must manage simultaneously to fulfill multiple roles for mixed constituencies.

Perhaps the greatest impulse behind New Museology has been the shift from maintaining museums as elite temples built upon the authority of select experts to establishing more inclusive and inviting forums for learning, dialog, and exchange. As crucibles of history, museums have the potential not only to represent but also to inform social attitudes, public opinion, and political debates. Because of the scale and the scope of its impact, nowhere is such work more important and necessary than in regard to the "difficult knowledge" that comes out of the perpetration of mass atrocity. But representing violence has always been fraught with ethical dilemmas. How can experiences of brutality and suffering be presented without minimizing, sensationalizing, or reigniting the sentiments behind them? Should painful materials be dutifully relegated to the dustbins or dark drawers of museums' storage facilities? If not, how can museum practitioners confront or display such content in ways that serve to diffuse or allay the divisions between people rather than reifying and perpetuating them?

Through a multi-pronged and multi-media approach, the Jim Crow Museum of Racist Memorabilia (JCM) at Ferris State University in Big Rapids, Michigan offers innovative strategies for addressing these and other difficult dilemmas. While the core physical exhibit room is diminutive in size and thus constrained to a limited audience, the museum's vision and unique methodologies deserve close attention, as it is poised to inform the field in significant ways. The JCM integrates a range of elements from recent theory and practice to produce a dynamic, diversified institution through a cluster of both virtual and real world sites. The museum's objectives are ambitious and wide-reaching. It aims to

> [c]ollect, exhibit and preserve objects and collections related to racial segregation, civil rights and anti-Black caricatures; Promote the scholarly examination of historical and contemporary expressions of racism; Serve as a teaching resource for Ferris State University courses which deal, directly or indirectly, with the issues of race and ethnicity; Serve as an educational resource for scholars and teachers at the state, national and international levels; Promote racial understanding and healing; [and] Serve as a resource for civil rights and human rights organizations.[1]

What is notable about this set of goals, for a university-based museum, is how explicitly they address both academic and more public domains. Reworking exhibitionary practices to more centrally integrate pedagogical methods and structured dialog, the JCM challenges many of the foundational binaries that have shaped museum work, including: old/new museology, object/narrative, didacticism/dialog, authority/multivocality, elite/masses, White/"Other," tangible/intangible heritage, center/margins, and individual/society.[2] As such, it resists simple categorization, but incorporates elements from a range of traditional museum types,[3] successfully operating as a history museum, a classroom laboratory, a research center, a space for dialog and debate, and a repository of powerful and hurtful objects that have not only served as reflections and records of racist attitudes, but also as conduits of ignorance and hate. Through its website and two traveling exhibits, which are often mounted in local community centers and accompanied by public openings and related events, the JCM also effectively serves as a public forum.

African-Americans have long been represented and defined in essentialized, hateful ways, and on others' terms. The JCM examines the historical roots of these images, contextualizes them, deconstructs them, and allows visitors to confront them first hand, powerfully connecting the United States' Jim Crow "past" with the ongoing present, and revealing the symbiotic relationship between life and representation. As stated on the website, "The dehumanization of African-Americans through caricature helped justify their political, social, and economic oppression. Common, everyday items, such as ashtrays, magazine advertisements, figurines, pencil holders, fishing lures, jewelry, board games and children's toys portrayed Blacks as happy servants, buffoons, savages and sexual deviants."[4]

The JCM is not a museum in the traditional sense. The core of the institution is its collection of more than 5000 historical and everyday objects representing Black stereotypes. Housed in a windowless room on the Ferris State campus, it is not publicly advertised or visible. This, of course, means that access to the permanent collection is extremely limited. The low-tech exhibit is presented in conventional glass cases mounted on the walls and in tables. There is no sophisticated lighting or soundtrack. The museum staff consists of faculty members at Ferris State who are trained facilitators interested in the race-based system of inequality known as Jim Crow. Many Ferris State students, the museum's primary constituency, are learning about this history in campus classes in which they are enrolled. Members of the general public may contact the museum in advance and arrange to join a university-approved class session, workshop, or seminar, and the museum also occasionally hosts researchers, clergy, civil rights groups, corporate groups, and human rights organizations.

Facilitators encourage visitors to share their own knowledge, thoughts, and impressions, along with their reflections on and experiences of racism in (American) society. The day that I visited with a group of University of Michigan undergraduates, three staff members were on hand to lead the kind of highly-interactive, class-based sessions their own students would experience preparing for and processing their site visit. In small groups of about 25 students each, we attended a lecture and discussion on the history of Jim Crow, a visual literacy workshop, and a screening and discussion of a 30-minute documentary on the genesis of the JCM, titled "Jim Crow's Museum."

A cornerstone of the JCM experience typically viewed by students before their visit, it features founder and curator David Pilgrim, who started the collection about thirty years ago. The documentary frames the viewers' experiences by presenting the "back-story" of the collection's creation and explores the connections between the socio-legal system of Jim Crow segregation and racist memorabilia. It takes historical contextualization seriously as an educational goal. At age 13, Pilgrim intentionally destroyed what he now regards as the first object of his collection. Immediately after purchasing a ceramic "Mammy" salt-shaker from a middle-aged White man at an Alabama flea market, he threw it to the ground where it shattered into many pieces. Over the next few decades, however, Pilgrim acquired much more of this kind of racist paraphernalia, and amassed a sizeable collection at Ferris State University in Big Rapids, Michigan, where he is a sociology professor and Vice President for Diversity and Inclusion.

At the museum, personal reflection is encouraged and there are many opportunities for both formal and informal dialog with friends, other visitors, and facilitators. Whether on-site or in preparatory class sessions, the structured pedagogical encounters around the JCM provide students and visitors with a personally mediated, historical context designed to equip them with the skills and knowledge needed to understand the objects that will eventually be viewed in the exhibit room. This contextualization and the discussion that emerges from it help to humanize the subjects of Jim Crow racist memorabilia. In classroom settings, faculty draw upon images, primary sources, historical scholarship, statistics, personal experience, and examples from popular culture. Open-ended questions are posed throughout, prompting conversation and inviting personal reflection, making everyone an "expert" on some aspect of this ongoing history.

Involving and engaging a diverse audience is one of the key challenges of tolerance work and education. Because inequality is produced and experienced in uneven ways, so too is everything that issues from it: the legacies, consequences, pain, stakes, and even awareness of and concern about inequality's very existence. Using a range of tactics and media, Ferris State faculty and JCM staff approach the Jim Crow material from various disciplinary backgrounds. For instance, in the visual literacy workshop I attended during my visit, a JCM facilitator began by demonstrating how to "read" images for historical significance and symbolic meaning, before inviting us to try out our developing skills together. The hands-on, pedagogical techniques employed by the JCM offer a radical departure from a long history of museum practice in which various (il)literacies have served to enhance the status of museums as gatekeepers for the maintenance of expert knowledge. The attendant exclusivity of this tradition has kept most people from stepping through museum doors as anything but passive recipients of pre-determined, dominant knowledge. Whether in on-site workshops or in preparatory class sessions, anchoring the JCM experience in a series of pedagogical encounters transforms visitors in powerful ways, deepening their engagement and maximizing the impact of what a museum can achieve.

While museums have historically traded in their presumedly singular ability to understand, interpret, and appreciate artifacts and works of art at a certain elite level, there has been a recent push to broaden presentational approaches to accommodate, interest, and reflect a wider audience.[5] Through its less formal, pedagogical, and dialogic approach, the JCM and affiliated faculty introduce and model the requisite skills of more traditional, elite and elitist, scholarly ways of knowing. Given its location at an institution of higher learning, the requirement of a pre-approved and typically school-group visit, and the reliance upon the Internet as an additional access point, the JCM does not entirely break free of museums' exclusionary traditions, but through its multi-sitedness it does intervene in important ways. For instance, the collection is in the process of being digitized, and many of the objects are available for viewing on the Internet. Online viewers can access exhibits, scholarly articles, and staff responses to the "Question of the Month"; watch film and video clips; and read letters (both supportive and critical) the museum has received (see Figure 3.1). The range of content in the letters speaks to both the success of the JCM in making visible and problematic deeply embedded forms of racism and prejudice, and also the continuing need to keep engaging these issues. With an estimated 3 million hits to its website, and as emailed commentaries and questions from people in many different countries demonstrate, the virtual museum has extended the JCM's impact across the world.

Contributing to social change and sociopolitical justice, the JCM approach equips constituents of all racial and educational backgrounds with tools to become more knowledgeable and comfortable in the historically exclusive domains of social and academic analysis, but also helps them shatter some of the prejudicial assumptions upon which these domains are premised. Through some of the techniques mentioned above, the JCM has actively sought to create opportunities for broader public access as part of its commitment to promoting diversity and understanding, as articulated in their statement of values: "We reject the 'ivory tower' model of scholarly life. We are a resource to universities, high schools, civic organizations, and human rights groups."[6]

The JCM provides practical, everyday evidence that substantiates scholarship illustrating that racism did not end in 1954 when the

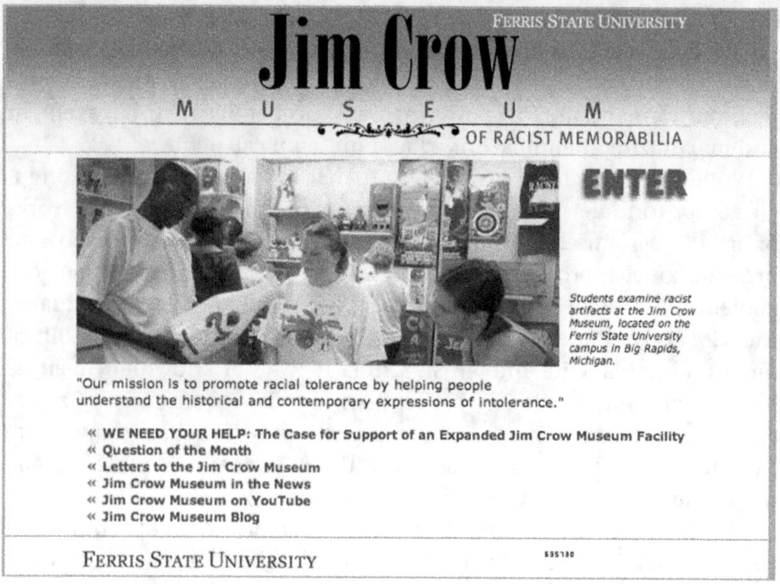

Figure 3.1 The Jim Crow Museum of Racist Memorabilia website home page.

Supreme Court ruled that segregation was unconstitutional. Nor did structurally embedded prejudice cease a decade later when Congress passed the 1964 Civil Rights Act. Jim Crow was much more than a set of legislation. It was a social order premised on the maintenance of a racially segregated system that placed Whites at the top of a hierarchy of humanity and Blacks at the bottom. This system had roots and repercussions in all aspects of society. As the JCM materials attest, Jim Crow was "a way of life" which excluded African-Americans from schools, stores, jobs, churches, public transportation, restaurants, public facilities such as bathrooms and water fountains, hospitals, cemeteries, militias, libraries, prisons, and neighborhoods. This exclusion was grounded and reproduced in social relations, personal attitudes, legal code, and social structures from the most minute to the most abstract and far-reaching levels.

The permanent collection consists solely of hateful, ugly, racist items. They convey racist meaning ranging from the overt to the subtle, and from more explicitly to implicitly demeaning and dehumanizing. Objects include an illustrated edition of the children's rhyme "Ten Little Niggers," a personal photo album with snapshots of Ku Klux Klan rallies and initiation ceremonies, and a postcard depicting four naked Black children on the bank of a river with a caption reading, "Alligator Bait."

The exhibit is organized thematically around a typology of stereotypes: "Coons" (as in raccoons), animals seen as "lazy, easily frightened, chronically idle, inarticulate buffoons;" "Toms" (as in Uncle Tom),[7] obsequious, affable, eager-to-please, faithful servants; "Mammys," their content, matronly, and loyal female counterparts; "Pickaninnies," the wild, disreputable, and disheveled child version of "coons;" "Jezebels," hyper-sexed, aggressive, often vengeful black women; and "Brutes," dangerous, savage, male predators. The range of historical and contemporary displayed materials contained under these headings effectively demonstrates that Jim Crow is alive and well in the contemporary United States and beyond. (Though most of the objects housed in the museum come from the US, the JCM has a small but growing international collection.) Objects are dated (although precise dates are often unknown), but they are organized by representational genre. Resisting an exclusively chronological ordering in favor of a thematic one makes the connections between past and present more clear, preempting any tendency among viewers to locate racial segregation and prejudice exclusively in the past. Visitors can trace the caricatures across time and (to a lesser extent) through space to identify the recurring themes in depictions of Black people.

On the collection he has amassed, Pilgrim notes, "I am a garbage collector, racist garbage. For three decades I have collected items that defame and belittle Africans and their American descendants."[8] Traditional modes of museological valuation, such as those that measure an object's rarity, workmanship, age, and condition are not relevant here. With a few exceptions, most of these objects are neither rare nor unique, nor do they have significant monetary value. In fact, Pilgrim claims that he could easily reproduce the collection in six months just by shopping on the international online marketplace eBay: most of the objects are still in circulation, and many are even still in production. Along with the surrounding infrastructure for engaging with them, it is the *assemblage* of these materials that makes them so valuable, as it repositions the framework of and for analysis by making the continuities of racism more visible.

To date, the collection also includes two traveling exhibits that help to expand the audience further. "Hateful Things" consists of a set of 39 racist objects and images accompanied by didactic panels explaining their historical and cultural significance. "THEM: Images of Separation" is a 35-piece exhibit with didactic panels that goes beyond Jim Crow issues to examine other forms of prejudice including the subjugation and stereotyping of women, poor Whites, gays, Jewish Americans, Native Americans, Mexican Americans, African Americans, Arab Americans, Asian Americans, and others. Both exhibits can be accessed online, although the explanatory panels are not included.[9]

3.1 Beyond new museology: creating space for difficult dialogs

When controversial materials or subjects surface within a museum setting, the tendency is to manage, diffuse, or stifle debate rather than harnessing it toward a productive end.[10] Through dialog JCM facilitators leverage the museum's miscellany of hate in an attempt to achieve something positive. It is a difficult, delicate process that does not work with everyone; the message or the approach occasionally pushes people further away. While creating space for dialog is often celebrated as a way of democratizing museums, this goal is constrained by a challenging reality: in any given social situation, not everyone feels equally free or comfortable to speak. Furthermore, as Silverman (1995) has noted, museum visitors bring their own experiences, perspectives, and worldview to exhibits and leave with varying messages.

JCM facilitators acknowledge the museum as a politicized space, and the unevenly painful nature of the objects on display. They recognize and openly address the thorny nature of collecting and exhibiting racist memorabilia. The museum presents a non-negotiable baseline to its visitors: racism is wrong. But the complex questions around this issue, including debates about what counts as racist, what one should do when one encounters racism, and how racism has shaped oneself as a person, are left provocatively open by the range of positions, feelings, and experiences that are allowed to surface.

New Museology has emphasized the discursive nature of objects (Taborsky, 1990). JCM objects do not just talk to visitors—they scream at them. The exhibit room invokes not so much cabinets of curiosity, with their intriguing jumble of rare and unique wonders, but closets of horror filled with the skeletons of centuries' worth of hate and hurt.[11] Much of the power and value of these objects is in their aggregation, their collective scope, and the perduring potency of what they represent. In this sense, the work of the JCM is akin to the practice of ethnography, in which a frame is both cast onto and emerges from the everyday flow of life by a researcher to highlight ongoing cultural patterns. Museum exhibits are often created as either object-centered or narrative-centered in their approach. The JCM transcends this division, using physical objects to intervene in pre-existing narratives, both social and personal. By carefully leveraging these objects, the JCM intervenes in deeply embedded historical, cultural, and socially reproduced racism and seeks to redirect visitors' thoughts to more reflective, informed, humane, and productive ends. In this way, troubling objects become vehicles for education, critique, self-reflection, dialog, personal growth, and social change.

Although debates and controversial exhibitions have been closely scrutinized in the often theoretical scholarship produced within the field of Museum Studies, museum visitors rarely have an opportunity to see into the decision-making processes that produce the exhibits they encounter (Butler, 2007; Linenthal, 1995; Linenthal and Engelhardt, 1996; Young, 1993). One of the most powerful ways that the JCM improves upon the traditional museum model and makes it more inclusive is through a commitment to candor and transparency. Given the emotional potency that many of the JCM's objects possess and the strong responses they provoke among viewers, it is important to witness the facilitators' own struggles in curating the racist memorabilia and the feelings and dilemmas that can arise—particularly in a field where curators are trained to work with cultural treasures. Difficult ethical questions come with the territory, and facilitators at the JCM do not ask more of their visitors than they are willing to give of themselves. In presentations they are often openly self-reflexive in sharing some of the challenges they have faced in working with racist materials.

In this era of "crisis" and reinvention for museums, curators are also being asked to relinquish some of their authority and share it with audience members who bring their own views and experiences to bear on the exhibits they visit. Some have been more amenable to this power sharing than others. Curator and founder Pilgrim leads his audiences by example. In talks, interviews, essays, and Internet postings, he often shares his personal experiences confronting and experiencing racism. Whether reflecting on the limitations of the name he chose for the museum (he feels that "Jim Crow" misleadingly suggests that the museum only deals with things from the past), the choices he has made in deciding which objects to exhibit (he hates having the Ku Klux Klan material on display because he feels it dominates and overpowers the other objects in the room), or sharing the frustrations, pain, and disappointments of his work as curator (having to watch his young daughter observe a demeaning imitation of Black people, losing his temper with the seller of an antique ink advertisement bearing the caption "Nigger

Milk," or confessing his gratitude for receiving an apology for racism from a White person that he never realized he needed), Pilgrim has proven willing to expose his own vulnerabilities, shortcomings, and self-doubts as curator (Pilgrim, 2007).[12] In ostensibly relinquishing the mantle of this "curatorial authority," he may command a much deeper appreciation and respect, and in allowing scholarly knowledge, pedagogical methods, and dialog to comingle, he seems to open far greater opportunities for learning than more traditional approaches have yielded in the past.

Pilgrim is also upfront about the ethical dilemmas involved in purchasing racist memorabilia. Some materials are donated, but others are bought. As previously mentioned, eBay has hundreds of listings of racist memorabilia at any given moment. The expansion of the collection through purchasing contributes to the trade in anti-Black caricatures, and through the market system not only rewards those who have come to possess such objects but provides financial incentive for them to acquire and produce more. Pilgrim is aware that in purchasing these items he is participating in a market economy based on racism (Pilgrim, 2007). He notes that generally, the more extreme the racism, the higher the value of the object. Once they are purchased his items are taken out of market circulation and are transformed into educational tools. Yet Pilgrim admits that for him, this does not fully mitigate his participation in an economy of violence and hate.

One of the most challenging objects in the JCM collection for Pilgrim is an airbrushed shirt featuring a Black "gangsta" figure in a ghetto. It raises complex and unsettling questions about the relationship between object, image, provenance, context, and meaning. It is also the first acquisition that he is certain was created by an African-American. Within the context of the museum experience, the shirt prompts a set of difficult questions: Is the (re)production of Black "gangsta" imagery by an African-American a co-optation or reappropriation of some of the tools of racism, a way to reclaim the visual language of the oppressor? Or is it evidence of a lack of consciousness at best and an internalized sense of inferiority at worst? Is it ironic, empowering, demeaning, or all of the above? Do the answers to these questions depend on context? The producer/wearer/observer's intent? Who decides? The power of this piece is its ability to unsettle and provoke, but most importantly to prompt discussion about racism among its viewers.

In his provocative film *Bamboozled* (2000), director Spike Lee plumbs the depths of these dilemmas through an exploration of the many meanings and valences implicating such objects, the circumstances of their production, the audiences that consume them (both intended and unintended), the larger economies (market and otherwise) in which they operate, and the complex emotional and psychological terrain of those who encounter them. It is in leaving such questions open that the JCM succeeds in meeting its most demanding objective: to promote racial understanding and healing. Through the practice of transparency, the museum workers avoid didacticism in favor of creating opportunities for dialog. Their main goal is not to create absolute consensus among visitors about the intrinsic, racist nature of each of the objects in their collection, or to agree upon a clear-cut line that should not be crossed in visual representations. In fact, one of the most discussed objects according to Pilgrim is a talking plastic cookie jar shaped like an alligator (Pilgrim, 2007). When opened, the alligator "talks" to the person looking for cookies in a heavily accented, caricatured voice, saying, "Mmmm mmmmm. Those sho' is some tasty cookies!" The discussions this contemporary item has inspired have found students arguing, from a variety of viewpoints, the importance of considering intent, humor, genre, historical context, cultural code, audience, and a variety of other factors to evaluate whether or not such a product is an example of a racist representation. Pilgrim likes the piece because it generates a range of responses, and sharing them makes people think more deeply about the legacies of racism in the present day.

3.2 The JCM as "counter-museum"

Museums have often sought to inspire and invoke a sense of internal transformation or even sublimation, typically by using rare or exquisite objects of display that may serve as examples of society's best achievements. But what approaches should be used when confronting and displaying the hatefulness and horror of our societies? Contributing to the emergent field of curating difficult knowledge, the JCM helps position visitors as participants in ways that enable them to inhabit educational, social, and personal spaces that link intangible and tangible culture and heritage. Some of the biggest difficulties in "collecting" and displaying intangible heritage have concerned how to document and represent it. The JCM uses various forms of knowledge generation, capture, and dissemination. Through multi-media technologies, including documentary film, object display, discussion, textual and visual analysis, historical contextualization, and an interactive web site, the JCM asks visitors to analyze images and objects in light of deeper contexts. The diversified JCM experience positions visitor-participants to engage and reflect upon the tendrils of culture that entwine us all in our mundane, everyday lives, including those legacies of violence and prejudice that we all inevitably navigate and sometimes perpetuate.

In Germany in the 1980s, a new genre of monument emerged that sought to reposition memory out of the stagnation of state custodianship and into the hands of citizens actively involved in memory work. These "counter-monuments," as they were termed by James Young (1992), spoke to the sense that memorials had become not receptacles for memory but rather tools for forgetting, their very existence excusing and enabling people to *dis*engage with the past.[13] This shift finds a suggestive parallel in the forefront of museum work today. For this reason, I propose the term "counter-museum" to designate museums like the JCM, which seek to engage visitors as active participants in dynamic, continuing memorial processes as opposed to presenting them with fixed or ossified history through the creation of monolithic, static representations of the past.

At the JCM, visitor-participants are encouraged and led to turn *themselves*—their values, their assumptions and beliefs, their community, their society—into the objects under scrutiny. This process of analysis can be private, internal, shared, and dialogic. It can be engaged in the present, and repeatedly revisited indefinitely into the future. With its innovative blend of curatorial and pedagogical strategies, the museum creates a space in which expertise, experience, and feeling can cross-fertilize. A model for what a successful counter-museum can be, the JCM examines and leads its visitors to engage in dialog and self-reflection on the fraught nature of racism as experienced by everyday people in real life. The JCM insistently inserts into view a shameful shard of American history that has been systematically swept under the carpet, cast far from center, and often belittled or denied through pronouncements that racism is a thing of the past, that racist caricatures are harmlessly humorous, or—worse yet—that they merely reflect the realities of racial difference. The collection of racist memorabilia at the JCM contests such arguments with a stockpile of evidence buttressed by analysis, scholarship, and reflection. As a collection, it demands that viewers acknowledge not only the deeper historical genealogies of these images, but their centrality in both American history and contemporary life. While the JCM uses its authority to situate material in relation to Jim Crow history and culture, visitors are encouraged to apply and reflect upon the implications of this history on their own terms.

The day that I visited, I observed and participated in several discussions with the group of (mainly White) University of Michigan undergraduates with whom I had come. For the most part, students seemed to stay in previously established social groupings, and our subgroup of about twenty all maintained a rather somber demeanor in the presence of these objects. There was some interaction across groups, however, mainly facilitated by the physical movement through the space itself: sometimes people would point to particular representations behind glass and individuals would reposition themselves for better viewing. In contrast to the more energetic exchanges that had taken place in the structured sessions before, there was a lot of silence in the gallery room itself, and the conversations that did take place began in hushed tones with facilitators speaking more loudly as interested visitors clustered around to listen in. Within the gallery, conversations ranged from one-word exclamations ("Damn!" and "Geez!"), to shared memories of encounter with similar objects, to references back to the images we had viewed in the facilitated sessions, to questions about why someone would choose to part with a photo album of KKK activities and rituals, to debates about the talking alligator cookie jar, to audible sighs.

JCM staff interact with visitor-participants, putting their knowledge and theory into practice through teaching, dialog, counsel, and facilitation. Witnessing varying responses on the part of fellow visitors is part of the learning process too. Invariably, some visitors are emotionally affected more immediately and profoundly than others. As a result of viewing the collection, tears have been shed across the racial spectrum, and academic and emotional support is available in person from trained professionals who are prepared to address any personal or interpersonal issues that may arise. The website also offers opportunities for anyone with Internet access to write to the museum staff whose email addresses and phone numbers are publicly available, as are messages from contributors who have agreed to have their writings published. Several letters have been posted by visitors who weeks and even months after their visit are still processing the experience, attesting to new understandings of the world due to their encounter with the JCM. There are also letters from skeptics and critics: people who oppose everything from the museum's existence, to the presence of specific items in the collection, to the preoccupation with racism as a topic of inquiry and debate. Pilgrim, along with other museum staff, regularly answers emails, posts essays (both academic and personal), and provides researchers, students, or people who are just curious with references and research advice.[14]

Attempts to address racism in society today have often been stymied by accusations of "political correctness." Rather than engaging in substantive debate, such critiques foreclose dialog before it has even begun based upon a dubious claim to authority that delegitimizes the purported (and purportedly knowable) intent of the person deemed "PC" without addressing the content that he or she is putting forward. This is a cowardly response to those who think seriously and care deeply about words, images, and representations, and their power to harm, and is itself an example of how inequity is deeply imbricated in not only the words and concepts we use but also the things we assume and the way that we speak (Patterson, 2004: 77).

The JCM offers a way out of the "PC" proponent vs. critic polarization that often underlies the limited discussions of race in the US today. Through the museum's multi-faceted approach, theory and practice inform one another in a continuing, symbiotic relationship that remains relevant to the scholarly world of academe and to the everyday realities of society at large. Through the amassing of a sizeable collection of racist memorabilia, the pursuit of scholarly inquiry, and a commitment to continuing engagement and debate, the JCM is a museum, educational facility, archive, and ongoing experiment that critically complicates—while rendering irrefutably relevant—what "culture wars" rhetoric has denigrated as "political correctness."

When asked by S. C. Dubin what museums are for, the British Museum's director Neil MacGregor answered, "[Museums are] about serious engagement with objects and the ideas that they embody." He also said that they should "inspire a sense of wonder." But at heart, he argued, "a museum's job is to serve a far more radical function: to create the 'right level of doubt' in its audience, to cause them to question the very nature of their society and ultimately to 'change the citizen'" (Dubin, 2006).

The Jim Crow Museum of Racist Memorabilia answers both of these calls with courage, compassion, and a commitment to making the world a better place. By inviting viewer-participants into its learning laboratory, the JCM explores the possibilities for engaging with historically contentious objects in new ways, and toward new ends. As such, the JCM is not a traditional museum, but a *counter-museum* that seeks to use products of intolerance to teach understanding, leveraging the detritus of hate to encourage, assist, and provoke visitors to turn their gazes inward to scrutinize themselves and their society, examining the lasting ways in which images of racist and anti-Black ideas have permeated American culture and beyond. Ultimately, perhaps the small, university-based museum can be the most effective space to invert the big monster that is racism.

Notes

I would like to thank Bradley Taylor for allowing me to accompany him and the members of his Communication Studies 468: Visual Communications class on a field trip to the Jim Crow Museum of Racist Memorabilia on October 25, 2008, and Alice Goff, Bridget Guarasci, Andy Karafa, Erica Lehrer, Cynthia Milton, Lewis and Sheila Patterson, David Pilgrim, Raymond Silverman, Bradley Taylor, and Beatriz Zengotitabengoa for their helpful comments on early drafts of this chapter.

1. Available at http://www.ferris.edu/news/jimcrow/menu.htm [Accessed November 2, 2010].
2. As discussed by Foster (2003), whether to capitalize the terms "Black" and/or "White" continues to be a question of open debate among scholars of race and racism, with compelling and contradictory arguments on all sides. For the purposes of consistency, I capitalize both terms, in keeping with most of the references I quote here.
3. Elaine Gurian identifies the following five categories of museums: object-centered, narrative, client-centered, community, and national (Gurian, 2006 [2002]).
4. Available at http://www.ferris.edu/htmls/news/jimcrow/menu.htm [Accessed July 1, 2010].
5. Not without significant criticism: consider, for instance, Detroit Institute of Arts director Graham Beal who was impugned for leading the recent overhaul of the museum's exhibited content and display, reflecting a conscious shift in the DIA's orientation to appeal to a broader, more inclusive, and local public. See visitor reviews posted on "Yelp.com," available at http://www.yelp.com/biz/detroit-institute-of-arts-detroit [Accessed July 1, 2010]. National Public Radio's 2007 segment "Detroit Museum Accused of 'Dumbing Down' Art," as heard on "Day to Day" from NPR News with host Alex Cohen (November 27). http://www.npr.org/templates/transcript/transcript.php?storyId=16655747 Copyright ©2007 National Public Radio, and Penney, 2010.
6. December 17, 2007. http://www.ferris.edu/jimcrow/values.htm [Accessed July 1, 2010].
7. A dutiful, loyal, and long-suffering house slave, Uncle Tom is the central character in Harriet Beecher Stowe's 1852 novel titled *Uncle Tom's Cabin, or, Life Among the Lowly*. Although the novel played an important role in bolstering the abolitionist movement that was working to end slavery, and even in helping to foment the Civil War, it features highly sentimentalized, stereotypical characters (including the Mammy and "pickaninny" figures).
8. Pilgrim, David. "The Garbage Man: Why I Collect Racist Objects," http://ferris.edu/jimcrow/collect/. Accessed July 1, 2010. Referencing C. Vann Woodward (1974). *The Strange Career of Jim Crow*, 3rd edn. (New York: Oxford University Press). http://www.ferris.edu/jimcrow/collect/ [Accessed July 1, 2010].
9. "Hateful Things" is available at http://www.ferris.edu/htmls/news/jimcrow/traveling/. "THEM" is available at http://www.ferris.edu/htmls/news/jimcrow/traveling2/ [Accessed July 1, 2010].
10. A phenomenon identified and incisively critiqued by Fred Wilson in his 1992 exhibit "Mining the Museum" drawn from the Maryland Historical Society's collection.

11. Seen by many as the precursor to the modern-day museum, curiosity cabinets date back to the Renaissance. These collections of objects were meant to inspire wonder, but also served to order, control, and catalogue otherness, offering owners a platform for sharing personal vignettes and knowledge.
12. A video of this talk is available for viewing on the University of Michigan's Museum Studies Program webpage at: http://www.umich.edu/~ummsp/events/controversy_pilgrim.htm [Accessed July 8, 2010].
13. Parsing Martin Broszat, Young writes that "monuments may not remember events so much as bury them altogether beneath layers of national myths and explanations. As cultural reifications, in this view, monuments reduce or, using Broszat's term, 'coarsen' historical understanding as much as they generate it." (1992: 272)
14. Letters may be found at http://www.ferris.edu/jimcrow/letters/ [Accessed July 1, 2010].

Works Cited

Bamboozled (2000). Dir. Spike Lee. New Line Cinema.

Butler, Shelley Ruth (2007). *Contested Representations: Revisiting "Into the Heart of Africa."* Toronto: University of Toronto Press.

Dubin, S.C. (2006). "Incivilities in Civil(-ized) Places: 'Culture Wars' in Comparative Perspective." In S. Macdonald (ed.). *A Companion to Museum Studies*. Oxford: Blackwell: 477–93.

Foster, Lorne. "The Capitalization of Black and White." *Share: Canada's Largest Ethnic Newspaper*, August 21, 2003, vol. 26, no. 18.

Gurian, Elaine (2006 [2002]). "Choosing Among the Options: An Opinion about Museum Definitions." *Civilizing the Museum*. London: Routledge: 48–56.

Jim Crow Museum of Racist Memorabilia website: http://www.ferris.edu/htmls/news/jimcrow/menu.htm. Accessed July 1, 2010.

Jim Crow's Museum (2004). [DVD] Big Rapids, Michigan: David Pilgrim and Clayton Rye.

Linenthal, Edward T. (1995). *Preserving Memory: The Struggle to Create America's Holocaust Museum*. New York: Columbia University Press.

Linenthal and Tom Engelhardt (1996). *History Wars: The "Enola Gay" and Other Battles for the American Past*. New York: Henry Holt and Company, LLC.

National Public Radio (2007). "Detroit Museum Accused of 'Dumbing Down' Art," as heard on "Day to Day" from NPR News with host Alex Cohen (November 27). http://www.npr.org/templates/transcript/transcript.php?storyId=16655747 *Copyright ©2007 National Public Radio.*

Patterson, Monica Eileen (2004). "Interventions," in David William Cohen and Michael D. Kennedy (eds). *Responsibilities in Crisis: Knowledge Politics and Global Publics*. Ann Arbor: University of Michigan University Library Scholarly Publishing Office, 77.

Penney, David (2010). "Reinventing the Detroit Institute of Arts: The Reinstallation Project 2002–2007." *Curator: The Museum Journal* 52(1): 35–44, 15 Jan.

Pilgrim, David. "The Garbage Man: Why I Collect Racist Objects," http://ferris.edu/jimcrow/collect/. Accessed July 1, 2010. Referencing C. Vann Woodward (1974). *The Strange Career of Jim Crow*, 3rd edn. (New York: Oxford University Press).

Pilgrim, David (2007). "Spoiling Public Spaces: Exhibiting Racist Artifacts in a public Museum," public lecture, University of Michigan Museum Studies Exhibiting Controversy Colloquium, April 5. Also accessible at http://www.umich.edu/~ummsp/events/controversy_pilgrim.htm. Accessed July 8, 2010.

Silverman, Lois (1995). "Visitor Meaning Making in Museums for a New Age." *Curator* 38: 161–70.

Taborsky, Edwina (1990). "The Discursive Object." In Susan Pearce (ed.). *Objects of Knowledge, New Research in Museum Studies, Vol. 1.* (London: The Athlone Press Ltd), 50–77.

"Yelp.com": http://www.yelp.com/biz/detroit-institute-of-arts-detroit. Accessed July 1, 2010.

Young, J. 1992. "The Counter-Monument: Memory against Itself in Germany Today." *Critical Inquiry*, 18(2) (Winter): 267–96.

Young, J. 1993. *The Texture of Memory: Holocaust Memorials and Meaning.* New Haven: Yale University Press.

4
Politics of the Past: Remembering the Rwandan Genocide at the Kigali Memorial Centre

Amy Sodaro

In April 2004, the Kigali Genocide Memorial Centre was dedicated to commemorate the tenth anniversary of the Rwandan genocide. Perched on a hill overlooking the city of Kigali, the center houses a museum with a permanent exhibition, a memorial garden, a small library and nascent documentation center, and mass graves holding the remains of over 250,000 genocide victims. While the museum is built on a neutral site, chosen for its striking location and its availability rather than its meaning to genocide memory, the Kigali Centre strives to be the center of Rwandan genocide remembrance. In this country that is both deeply wounded by the devastation of the genocide, but also furiously trying to put the past behind it in a flurry of development projects, the Kigali Centre seeks to be both a solemn and enduring site of commemoration for survivors and families and an active partner in Rwanda's development.

The Kigali Centre was created under the leadership of a British anti-genocide organization, the Aegis Trust, at the behest of a Rwandan government that was deeply uncertain about how best to memorialize and come to terms with the genocide. Inspired by the UK Beth Shalom Holocaust Centre, which was inspired in turn by Yad Vashem, the Kigali Centre is one of the latest iterations of an international trend in commemorating genocide and atrocity: the memorial museum. More than a museum or a memorial, memorial museums work both to commemorate and to educate, as well as document and preserve the past, collect survivor testimony and details about victims, influence national and international policy to prevent genocide and human rights abuses, and, ultimately, foster democratic culture. Unlike other memorials in Rwanda, which are raw sites of massacre and murder, where the gruesome evidence of the genocide is placed on display and which serve as spaces of mourning and remembrance for their local communities, the Kigali Centre actively engages and utilizes the "difficult knowledge" of the genocide to educate visitors to prevent future genocide, and it ultimately seeks to do this on a regional and international stage.

Memorial museums have emerged out of a newly-perceived obligation on the part of today's nations to face the past—as dreadful as it may be—in the effort to learn its lessons and use its memory to strengthen democratic culture and prevent future violence. Increasingly, the effort to confront the past is tied to democratic aspirations, especially in countries transitioning from conflict and looking to the liberal democratic model for guidance. Collective memory of a shared past, always a tool for nation building, has remained such but has shifted its focus; as Jeffrey Olick writes: "political legitimation depends just as much on collective memory as it ever has but the collective memory is now often one disgusted with itself, a matter of learning the lessons of history more than of fulfilling its promise or remaining faithful to its legacy" (2007: 121–2). As mechanisms of political legitimation, memorial museums seek to address broad, international audiences and issues as they strive to play active roles in development, transition, and democratization. In this the Kigali Centre departs sharply from other memorial efforts throughout the country, which are somber, funereal spaces more akin to graveyards than the active "memory entrepreneurship" model with its broad agenda offered by the Kigali Centre.

This chapter examines the Kigali Memorial Centre as one of the latest examples of this transnational trend in memorialization, which dramatically departs from other genocide memorials in Rwanda; the Kigali Centre was, after all, designed and built by a British organization, whose genesis and inspiration lie in commemoration of the Holocaust. At the same time, as memorial museums are political tools used to legitimate regimes and advance political agendas, the particular Rwandan context cannot be ignored. The Kigali Centre seeks to negotiate the difficulty of genocide remembrance in a country in which perpetrators continue to live next door to victims, justice and reparation have been agonizingly slow, the divisions in society that caused the genocide have not been addressed but simply forced out of sight, and the Tutsi government rules with an iron fist to maintain the precarious peace, often exploiting memory of the genocide to support its political and militaristic agenda. The political and social context of genocide remembrance in Rwanda compromises the Kigali Centre's ambitious goals of fostering tolerance and reconciliation and working to prevent genocide. Rather, this chapter argues, genocide memory in Rwanda—and specifically in the Kigali Centre, as the "official" site of genocide remembrance—is often politicized by the current regime to legitimate its anti-democratic policies and advance its political agenda, often at the expense of the victims and survivors.

4.1 After the genocide: Rwanda sixteen years later

In Rwanda the genocide is everywhere—in the purple banners that dot the country, imploring Rwandans never to forget; in the ubiquitous churches where bones are stacked as testament to what happened; and in the haunted look of survivors who are not only trying to deal with their memories, but with the day-to-day struggle to survive. But in many ways, it is also hardly visible, especially in Kigali: as the Rwandan government tries to put the genocide behind it, the fast pace of development means that new buildings, roads, and commercial complexes have obliterated many sites of massacre and conceal the devastation of what happened so recently. However, the official government position, which claims that there are no Hutus and Tutsis, only Rwandans, and zealously privileges looking forward into the future (as opposed to back into the past) under the guise of national unity,[1] belies the truth of Rwanda's precarious situation and masks what is often an authoritarian, highly controlling, exclusively Tutsi, and fundamentally undemocratic government (Reyntjens, 2004).

Immediately after the genocide, Rwanda experienced massive displacement and chaos. Up to two million Hutus fled the country fearing revenge, most settling in refugee camps in Congo, then Zaire; many others were slaughtered by the Rwandese Patriotic Front (RPF)[2] as they took the country and stopped the genocide; over one million Rwandans were internally displaced; and over half a million Tutsis that left the country following the independence of 1959 returned to Rwanda from exile, called back by the newly victorious RPF government. While trouble brewed in Congo as the Rwandan *interahamwe*[3] terrorized the population and thousands of Hutu refugees died in the abhorrent camp conditions, the new Rwandan government set about trying to rebuild a country that was literally in ruins.

Foreign aid poured in, "driven by an acute guilt syndrome after the genocide," and the West stood firmly behind the victorious RPF (Reyntjens, 2004: 179). Meanwhile, the Tutsi government has consolidated power—a fact that became strikingly obvious in August 2010 when Paul Kagame won re-election with 93 percent of the vote, after effectively eliminating all opposition. Since 1994, in the name of unity and reconciliation, the government has forbidden mention of ethnicity, and continues to accuse anyone who opposes or questions its policies of genocide ideology—a very serious accusation (Reyntjens, 2004). Increasingly, any action or speech against the government, especially mention of the RPF's human rights abuses,[4] is deemed "divisionism" and is subject to punishment. While the international community pours money and aid into the country to support the government's ambitious development plans,[5] human and civil rights have come under increased pressure in the purported fight against divisionism and genocide ideology. There is concern today that Rwanda "is experiencing not democracy and reconciliation but dictatorship and exclusion" and that it is strikingly similar politically and socially to pre-genocide Rwanda (Reyntjens, 2004: 177).

In addition to the troubling anti-democratic tendencies of the Tutsi government, the problem of justice in post-genocide Rwanda is far from resolved and is further straining ethnic tensions. With over 100,000 individuals accused of crimes related to genocide, both the International Criminal Tribunal for Rwanda and Rwanda's broken judicial system are wholly inadequate. To attempt to overcome this problem, in 2000 the Rwandan government decided that the vast majority of those accused would be tried in local or provincial *gacaca*,[6] a traditional form of dispute resolution adapted in the post-genocide context, which many today see as a tool for reconciliation and truth-telling in addition to delivering justice. However, the process has been laden with problems and outsiders and Rwandans are increasingly skeptical that they are indeed contributing to reconciliation *or* justice. Many worry that they are instead fueling the flames of residual ethnic tensions (Rettig, 2008; Buckley-Zistel, 2006).

Within this post-genocide context, survivors and their families often feel forgotten and disenfranchised (Buckley-Zistel, 2006). Many who continue to live in fear of the other group have no option but to return to their village and live among those who tried to kill them. The country's rapid pace of development and the ambitious plans of the government have left many survivors behind in abject poverty. Many lost everything in the genocide—not just family and loved ones, but their homes, farms, and livelihood. The government has enacted very limited material reparations for the survivors, but they are grossly insufficient in regard to actual need. Symbolic reparations have also been lacking.

Throughout the country there are numerous memorials. The most prominent are schools and churches where some of the largest massacres occurred when Tutsi and moderate Hutu families from the surrounding hills sought protection from their murderous neighbors. These memorials are mostly left as they were found—they have been cleaned up, but the bones or bodies and clothing have simply been piled on shelves or benches (see Figure 4.1). They are raw and incredibly powerful. In Murambi, one roams through the now-silent school grounds, uncertain of what to look for; then a strange smell slowly grows stronger until the visitor comes across room upon room of desiccated bodies, preserved in lime and laid out, grotesque and prostrate, on never-ending pallets in a terrible and tangible portrait of genocide. In Nyamata, one wanders the church pews heaped with clothing, stained with blood, able to touch this or that personal belonging, before descending into a crypt stacked with bones. In Ntarama, one stands in the ruins of a room that was filled with terrified people and burned almost to the ground; bits of bone and hair litter the blackened floor and next door, in the Sunday school, blood still stains the wall.

These memorials are very much local sites; they were established and continue to be used as spaces of remembrance primarily by survivors and victims' families from the surrounding hills. Occasionally international visitors or groups from different provinces visit, but the memorials are principally the cemeteries of those killed in the genocide and their purpose is mourning first, warning against genocide second. Their display of bones and bodies is also completely unlike Western forms of memorialization, which typically do not display human remains. The very raw, unsanitized nature of the Rwandan memorials and especially the stacks of human bones has perhaps as its only form of comparison the killing fields of Cambodia, especially Choeung Ek, where visitors walk over bones, teeth, and other remains, to a stupa stacked with skulls. Both the Rwandan memorials and Choeung Ek lay the gruesome evidence out in a shocking and damning condemnation of the brutality of the genocide. And indeed, the bones and bodies are evidence; while arguments about whether the remains should be buried abound, the tangible fact of their existence would seem to preclude any form of denial or revisionism.[7]

The Rwandan memorials come alive during the period of mourning, when some of the bones are ceremonially buried in mass graves and commemorative ceremonies are held. However, there is little "curation" by the government and virtually no interpretation for visitors who are not familiar with the events of the particular site. Maintenance of the sites is essentially left up to the surrounding community and guides or caretakers are very poorly paid if at all. One does find the occasional guide, usually a survivor from the site, but it is clear that these are spaces of remembrance and mourning—graveyards—for those who

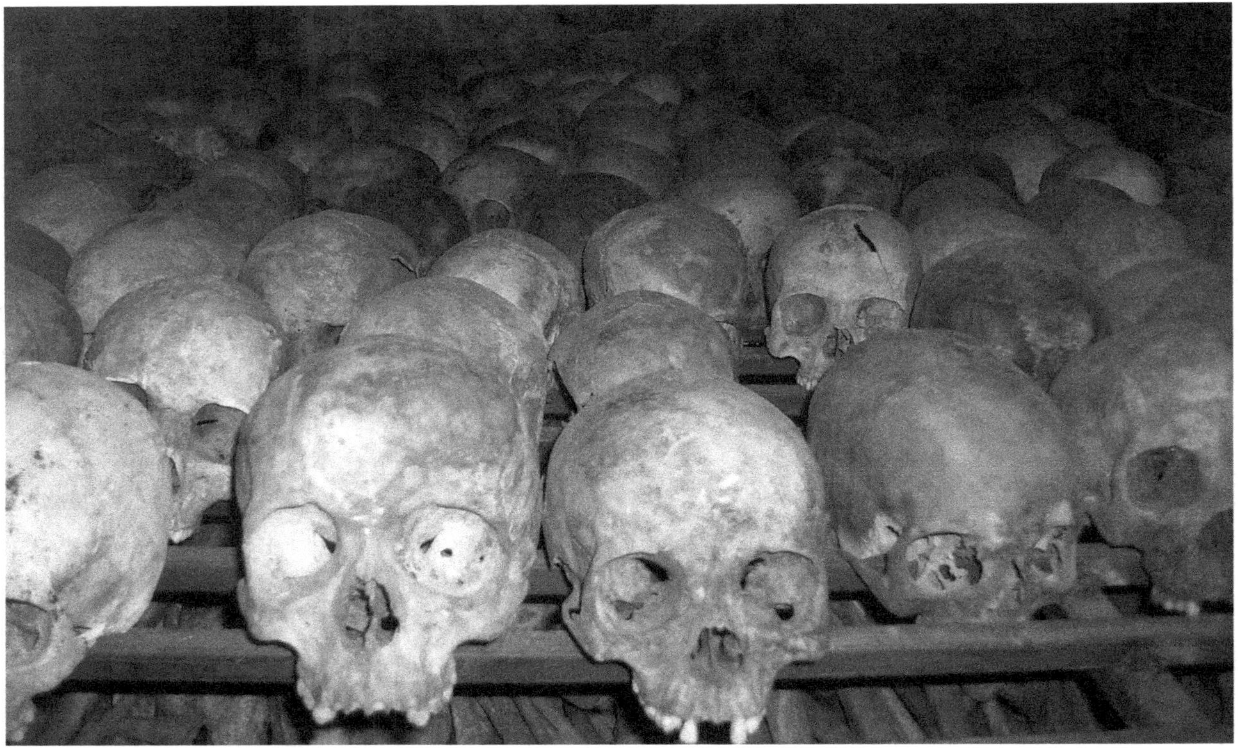

Figure 4.1 Nyamata Memorial, Rwanda. (Photograph by Amy Sodaro.)

survived the massacres. And at each memorial there are concerns about upkeep and maintenance, a lack of funds, and worry about what will happen in the future to these very important spaces of memory.[8]

It is in this complicated environment that the Kigali Genocide Memorial Centre was conceived to give voice and acknowledgment to victims and survivors, to educate future generations against the divisions that sparked the genocide, to preserve the truth of what happened, and to foster reconciliation, forgiveness, and democratic culture. However, as memory of the genocide is often wielded by the government to enforce dictatorial policies and many Rwandans feel that national unity is a myth, the Kigali Centre, as Rwanda's national memorial, is often compromised in its efforts.

4.2 The Kigali Genocide Memorial Centre

While across the country, the sites of massacres and death were preserved as simple and often crude memorials, in Kigali, Mayor Theoneste Mutsindashyaka had plans for something different: a national site of genocide remembrance.[9] The Kigali City Council donated the Gisozi site, which, unlike the other memorial sites, has no particular importance vis-à-vis the genocide, and the mayor and officials in the Ministry of Culture immediately set about trying to determine what kind of memorial would be appropriate. As they began to conceptualize a Rwandan memorial, they visited Yad Vashem in Jerusalem and several Holocaust sites in Europe, which they considered too large, elaborate, and expensive for Kigali. They also visited the Beth Shalom Holocaust Centre in the UK and there found a much better approximation of what they were looking for.

The Beth Shalom Holocaust Centre was created by brothers James and Stephen Smith who, moved by a visit to Yad Vashem, decided that the UK needed a similar site of remembrance. They created the UK Holocaust Centre in the mid-1990s to be a place for survivors to tell their stories and for young generations to learn the history of the Holocaust and the dangers of racism and intolerance. Together with the Holocaust Centre they founded the Aegis Trust, an organization focused on preventing contemporary genocide. With Aegis, the Smith brothers visited Rwanda in 2000, traveling the country to speak with survivors and visit sites of the genocide. They were not new to working in Africa, and had helped to develop the Cape Town Holocaust Centre, which opened in 1999 as the first Holocaust museum in Africa, for which they had created a small exhibit on the Rwandan genocide. Their familiarity with the Rwandan genocide and their experience in Cape Town, as well as the UK Holocaust Centre's small scale and focus on survivors, made the Aegis Trust a natural choice to lead the development of a Rwandan memorial in the eyes of Kigali's mayor. The Smith brothers were concerned that it was too early to create a memorial and were ambivalent about the idea of a Western organization imposing ideas about how to memorialize Rwanda's tragedy. But at the same time they were convinced that memorials can help heal a community and prevent future violence, especially in the case of Rwanda, and warily agreed to participate in planning discussions about the Rwandan memorial.

Mayor Mutsindashyaka described his plan for the memorial: a darkened crypt filled with bones; in the darkness, a soundtrack of screaming, pleading, and machetes falling on their targets that would make the visitor experience that horror of those 100 days. Worried that this was not the proper reparation and acknowledgment that the survivors needed, and that it would inadequately educate younger generations about the genocide, the Smith brothers agreed to take control of the project. As part of the agreement, the city of Kigali donated the land and agreed to cover the cost of maintaining the building. Aegis was responsible for raising money for the museum and education center, and the center's operation. Money began to trickle in, with the first donation coming from Bill Clinton's foundation, but it was not until December 2003, just four months before the planned anniversary dedication, that enough funds were secured to complete the project.[10] Working day and night, the Smiths and a team of 50 Rwandans drafted the exhibition narrative in Kinyarwanda, English, and French; installed the exhibition panels, which had been constructed in the UK; built the first of the mass graves;[11] planted the memorial rose gardens, and finished the entire museum and complex in time for a ceremonial opening in April. (See Plate 4.1.)

4.3 The permanent exhibit

The permanent exhibition of the Kigali Centre has three parts: "Wasted Lives," which examines genocide around the world; "Genocide," which tells the story of the Rwandan genocide; and a memorial to the children killed in the genocide. The purpose of the exhibition is to tell the story of the Rwandan genocide and place it within the broader history of genocide. This contextualization is intended to aid the visitor in understanding how the genocide could have happened:

> It attempts to show the complexity, rather than the polarity, of human interaction, but with the underlying intent to demonstrate

> that racism and discrimination create conditions for violence and mass murder. It demonstrates that there was a series of choices that people faced rather than their being subject to inevitability.[12]

"Wasted Lives" contextualizes genocide internationally and historically through a chronological description of the major genocides of the twentieth century, including the genocide of the Hereros in today's Namibia, the Armenian genocide in 1915, the Holocaust, the Cambodian genocide, and genocide in former Yugoslavia. Beginning with the UN definition, the exhibit attempts to distill the elements that these genocides have in common and to detail the background and history of each. Through the use of texts, photographs, and film, the exhibit takes the visitor through the violent twentieth century.

The exhibit consists of only three small rooms and therefore cannot address the complexity of each genocide. However, certain themes are emphasized to connect these genocides to what happened in Rwanda, such as the fact that genocide is not the result of a spontaneous hatred but relies on planned and sustained processes of dehumanization, and that genocide destroys many more lives than those who are murdered. Because of the amount of information and the limited space, the exhibit is dense and sometimes seems arbitrary; nevertheless, its point is to demonstrate the waste and horror of genocide, which becomes evident as the visitor tallies the sum of its destruction in the twentieth century. It also reminds the visitor that genocide is not unique to Africa or the "ancient tribal hatreds" in Rwanda, as the international community might like to think, but has occurred in the most civilized counties in the West and results from planned and meticulous policy decisions.[13]

After "Wasted Lives," the visitor is led to "Genocide," which radiates out from a memorial rotunda in three sections: "Before," "During," and "After." Like "Wasted Lives" and following the curatorial and exhibition strategies of memorial museums around the world, "Genocide" uses a combination of text, photographs, film footage, artifacts, and recorded survivor testimony to tell a narrative history of what happened. It also follows a controlled path that leads the visitor chronologically through the build-up to and aftermath of the genocide. "Before" starts with the history of Rwanda before colonization and depicts a harmonious Rwanda of one people peacefully co-existing. The language is that of unity: "We held elections [. . .]," "We did not choose to be colonized [. . .]" and the point is clear that the white colonizers destroyed this harmony. Under colonization, first at the hands of Germany then, after World War I, Belgium, race science and ethnic classifications enforced by identity cards were introduced into Rwandan society, beginning the dangerous division of the Rwandan people. Following the current government's explanation of the genocide, the museum's narrative emphasizes that ethnic division and strife were imposed top-down by the colonists (Reyntjens, 2004).

The exhibit goes on to describe Rwanda's independence of 1959 and the further divisions in society that it wrought. Tracing the rise of genocide ideology in Rwanda post-independence, the exhibit brings the visitor to what it calls the "Path to the Final Solution," drawing explicit parallels to the Holocaust and reminding the visitor of the museum's provenance out of the (Western) tradition of Holocaust memorialization. Here, the exhibit tells of the 700,000 Tutsis exiled from Rwanda between 1959 and 1973, the periodic massacres of those remaining, the RPF's heroic struggle for rule of law and equality, the rise of propaganda such as the Hutu Ten Commandments, and the incipient use of radio to spread hatred. "Path to the Final Solution" tells the tale of genocide carefully planned and methodically executed, stressing that the genocide had been brewing since before Rwanda gained independence. "Before" brings the visitor to that April night when the President's plane exploded over Kigali, before the country was plunged into 100 days of horror.

"During the Genocide" seems to stick most closely to the mayor's initial idea of the dark labyrinth of terror and attempts to convey the absolute horror of the genocide. Terrifying testimony from survivors plays in the background and video screens vividly depict the violence and brutality: bodies lying in the waterways, machete wounds, and burned villages, churches, and schools. There are display cases stacked with machetes and panels describing the evils inflicted on women and children and the torture of many victims before their slaughter. There is a wall of panels describing some of the most chilling massacres in the churches of Rwanda where families gathered, seeking shelter in the house of God.

Leaving this part of the exhibit, the visitor encounters a few panels about resistance and the silence of the international community. It is at this point that one realizes that throughout "During" despite the horror, graphic details, and incomprehensible brutality, very little blame has been ascribed at all. Not only is the role of the international community and the church minimized in the permanent exhibit, but any sense of collective blame is missing. The exhibition tells of the *interahamwe* and it describes some of the most influential individual perpetrators, but on the whole there is a noticeable lack of blame ascribed to Hutus—even extremists—or anyone else in Rwanda. Rather, the exhibit depicts the collective victimization of a Rwandan people torn apart by colonial forces.

"After" takes the visitor through the chaos and upheaval immediately following the genocide as millions of refugees fled the country, plagued by guilt, fear, and confusion. It describes the refugee camps in Congo, where international aid was finally delivered—to those who had perpetrated the genocide—and which quickly became hotbeds for the dissemination of genocide ideology as well as deadly diseases like cholera. It tells of survivors' attempts to rebuild their lives and of the long-term consequences, such as the alarming rates of HIV/AIDS in the tens of thousands of women who were raped. It describes the efforts to enact justice through the International Criminal Tribunal for Rwanda (ICTR) and the gacaca, while highlighting the impossibility of justice ever being fully delivered. "After" ends with a few panels on the need to confront and remember the past, which read as a justification for the memorial center's existence. The panels remind the visitor that although it is painful to remember, memory may serve as a form of redemption if it acts as a warning that prevents future violence. They also stress the center's prioritization of education as the way forward and underline the dual goals and necessities of education and commemoration.

With this, the visitor leaves the interpretive parts of the exhibit and enters the dimly-lit and eerie memorial rooms. The first has a large screen showing survivor testimony and the walls are covered in photographs. There are family photos, ID cards, and candid snapshots—thousands of them. They are loosely clipped to wires, and are often taken by visitors who know the individual or who are reminded by the photo of lost loved ones. Unlike the photos from the Nazi concentration camps or the Cambodian detention center, Tuol Sleng, which seem distant due to their black and white, grainy quality, these photos are in color and feel immediate.

In the next memorial room, the walls are lined with bones laid out in well-lit display cases. Like the other genocide memorials throughout Rwanda, this room depicts the extreme violence of the genocide; however, by placing the bones behind glass in a neat and symmetrical display, the effect is much more sanitized and orderly than the gaping wounds of the other memorials. Long bones methodically line the room, with skulls in a row in the center; some have visible fractures, perhaps caused by machetes. There is a display case filled with personal artifacts: shoes, a pipe, keys, a rosary. In the background the names of the victims are read by a disembodied voice, giving the visitor a sense of the scale of the genocide. The final memorial room also screens survivor testimony and here the walls are hung with clothing from the victims, another trope referencing the other memorials throughout Rwanda, but sanitized and hauntingly beautiful in the Kigali Centre. Together with traditional Rwandan clothing are modern, familiar touches for the Western visitor: a Superman sheet, a Cornell sweatshirt. Again, this memorial room seeks to draw the visitor in and demonstrate that this did not happen in some distant place long ago, but to people *just like you.*

The final element of the permanent exhibit is the memorial to the children, which consists of about a dozen large photographs of Rwandan children accompanied by plaques listing the child's name and age and a few facts about the child: favorite food, favorite sport, best friend, last words, and a short description of how the child was killed ("hacked to death by a machete," for example). The simplicity of the memorial and the unthinkable brutality that it conveys is particularly powerful. The visitor exits through another room of photos, which are there for the taking, if a photograph can be any consolation. This is the most emotionally powerful part of the exhibition and elicits a deeply affective response in the visitor not unlike the memorials in Murambi or Ntarama; in this way it complements the historical and intellectual experience of the exhibit and provides the affective commemorative counterpart to the pedagogical strategies used in the rest of the museum.

4.3 The politics of Rwandan genocide memory

Beyond the permanent exhibit, the Kigali Centre has ambitious plans to become the first genocide studies center in Central Africa, with robust documentation, education, and conference facilities. These plans reflect the current global need to create memorials that do more than solemnly remember the past, instead using the "difficult knowledge" of genocide for education and prevention on a national and international scale. However, despite the center's ambitions, only an estimated 20 percent of the Rwandan population visited the center in its first five years because it is simply too expensive to get to Kigali; and even though the center has a sophisticated website, most of the population relies on radio for information and has no Internet access. There is clearly a disconnect between the international ambitions of the Kigali Centre and the reality in Rwanda, though the goals are admirable and the center is doing what it can to advance them. However, despite these obstacles, it is Rwanda's political situation that presents the greatest challenge to the center's efforts to translate memory of the genocide into education, peace, and democratic culture.

In any memorial museum, there is both a danger and an inevitability that the museum will serve as an alternative to material reparation, justice, and an actual confrontation of the past, becoming instead a symbol onto which a society can project its memory and divest itself of the burden of the past. As James Young has noted, there is "an inverse proportion between the memorialization of the past and its contemplation and study . . . In shouldering the memory-work, monuments may relieve viewers of their memory burden" (Young, 1993: 5).

Though Rwanda presents a very different context than the late-twentieth-century Holocaust memorialization to which Young refers —in fully reconstructed societies in which there is a real threat that the Holocaust will be forgotten—in Rwanda the danger of allowing the Kigali Centre to replace genuine efforts to deal with the past is real. It is a distinct possibility that the center is indeed intended as some kind of alternative to actual confrontation of the present-day reverberations of the past and meaningful acknowledgment and concern for the victims. The government, in its effort to move forward, stifles or simplifies any nuanced discussion of what caused the genocide. It has failed to address adequately even the most basic needs of the victims of the genocide, such as housing, land, and livelihood, not to mention its failure to attend to the deep psychological wounds that will haunt generations, and it has neglected the memorial sites throughout the country like Murambi, Nyamata, and Ntarama, which are sacred to the individuals who live near them. In some ways the Kigali Centre appears to be a Band-Aid applied by the government to soothe the international community and its own people, legitimate its standing as a "democratic" nation that has come to terms with its past, and avoid addressing the complexity of pre- and post-genocide Rwanda as well as ethnic conflict in the region.

It is essential to remember that in the case of the Kigali Centre, to prevent genocide means something different than it does at other Holocaust and genocide museums around the world: it means to prevent *the very same* (or directly inversed) genocide from occurring again. This is a burden that other memorial museums do not have; for them to prevent genocide is an abstract mandate with room for flexibility. For the Kigali Centre, to prevent genocide means to prevent or hinder the violent resurgence of genocidal ideology that led to the massacre of almost one million people in 100 days. This ideology still exists in the schools and homes of many Rwandans[14] and continues to take countless lives in the region every day.

The challenge of prevention in the Kigali Centre is enormous, and it is dangerous. As we have seen, the government has imposed a version of the past and the present that at times diverges from reality. The genocide, according to both the government and the narrative of the museum, was caused by divisions in Rwandan society forced by colonial rulers who planted seeds of hatred. This narrative creates a sense of collective victimization that places the blame for the genocide largely on a few "bad apples" and a deadly and pervasive ideology emerging from colonization. Meanwhile the government claims that there is no ethnicity in Rwanda—just one people, reunited after a century of division wrought by the white colonizers. Both of these narratives avoid discussion of ethnic divisions that have plagued the country since before 1959 and that have not disappeared in the present, but have been forced out of sight—perhaps the most dangerous place for such divisions. The narratives also obscure the fact that countless Rwandans murdered their neighbors at the command of an overpowering, mono-ethnic, all-controlling government, which sounds disturbingly similar to the present Kagame regime in Rwanda, especially in light of recent revelations about its actions in the Democratic Republic of Congo (DRC), where the Kagame government is committing human rights abuses in the name of genocide prevention.

There are serious, lasting implications of the genocide that continue to play out in the region that are overlooked in both the Kigali Centre and the government's vision of the future. By packaging genocide remembrance in a well-curated, compelling, and sophisticated museum, the genocide itself becomes a moment in time; it is contained and discrete. Not only does the museum potentially bear the burden of memory of—and confrontation with—the genocide, it establishes the genocide as a distinct event with a beginning, middle, and end, and firmly sets its precedents in the Holocaust and other twentieth-century genocides. This narrative erases any urgency or historical connection with what is happening in the region today as the Rwandan Patriotic Army (RPA), the current manifestation of the RPF, takes its fight into neighboring countries—especially the DRC, where millions have died in the years since the genocide.

The danger in Rwanda, with a government that has such total control of society and state, is that genocide remembrance in official spaces like the Kigali Centre can be manipulated in a way that advances the government's political and military goals rather than seeking redress for the victims and attempting to learn from the genocide. Claudine Vidal has written about the politicization of genocide commemorations by the regime in Rwanda, commenting that:

> The ceremonies organized by the regime reveal an inevitable relation of power, first because they capture the silent words of the victims giving them a meaning determined by contemporary goals, and

> second because they take over the private mourning of the survivors and transform it into a collective mourning in the name of considerations that are not theirs [. . .] at every commemoration, those in power have instrumentalized the representation of the genocide in the context of the political conflicts at the time.
>
> (Cited in Reyntjens, 2008: 201)

While the Kigali Centre is not fully under the auspices of the government, it is a public-private partnership and the government has a strong say in how—and whether—it operates. It is very likely that in the acknowledgment and remembrance that it promotes and provides, it has done more good for the Rwandan people than harm. But the past is always remembered according to the dictates of the present and there is real danger in Rwanda that remembrance of the genocide in the national memorial museum is not about the victims and survivors, but about the present political agenda of a borderline dictatorial regime.

4.4 Conclusion

A number of scholars of memory have written about the late-twentieth-century shift from hegemonic narratives used to underpin the power of the nation state to the emergence of alternative narratives and a democratic fragmentation of memory (Le Goff, 1996; Torpey, 2003). At first glance, the Kigali Centre is troubling because it was designed and conceived by a British organization, implying an imperial memory project foisted on Rwandans—the internationalization of memory gone wrong. And indeed, it is not at all evident that a museum is how Rwandans would choose to remember the genocide, especially when considering the other sites of remembrance in the country. However, there are strong national forces at play in the museum as well, and these are perhaps more troubling. The Kigali Centre, rather than self-reflexively facing the past and trying to learn from it, in many ways simply reinforces the government's hegemonic narrative of the genocide. Rather than fragmenting memory and narratives, including those that look critically at the causes and effects of the genocide, in the Kigali Centre genocide memory appears consolidated into the single, dominant version that reinforces the goals and dogma of the government. This consolidation threatens to usurp for political purposes the memory of those who most need remembrance and acknowledgment, and potentially undermines the Kigali Centre's goals of learning from the past, preventing genocide and human rights abuses in the future, and healing this country that is so deeply wounded.

Genocide remembrance in Rwanda is a difficult project, and the Kigali Centre is ambitious in its attempts to negotiate it. Part of the transnational trend toward memorial museums, it attempts to come to terms with the past and rise to its present-day demands in an effort to build a better future. At the same time, remembrance alone in Rwanda is not enough to guarantee a peaceful future. At the moment, the anti-democratic inclinations of the current regime are deeply troubling and indicate that perhaps the genocide is not so far behind Rwanda, and that "never again" might be more urgent than ever before.

Notes

1. In 1998 the government created the National Unity and Reconciliation Commission (NURC) as a semi-autonomous body intended to educate about and promote unity and reconciliation. Available at http://www.nurc.gov.rw/index.php?option=com_content&view=article&id=73&Itemid=58> [Accessed October 22, 2010].
2. The Rwandan Patriotic Front was formed in the 1980s by Tutsi refugees living in Uganda. The RPF invaded Rwanda in 1990, beginning the civil war that would end in the 1994 genocide.
3. In Kinyarwanda, *interahamwe* means "those who stand together" and refers to the armed Hutu militias which were largely responsible for perpetrating the genocide.
4. The October 2010 UN report about atrocities committed in Congo by the Rwandan army is perhaps the most serious international test of the Kagame regime, which has enjoyed relative impunity for crimes committed in post-genocide Rwanda and Congo.
5. These ambitious plans include Rwanda's Vision 2020 (see http://www.enterprise-development.org/download.aspx ?id=548 [Accessed October 22, 2010]); recent events, however, such as the election and the UN report may slow international aid as Rwanda's human rights records comes increasingly under scrutiny.
6. *Gacaca*, which comes from the word for "lawn," were used traditionally to mete out restorative, not punitive, justice; following the genocide they are used to gather evidence, judge the accused, and hand down criminal sentences (Rettig, 2008).
7. For a discussion of the display of bones in Rwanda, see Anna Maria Brandstetter (2010), "Contested Pasts: The Politics of Remembrance in Post-Genocide Rwanda," Sixth Ortelius Lecture, Netherlands Institute for Advanced Study in the Humanities and Social Sciences. Available at http://www.nias.knaw.nl/Content/NIAS/Publicaties/Ortelius/ Ortelius_Lecture_6.pdf [Accessed October 28, 2010].
8. Guides at Ntarama, Nyamata, and Nyarubuye described the lack of funds to maintain the sites and their resultant inability to follow through on plans to create more interpretive memorials.

9. Research for this chapter was conducted in Rwanda in June 2008. Much of the detail about the Kigali Centre comes from the author's interviews and discussions with staff of the Kigali Centre and Aegis Trust, including: James Smith, Director, Aegis Trust; Freddy Mutanguha, Director, Kigali Memorial Centre; Steven Robinson, Rwanda Development Officer, Aegis Trust; Honore Gatera, Head Guide, Kigali Memorial Centre.
10. Additional funding was secured from the Waterman foundation in the UK, the Swedish and Belgian governments, the British department of education, and others.
11. The mass graves at Gisozi hold remains that have been uncovered throughout Kigali. Each year during the period of mourning additional remains that have been discovered are buried at Gisozi and other memorial sites.
12. Available at http://www.kigalimemorialcentre.org/old/centre/exhibition.html [Accessed October 20, 2010].
13. Samantha Power, in *A Problem From Hell*, describes how Western journalists and officials chose to frame the Rwandan genocide as a product of "ancient tribal hatreds" that go back far beyond colonialism in order to avoid using the term genocide and absolve the West from any blame or any obligation to intervene (Power, 2002: 355).
14. See, for instance, http://news.bbc.co.uk/2/hi/africa/7194827.stm [Accessed October 20, 2010].

Works cited

Buckley-Zistel, Susanne (2006). "Remembering to Forget: Chosen Amnesia as a Strategy for Local Coexistence in Post-Genocide Rwanda." *Africa* 76(2): 131–50.

Halbwachs, Maurice (1980). *The Collective Memory*. Translated from French by Francis J. Ditter Jr and Vida Yazdi Ditter. New York: Harper & Row.

Le Goff, Jacques (1996). *History and Memory*. Translated from French by Steven Rendall and Elizabeth Claman. New York: Columbia University Press.

Olick, Jeffrey, K. (2007). *The Politics of Regret: On Collective Memory and Historical Responsibility*. New York: Routledge.

Power, Samantha (2002). *A Problem from Hell: America and the Age of Genocide*. New York: Harper Perennial.

Rettig, Max (2008). "Gacaca: Truth, Justice, and Reconciliation in Postconflict Rwanda?" *African Studies Review* 51(3): 25–50.

Reyntjens, Filip (2004). "Rwanda, Ten Years on: From Genocide to Dictatorship." *African Affairs* 103: 177–210.

Torpey, John (2003). "Introduction." In John Torpey (ed.). *Politics and the Past: On Repairing Historical Injustices*. Lanham, MD: Rowman and Littlefield: 1–34.

Young, James E. (1993). *The Texture of Memory: Holocaust Memorials and Meaning*. New Haven: Yale University Press.

Part II
Visualizing the Past

Introduction

Monica Eileen Patterson

Calls to confront the atrocities of the past face many challenges. Publics may resist feeling implicated or held accountable for others' suffering, or be simply indifferent to it. Even among sympathetic constituencies, there is the danger of oversaturation and fatigue; a sense of numbing or even paralysis can result from "overexposure." Of course the thresholds for each of these domains vary considerably among individuals and groups, and these three responses are by no means exhaustive or mutually exclusive. But as the authors in this section discuss, visual materials and images can provide unique ways to breach or circumvent these barriers.

In many societies, the visual possesses significant truth-value in its capacity to represent both the irrefutable facts of violence and the interpretative dimensions of its emotional and (inter)personal impact. For instance, documentary photography has considerable evidentiary authority when it comes to providing proof of historical abuses. Along with artistic renderings in a variety of mediums, photographs can evocatively portray the humanity of victims, and open avenues for empathic connection between viewer and subject. But they can also overwhelm and alienate. Ethical issues abound in the reproduction and (re)presentation of images of human suffering and there is always a danger that for some, further violence is produced by displaying or looking. Visual art has the potential to explore perspectives, experiences, and the feelings that emerge from them. As a more open-ended, often less literal form of expression, art can provide a safe(r) space for addressing challenging issues. But it can also be powerfully persuasive and productive, even playing a role in complex processes of nation building, as the authors in this section reveal.

Consciously constructed as alternative spaces, exhibits can serve as important social arenas and performative sites where social and personal silences can be broken, offering a model for curation as an aide to other related representational and activist practices. It is in the constellation of features—photographic evidence, narrative, written testimony, oral interpretations offered by memory workers at display venues, and the dialogue and exchange between them and their viewers—that the possibilities for change are the greatest. But the benefits of witnessing are unevenly spread across varying vectors of access, representational power, control, and authority. In expanding the "contact zone" of an experience, exhibits can seed broader, more inclusive conversations and prompt reflection about experiences that are removed from one's own first-hand encounters.

5
Living Historically through Photographs in Post-Apartheid South Africa: Reflections on Kliptown Museum, Soweto

Darren Newbury

Established at the beginning of the twentieth century, Kliptown is among the oldest of the urban settlements that comprise the vast township of Soweto, which lies to the south-west of Johannesburg. Together with townships such as Sophiatown and Alexandra, Kliptown was one of the few places in South Africa where blacks could own property, and for the first part of the century it was home to a rich mix of different cultural and racial groups. Its national historical significance derives, however, from the mass political gathering that took place there on an abandoned patch of land during two days in June 1955. The Congress of the People was convened by a coalition of anti-apartheid organizations led by the African National Congress (ANC), known as the Congress Alliance. Other members of the alliance were the South African Indian Congress, the South African Congress of Trade Unions, the Coloured People's Congress and the Congress of Democrats. The meeting represented the culmination of a year's work gathering views from across the country and across racial lines that were synthesized into a declaration of political values and human rights to form the basis of collective opposition to apartheid. Nearly 3000 delegates were elected to attend the meeting in Kliptown, which would ratify the final form of what was known as the Freedom Charter. Enshrined in the Charter were commitments to equality, access to education, trade union rights, the redistribution of wealth, and, most importantly, a non-racial democracy in South Africa: "We, the People of South Africa, declare for all our country and the world to know: that South Africa belongs to all who live in it, black and white, and that no government can justly claim authority unless it is based on the will of all the people." Just under a year later the Charter was officially adopted by the ANC, providing the cornerstone of policy throughout the struggle against apartheid, even if its more socialist commitments would be the subject of re-examination as the prospect of power became a reality.

The Congress of the People was without question an event of historical significance, but once the meeting had closed, the empty patch of land, subsequently known as Freedom Square, returned to its former abandoned state and would remain that way for the best part of the next 50 years. Not until the post-apartheid period, with the opportunities that have opened up in the space between tourism, development, and public history, would there be an attempt to reinvest the site with the memory of what took place on June 25 and 26, 1955.

In a series of faltering steps, the Kliptown Open Air Museum and the now renamed Walter Sisulu Square of Dedication have taken shape as a site of national memory.[1] New plans for the site were first mooted in the early 1990s, when proposals were put forward for commercial development. However, given the historic significance of Kliptown, these plans proved controversial and prompted the involvement of the National Monuments Council (Noble, 2008). In 2002, with the backing of the Johannesburg City Council, and funding provided through the Johannesburg Development Agency, a competition for the redesign of the square was launched and its development as a heritage site began to take shape, in the context of the regeneration of the wider area. The business plan focused on heritage, education, and tourism, and envisaged that, as well as responding to the local community, the site would attract visiting school groups from Soweto and Johannesburg, day-trippers from greater Johannesburg (including white South Africans who had never visited a township before), and international tourists. Visitor analysis suggested that Kliptown appealed mainly to independent travelers with a particular interest or prior knowledge of South African history, and therefore a key aim was to give the area a more prominent position in the Soweto heritage landscape for it to become a more mainstream tourist attraction.

The museum was joining a well developed post-apartheid heritage landscape, which now contains several substantial memorial museums as well as numerous smaller displays and sites of memory (Coombes, 2003; Marschall, 2010; Nieves and Hlongwane, 2007). The Hector Pieterson Museum (opened in 2002), which commemorates the 1976 Soweto Uprising, is situated in Orlando, a few miles from Kliptown, and just beyond Soweto on the outskirts of Johannesburg is the Apartheid Museum (opened in 2001). Contributing to a topography of struggle and resistance, the apartheid heritage trail (the "Struggle Route") around Soweto also includes the former houses of Nelson Mandela and Desmond Tutu, the Regina Mundi church and Avalon cemetery. Further afield, in Port Elizabeth there is the Red Location Museum (opened in 2005) and, in Cape Town, the District Six Museum (opened in 1994).

The museum represents a contribution to the presentation of national history. At the same time the curatorial team made a deliberate attempt to address local audiences. This is reflected in the use of isiZulu alongside English for the text panels in the museum. The dominant language in KwaZulu-Natal, isiZulu is also widely spoken in Kliptown and neighboring areas and has the most first-language speakers of South Africa's eleven official languages. Nevertheless, despite these efforts, the developments at Kliptown have proved controversial with the local community, both symbolically, through the imposition of a form of official national memory over a more local community memory, and materially, through the failure to provide an environment that serves the needs of local traders and residents: "the windswept terrain of the old square, with its seemingly endless hard paved surface, devoid of places to sit or opportunity for shade from the harsh sun, is quite uninhabitable, and one struggles to imagine how this space might be used by the residents of Kliptown on a daily basis" (Noble, 2008: 28; see also Peters, 2004). While the development does attract tourists, the distance of Kliptown from Soweto's other sites of historic interest, combined with its perception as a less safe place, means that a failure to engage the local community has practical as well as symbolic consequences.

Although it is important to understand this context, my purpose in this chapter is rather more circumscribed, and I want therefore to set aside, for the moment, the controversies that surround the Kliptown developments. I will return to the issue of context again in the concluding section. I want to concentrate, initially, on the place of photography within this national monument to the struggle against apartheid. Photography has played a central role in the presentation of apartheid histories and therefore an understanding of photography is central to the interpretation of post-apartheid museums (Newbury, 2009). Here I want to develop this argument, to consider how a set of archival photographs made at a moment of struggle and uncertainty, and whose creation and subsequent survival was itself contingent, are returned and reactivated in a narrative of continuity, linking past and present.

On Union Street, at the far corner of the square, the small Kliptown Museum is situated in a converted hardware store. The museum houses an exhibition display entitled "The People Shall Govern." It tells the story of Congress of the People meetings from their inception and planning through to the event itself, set within the context of apartheid and South African history up until the first democratic elections in 1994. The small size of the museum means that this history is rather abbreviated, but the narrative is sufficiently consensual (Coombes, 2003: 11), at a national level at least, that recognition can be triggered with the economical use of visual and textual elements. For example, the final image in the museum is a wall size photograph of Nelson Mandela among a crowd of supporters, accompanied by a quotation from his presidential inauguration speech, leaving little doubt as to the way this story ends. The exhibition situates the square historically in the dominant South African narrative of struggle and liberation.

The museum deals with "difficult knowledge" in a way that is closely controlled. Conflict and oppression are framed as things of the past and set within a positive narrative of democracy achieved. There are visual references to the brutality of apartheid: for example, one panel includes photographs of the Sharpeville Massacre of 1960 and the mass funeral that followed (see also Newbury, 2011). There are also references to the daily humiliation and oppression that characterized the apartheid regime, represented by Ernest Cole's photographs of the ubiquitous signs of segregation, from park benches to public toilets. But these images do not dominate the museum. The impact of Ian Berry's photograph of Sharpeville, which one might consider the most difficult in the museum, is in fact muted by its use as the background for a densely packed information panel on the founding of Umkhonto we Sizwe, the armed wing of the ANC. The viewer is not invited to confront the image in itself, as is the case at the nearby Hector Pieterson Museum, where the iconic photograph of the lifeless body of Pieterson is displayed outside the museum alongside the memorial headstone. Neither does the museum refer to the extent of the violence that accompanied the eventual transition to democracy, of which there is of course an extensive visual record (Marinovich and Silva, 2001). No doubt this could be partly attributed to lack of space (the much larger Apartheid Museum, for example, does devote space to this period); however, the place of this museum in the post-apartheid landscape of memory points in a different direction. The main visual and historical point is to offer a positive counter-narrative to the systematic denial of the humanity of the other that was the driving ideology and practice of apartheid. The museum does not emphasize the victims of apartheid, but rather the historical actors who opposed it, individual and collective.

Situated in post-TRC (Truth and Reconciliation Commission) South Africa, the museum contributes, in principle, to the work of symbolic repair and national reconciliation following a violent and divided past. If difficult knowledge is knowledge which is damaging to the self-perception of the viewer/knower, then this museum display might also be considered to provide restorative knowledge: knowledge which, rhetorically at least, offers the opportunity to repair that damage through a return to the past, and a renewal of the self and nation. This interpretation is open to white South African visitors, including those who feel a burden of "collective shame" (Blustein, 2008: 152–8) for the brutality and oppression of the apartheid regime. Whether such a reading could also extend to those centrally involved in the creation of the apartheid state and the perpetration of acts of violence in its name is more debatable, but it could at least be left open. After all, the reconciliation process in South Africa was intended to look beyond retributive justice in order to build an inclusive national identity.

In what follows, I offer a close reading of the place of photography in the representation of this moment in South Africa's past. This is not as straightforward as it might at first appear; there are a number of layers of photographic meaning within the museum, which can be read through and against each other. First, I argue that the museum can be understood as an invitation to live historically through photographs. This represents a central curatorial strategy of the Kliptown Museum display. Second, this museum, unlike a number of its counterparts, acknowledges the figure of the photographer and, intentionally or not, provides a space for reflection on the work and politics of representation. The creation of the museum display was contingent on the availability of a particular set of photographs, and I want to bring to the surface this photographic narrative. It is possible to read the museum as a memorial to the work of one photographer, Eli Weinberg, whose photography as well as his political activism would eventually lead him into exile. Finally, I shall return to the question of context in order to understand the interpretive challenge presented by situated readings of the museum.

The Union Street entrance to the museum building is rather unassuming, having retained the now faded and peeling shop front of Jada's, "Soweto's 1st Hardware Store." In contrast, the two sides of the museum that face on to Walter Sisulu Square are dominated by a large photographic installation. Mounted on vertical panels are a series of larger than life-size full-length montage portraits. (See Plate 5.1.) Against brightly colored backgrounds, a reference to the idea of diversity, and the "rainbow nation" more specifically, are superimposed silhouettes of what appear to be contemporary South Africans, a chic young woman, a man in a hat, and so on. The figures are not posed for the camera; these are people on the move. Filling the bodies of these silhouetted figures are images selected from the archive of black and white photographs of the crowds gathered at the Congress of the People. The sense of movement conveyed by the figures is significant, appealing to the self-perception of a youthful, dynamic, and vibrant Sowetan and, by extension, South African population. In this installation, the black and white photographs of past struggles do not stand over this population offering a lecture on the past, but instead represent something that the individual is urged to recognize and nurture within themselves and carry forward into the future.

This visual mode of address represents a development, rather than simply a reiteration, of the use of photographs in earlier museums such as the Apartheid Museum and the Hector Pieterson Museum, with which Kliptown has much in common. For many young South Africans, particularly those involved in photography and the visual arts, black and white documentary photography is associated with the struggle years and is seen as an austere and rather worthy esthetic, and therefore something from which they want to mark their own distance.[2] The development of a more overtly creative and performative approach to the Kliptown display might therefore be interpreted as a deliberate attempt to engage a more youthful audience. Nevertheless, the address of the installation remains inclusive. The text surrounding the visual panels contains an appeal—"Let Us Speak Together of Freedom"—cited from a call issued by the National Action Council of the Congress of the People in 1955. The rhetorical appeal is clearly to South Africans of all colors and races; the symbolic message that this history of democracy dwells in you.

In her study of the "civil contract of photography," Ariella Azoulay reflects on the idea of the "pure spectator who will encounter the image, be appalled by what is revealed, and successfully change the world through her active response to it" (2008: 191). Notwithstanding the fact that this idealized spectator does not exist, she has long been the object of desire of a certain kind of photography, including anti-apartheid struggle photography, particularly during the later apartheid years when its principal audience was the wider international community. However, in the South African case, the time for this kind of appeal has now passed; the brutal apartheid state has given way to a new democracy. Therefore, if photographs of the struggle for liberation have a social and cultural significance in contemporary South Africa, which their very ubiquity suggests they have, then their form of address must be rather different. The photographic installation on the exterior of the Kliptown Museum represents one such proposal. Following Nietzsche, it can be understood as an invitation to live historically, not to the detriment of the individual, "like one forcibly deprived of sleep" (1997 [1874]: 62), but in good measure. This is history contained, the promise of the TRC realized: no longer is the past the subject of nightmares, but instead it is made usable by the present. The movement of the figures symbolizes their productive relation to the past, what Nietzsche refers to as "the plastic power of a man, a people, a culture . . . the capacity to develop out of oneself in one's own way, to transform and incorporate into oneself what is past and foreign, to heal wounds, to replace what has been lost, to recreate broken moulds" (ibid.). The past is not a burden on the present, but travels optimistically with it. The proposition installed on the exterior of the museum is that Kliptown can serve as a foundational conjunction of place and time to which it is possible to return in collective memory, reconnecting past and present, and from which a new democratic South Africa can be imagined, one which will overcome the suffering and injustice that dominated the apartheid period. At least that is the promise, though of course to deconstruct the rhetorical strategy of an image is not to speak of its success, nor to discount the existence of counter-narratives.

This enclosure of the troubles of the past within the projection of history as collective memory is continued inside the museum. Photographs are used in two ways. First, there are the images, such as those of Sharpeville and the images by Ernest Cole, that reference historical moments in the struggle against apartheid. These images are reproduced small, and integrated as part of image and text informational panels. This is photography framed as historical evidence. In contrast, there is a second and altogether different use of photography. These images, almost exclusively taken by Eli Weinberg, are printed life-size, some filling entire walls. (See Figure 5.1.) All of these photographs relate directly to the Congress of the People meeting or its organization. And they are used with a theatrical intent.[3] They do not simply represent images of the past, but attempt to recreate the space and experience of the events they depict. In conjunction with a series of sculpted life-size wire figures that populate the museum, they create a kind of historical tableau. The figures, which in their style of construction resemble objects that can be found for sale to tourists on the streets of Johannesburg, represent the delegates who attended the Congress of the People. Each is identified by a name tag, and some can be recognized by their dress. For example, Z. K. Matthews, the prominent black academic who first mooted the idea of convening a national congress to draw up a Freedom Charter in 1953, is portrayed in full academic garb and holding a violin. (See Plate 5.2.) The figures provide the foreground through which the museum visitors pass, sharing the space metaphorically, and literally (as after all the museum is situated on Freedom Square), with those who came to Kliptown in June 1955 collectively to endorse a non-racial democratic vision of their country.

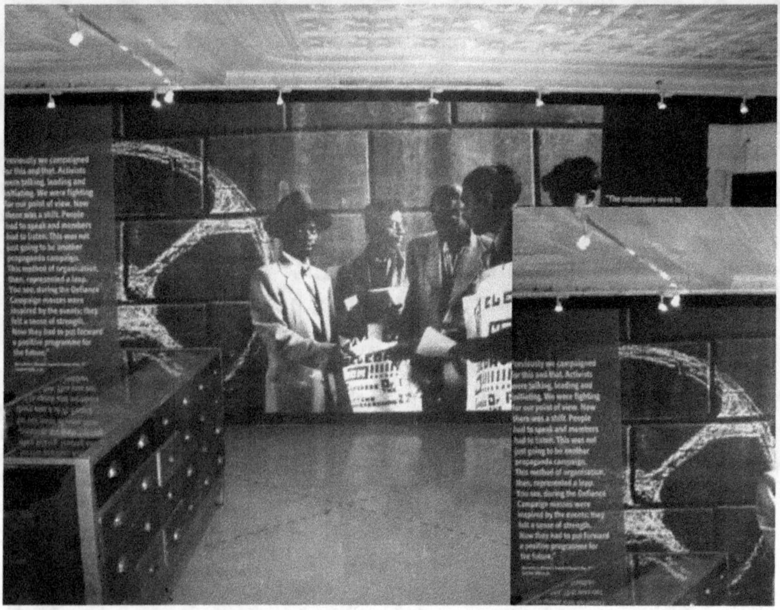

Figure 5.1 Exhibition display: Photograph of freedom volunteers by Eli Weinberg. Kliptown Museum, Johannesburg, South Africa, 2008.

This scenographic staging, in which the images participate with the sculpted wire figures and come to life so to speak, invites the viewer to suspend the present and imagine themselves in the historic moment. The exhibition guide invites visitors to "meet the different organizations that came together to form the Congress Alliance," to "take the final road to Kliptown and meet with the delegates," "to interact with the figures and engage with the Freedom Charter," all the time "immersed in an atmosphere that evokes the big gathering." To rework Azoulay's definition, the ideal spectator imagined by the museum encounters the image as history, recognizes this history as her own, and dedicates herself to the realization of its promise: "Now you are invited, having *experienced* the Congress of the People, to dedicate oneself to freedom by signing the Freedom book" (exhibition guide; emphasis added).

At this point I want to suspend my reflections on the dominant visual and performative rhetoric of the museum and follow a different path in my reading, one which opens up a little the grand narrative of the struggle for liberation and democracy, and provides an opportunity for reflexive engagement with the work of representation.

In the largest of the rooms, representing the Kliptown gathering, there is a life-size sculpted wire figure perched high above on a display plinth topped with a piece of corrugated metal roofing, surveying the scene with camera in hand. (See Plate 5.3.) This is Eli Weinberg. Visitors who take the trouble to read the small print on the photographic displays throughout the museum will notice that many are credited to Weinberg, including the wall-size images of the crowd assembled at Kliptown which provide a backdrop for the figures. But the link between this figure and the photographs could easily be missed by casual visitors. The figure itself is not labeled and one would have to read the text on the ribbons hanging down from the display to gain some understanding of his significance. The speed with which a group of tourists, on one of the Soweto townships tours that includes Kliptown on its itinerary, moved through the museum when I was there in June 2008 suggests visitors paying this amount of attention may be the exception rather than the rule. One can only speculate on what they make of the curious figure hovering over the historical tableau through which they pass.

However, not only do Weinberg's photographs make possible the museum display, but, as the presence of the figure suggests, he is also a part of the layered narrative of the event. Furthermore, this staging of the photographic act as part of the museum display invites, demands even, attention to the social relations that shape this particular visual record. Stepping out of the historic moment, one is confronted by the event as spectacle, both then, at the moment of recording, and now, in the moment of viewing. Weinberg is a significant figure in the history of political "struggle" photography in South Africa. He was born in Latvia in 1908, but after having been imprisoned as a young man for his political activities and faced with rising anti-semitism he fled Europe. He arrived in South Africa in 1929, joined the South African Communist Party (SACP) in 1932 and became a prominent trade union activist. In 1948, when the National Party came to power in South Africa, he, along with many others in the SACP, was subject to various restrictions and banning orders. He turned increasingly to photography, working both as a professional photographer, recording weddings, portraits, and so on, and as a photojournalist for the left wing newspaper *New Age*. As fellow anti-apartheid activist Albie Sachs recalls, Weinberg enjoyed declaring that "he made his living with pictures of weddings, and made the Revolution with images of struggle" (Sachs, 2009: vii).[4] Following the Soweto Uprising in 1976 he went into exile in Tanzania, where he died in 1981. A book of his photographs, *Portrait of a People*, was published by the anti-apartheid movement in 1981. As is evident in many of his photographs, Weinberg was photographing from within the anti-apartheid struggle, not merely as reporter. The social biography of the images is no less important. The majority of Weinberg's photographic archive was lost or destroyed, but the remaining work went into exile along with the photographer. Following his death, the photographs were donated to the photographic archive of the International Defence and Aid Foundation (IDAF), the hub of the international anti-apartheid movement, based in London (Newbury, 2009: 220–32). IDAF facilitated the publication of Weinberg's book, and used many of his images in anti-apartheid publications. His photographs were banned in South Africa and it was a serious offense to be found in possession of a copy of his *Portrait of a People*, even though it did circulate within the country. Following the demise of apartheid in 1990, the archive was returned to form part of the Mayibuye Archives—Robben Island Museum at the University of the Western Cape. Only as a result of deliberate acts of preservation and return within a committed politics of representation did they become available to create the display in Kliptown, and contribute to the project of reimagining South African national identity.

The presence of the figure of the photographer in the museum display is striking and stands in contrast to the transparency accorded to the photographic image in several other post-apartheid museums.[5] Neither the Apartheid Museum nor the Hector Pieterson Museum gives this degree of acknowledgment to the photographers, despite both museums being heavily dependent on the photographic archive for the creation of their displays. Although the tradition of anti-apartheid "struggle" photography does have a significant degree of recognition in South Africa and internationally, the prominence of the figure effects a kind of pause in the narrative of the display, as one is prompted to look back and forth between the photographer and the photographs he is displayed in the act of making. The minimal contextual information available to visitors accentuates this momentary sense of disruption. At one level the display seems curiously equivocal. The plinth carries a photograph of the mass political meeting with a text panel, titled "The Onlookers" ("Izibukeli"), which makes reference to the journalists, photographers, Special Forces police, banned leaders, and ordinary people who came to observe the meeting. Although Weinberg is not mentioned by name, to describe his participation in the same breath as that of police observers is, to those who are aware of his life and work, slightly unsettling and seems to contradict the nature of the display itself, which presents him as both a spectator *and* an actor within the scene. The latter is signified by his presentation as a figure in the same style as the delegates.

His elevated position may provide a metaphor for the omniscient gaze of the spectator, but in Weinberg's case it also has a more literal point of reference: he was banned from attending political gatherings and had literally to photograph events from a roof overlooking the main assembly. This was a familiar story of photographic defiance. Weinberg had resorted to similar tactics a year earlier at an ANC meeting in Sophiatown, leading in that case to his arrest and his prints and negatives becoming part of the court record, although ultimately he was acquitted. In Kliptown he left the scene just in time to avoid the security police (Weinberg, 1981: 144).

Although Weinberg photographed numerous mass political gatherings, the distanced viewpoint was not his only, or even his main, way of working. He regularly made photographs close up, often in a portrait mode, an indication of his close involvement with, and acceptance by, his subjects. Such images were intended to convey the commitment and humanity of those involved in the struggle against the apartheid system. Photographs such as the one of Freedom Volunteers (see Figure 5.2) are typical of this kind of image: the subjects present themselves directly to the camera, making the ANC salute, testifying to

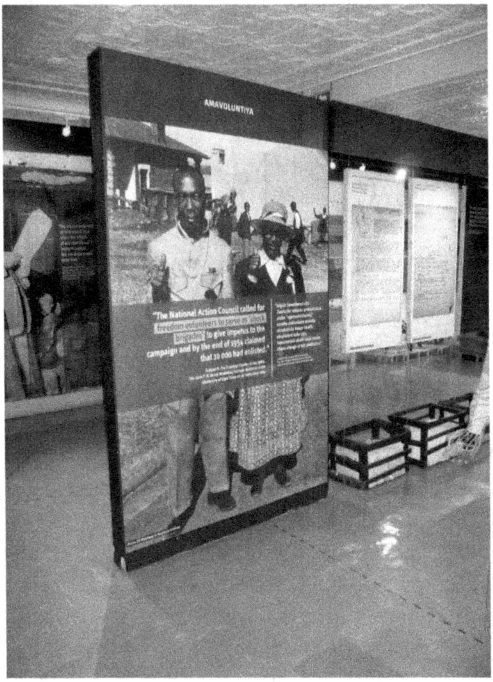

Figure 5.2 Exhibition panel: Photograph of freedom volunteers by Eli Weinberg. Kliptown Museum, Johannesburg, South Africa, 2008.

their political commitment and entrusting to photography the act of bearing witness to this commitment beyond the space and time of the photographic moment. Interestingly, perhaps being more conscious of making equal acknowledgment of women in the struggle, the museum chose to include the photograph of the Freedom Volunteer couple, as opposed to the image made at the same time of the man on his own, which appears in *Portrait of the People*. In order further to circumvent the restrictions placed upon him, and to capture images of the gathering up close, at Kliptown Weinberg had two photographers working under his instruction among the crowd.

Given Weinberg's commitment to the political movement displayed in the museum, why the ambivalence about the role of the photographer as spectator? Possibly, while acknowledging the importance of Weinberg as a witness, the museum did not want his story to distract from its main goal of presenting Kliptown as a founding moment for a democratic vision of South Africa. But perhaps this display also dramatizes a structural contradiction that besets photography, and by extension the museum itself: the danger of turning history and memory into spectacle; the incompatibility of looking and acting. This danger has been commented on by many photographic critics, but I want instead to quote from Aimé Césaire: "Beware of assuming the sterile attitude of a spectator," Césaire says, "for life is not a spectacle, a sea of miseries is not a proscenium, a man screaming is not a dancing bear" (cited in Walker, 2002: 183).[6] Significantly, this is not a rejection of representation per se. The poem from which this excerpt comes was composed as Césaire contemplated his return to immerse himself in the political and cultural life of Martinique. The words were a reminder to himself of the difficult line that the artist or poet must tread as he seeks to represent the troubled world before him. Césaire believed in the social and ethical responsibility of the artist "to rouse the modern world from its indifference to human suffering": "if all I can do is speak, it is for you I shall speak . . . My mouth shall be the mouth of those calamities that have no mouth" (ibid.). Yet at the same time he draws attention to the ethical danger inherent in this position, the danger of turning suffering into spectacle. Césaire is not proposing a turn away from representation, but rather posing with poetic clarity the dilemma that will always confront photographers, artists, and curators who deal with the representation of societies in conflict and troubled pasts.

Césaire's words also serve as a critical reminder that, through Weinberg, we are onlookers and would do well to reflect on the structural ambivalence of our privileged position, at least those of us who leave Kliptown at the end of our visit. But such reflexivity should not lead us to align our view completely with that of the photographer, thereby obscuring his specific attempts to resolve this dilemma of representation for the particular historical moment and political circumstances in which he lived. The equation that the museum posits between political and photographic representation is made possible by Weinberg's treatment of his photographic subjects as political actors, and as citizens, in spite of the apartheid state's reduction of a majority of the population to little more than units of labor, and its ultimate goal of rendering black South African citizenship a contradiction in terms. The presence of the Freedom Volunteers directly facing the camera stands as a metaphor for the presence required in the act of voting—what was once denied and has now been achieved. Only photographs made on the terms of the contract Weinberg established with his subjects can achieve this effect, establishing visually the connection between the struggles of the past and the democratic rights of the present. Weinberg's own presence in the museum reminds visitors not only of the work of collective memory in which, if successful, the museum engages them, but also the work on which memory depends, and which enables the past to speak to the present.

The Kliptown display represents an important restoring of history to vision, the survival of the images across time and space is itself a narrative of struggle, exile and return, albeit writ small when set against the momentous political struggle and ultimate transformation of South Africa from an international pariah to a country with one of the most progressive constitutions anywhere in the world. The re-placing of the photographs in Freedom Square is a move of symbolic significance, and in many ways a deserving tribute to the photographer, who lived his last years in exile from the country he regarded as his home, despite never achieving South African citizenship. Also important is the development of strategies of display that seek to engage younger audiences as well as those for whom the struggle against apartheid was a lived reality. However, important as it is to consider the visual narrative on its own terms, ultimately the museum cannot be considered in isolation from the social context in which it is located; no adequate account can ignore those situated readings which challenge its claims on the present, symbolic and material. In conclusion, then, I want to return the museum display to its context, on the edge of Walter Sisulu Square in Kliptown in the second decade of the new South Africa, and consider two arguments that represent significant challenges to its authority. First, that the message of the museum is contradicted by the urban environment in which it finds itself. Second, that, in the effort to present a national narrative of struggle and liberation, the space has been overwritten, obscuring other narratives and lives that have a valid claim to be represented.

Important as it is to restore previously hidden histories to public vision through the institution of the museum and to find ways to communicate these histories to as wide an audience as possible, this alone does not equate to the social justice demanded by those who came together in Kliptown in 1955. Social justice imagined is not social justice achieved. And, as Amy Sodaro points out in her contribution to this volume, there is a further risk that the institutionalization of memory, especially in monumental forms, divests individual social actors of the need to reflect critically on the past as they engage with the present. As Kliptown Museum's chief curator, Ali Hlongwane, acknowledged: "As well as stimulating dialogue on pressing social issues and promoting humanitarian and democratic values, the theory and praxis of memory making since 1994 may have included a triumphalism" (2008: 12). In this respect, and despite its successes, the museum is in danger of falling victim to its context; its rhetorical claims ringing hollow for those in its immediate vicinity, however much they may have national and international resonance.

Kliptown is an area of considerable deprivation and in recent years has seen protests around inadequate service delivery and lack of housing. It is unsurprising, therefore, that there has been criticism of the level of resources devoted to the redevelopment of the square and the creation of the museum versus the lack of resources and attention devoted to the material needs of residents. The completion of the museum and square has preceded the delivery of the much needed housing included in the development plan for the area, and the facilities provided for market traders have proved inadequate (Noble, 2008).[7] The fact that there is a Holiday Inn at the rear of the museum seems to underscore this disparity between the space of the museum and that of the surrounding area. Inevitably, the contradiction between the actual conditions in Kliptown and the promises of social and political justice enshrined in the Freedom Charter has served to heighten the location's symbolic importance in debates of where South Africa has come since the end of apartheid and how far it still has to go. This is a fact not lost on national politicians, who have chosen the site to renew the promise of democracy, and political activists, who have challenged their claim on this legacy. Association with Kliptown carries symbolic capital, but it also carries political risks. The Anti-Privatisation Forum, an activist organization opposed to many of the policies of the current South African government, organized demonstrations to coincide with the visit of ANC President Jacob Zuma to Kliptown in June 2008, and called for the people of Kliptown to boycott Nelson Mandela's birthday celebrations. Similarly, the political grouping that broke away from the ANC in 2008 called itself the Congress of the People (a move that was subject to legal challenge, albeit unsuccessful) in order to claim a democratic heritage going back to the 1955 meeting, and by implication to impugn the ANC's record in government.

This would be a difficult context for any museum to operate in; coupled with controversy over the consultation process and the development of the square it is clear that the museum risks overstretching itself in the attempt to invoke the sense of a single democratic community. The Congress of the People is presented as part of the collective memory of all South Africans, black and white, who are invited to imagine themselves as part of a single community of memory. And, by extension, the rhetoric of freedom and democracy invites international tourists into this same fold. In this sense, the museum represents what Margalit refers to as a "utopian universalistic project" (cited in Blustein, 2008: 207). But as he also points out, such projects are rarely the basis for collective action. It is difficult to see how the museum can truly be considered successful if it becomes insulated from the surrounding area, serving as a pleasurable or restorative experience for those living beyond Soweto, while failing to articulate the reality of daily life in Kliptown within its democratic national imagination.

The second charge laid at the door of the museum is that in inscribing the national narrative of South African democracy it obscures a more complex and layered historical reality. I want to turn here to a final photograph, one which is unacknowledged within the museum; indeed at one level it is not a part of the exhibition at all. It serves as another point of disruption, a discordant note more difficult to integrate into the narrative of the museum but nevertheless stubbornly present. The photograph (see Plate 5.4) is set into the wall near the beginning of the exhibition. It is an old black and white photograph showing a mosque in a style popular in late-nineteenth and early twentieth-century India. The Gujarati script at the bottom of the frame identifies the building as Lajpur's Jamia Masjid, the main mosque at Lajpur, a small town in south Gujarat.[8] Left over from the building's former use as a hardware store owned by the Jada family, this photographic remnant points to other narratives and histories latent in the space. Knowing that the shopkeepers of Union Street were displaced in the process of redevelopment (Noble, 2008: 25–7) adds an unsettling edge to any reading of this image. Beneath the newly inscribed surface of the museum display are complex histories of migration and identity, desires not wholly encompassed within the national narrative, which have the potential to render more complex the representation of Kliptown in the museum. Despite initial aspirations in this direction, the museum does not as yet appear to have found a successful formula for articulating local community histories, such as the photographic and oral history projects developed by the Kliptown Our Town Trust, with the national history represented by the museum.[9]

While there are many things in its social and political context that are beyond the museum's control, and for which it cannot be held accountable, it is clear that these criticisms are not entirely without warrant. Looking to the future, the challenge for the museum is two fold. First, to find ways of fulfilling the promise of the slogan emblazoned on its exterior—to speak together of freedom. It might be argued that in the past few years the history of the liberation struggle and the values it represented has begun to lose its purchase on the present. The violence in South African townships directed at migrants from other African countries undermines national identity and disregards the collective memory of struggle. As Hlongwane recognizes, this is a direct challenge to "memory activists and the museum community": "How has this society found it possible to trivialize the hardships of the 'other' exiles, the 'other' economic refugees and the 'other' immigrants? . . . Never again should those who have been degraded in return degrade those who have become the 'other'" (2008: 12). Although the worst of this violence has been in townships other than Soweto, which is comprised of more settled communities, the task for a museum such as Kliptown must be to explore how the history of the liberation struggle can be a resource for critical dialog with the present, but importantly this can only work though engagement with local as well as national communities of memory. Second, one might ask whether it is not possible to facilitate more complex layered forms of representation that open onto the past in less predictable and contained ways, that allow space for a multiplicity of narratives representative of the diversity that founded Kliptown and that lives on in its people and places. In these ways it may be possible to do justice to the aspirations of those who converged on Kliptown in 1955, and the efforts of those such as Eli Weinberg who ensured that a visual record of this event remains available to the present.

Notes

1. The Kliptown Museum was curated by a team from Ochre Media, who also worked on Constitutional Hill, a heritage site in central Johannesburg. However, it should be acknowledged that the Kliptown Our Town Trust had

been active over a longer period in the field of community history, including the presentation of photographic exhibitions at the Kliptown Community Centre, oral history projects, and the project to reconstruct the Sans Souci, a former Kliptown cinema (thesanssouci.org).

2. Although there is a creative and performative strand of photographic practice that can be traced back at least as far as *Drum* magazine in the 1950s, it does not mean the perception is less prevalent. For a discussion, and examples, of the importance of performance to contemporary South African art photography, see Douglas, 2009.
3. For a discussion of the idea of the "performing museum," see Williams, 2007: 96–102.
4. It is perhaps interesting to note that photography had a restorative role for Weinberg too. Albie Sachs recalls hiking in the hills of Lesotho with a small group of like-minded friends, including Weinberg with his camera: "we literally turned our backs on apartheid and sought fresh energy for our return to the struggle" (Sachs, 2009: vii).
5. Museum Africa provides an exception as it has a room dedicated to photographers, notably those who worked for *Drum*, but this is a much older display than either the Apartheid Museum or the Hector Pieterson Museum and lacks the performative, staged dimension discussed here.
6. The quote comes from the opening of Césaire's dramatic poem *Notebook of a Return to the Native Land* (1939).
7. These points are also informed by a discussion with the curator Ali Hlongwane (June 2008).
8. I am grateful to Marcus Banks for translating the script and offering some suggestions regarding the building.
9. Peters talks about shaping the "visitor experience of Kliptown through dispersed nodes in the community which allows visitors to move from the Freedom Square into the historic town of Kliptown" (2004, n.p.). It is not clear to what extent this concept has been realised, as the Kliptown Museum presents itself as a relatively self-contained experience. Ironically, this is despite Gene Duiker of KOTT being employed as researcher for Ochre Media during the making of the Kliptown exhibition (Ali Hlongwane, personal communication, October 26, 2009).

Works cited

Azoulay, Ariella (2008). *The Civil Contract of Photography.* New York: Zone Books.

Blustein, Jeffrey (2008). *The Moral Demands of Memory.* Cambridge: Cambridge University Press.

Coombes, Annie E. (2003). *History After Apartheid: Visual Culture and Public Memory in a Democratic South Africa.* Durham, NC: Duke University Press.

Douglas, Anna (2009). *Life Less Ordinary: Performance and Display in South African Art.* Catalogue of the exhibition held at Djanogly Art Gallery, September 5—November 15. Nottingham: Djanogly Art Gallery.

Hlongwane, Ali Khangela (2008). "Never, Never and Never Again: Realising a Dream or Chasing a Mirage." In *Programme for the 6th Nelson Mandela Annual Lecture,* Walter Sisulu Square, Kliptown, Soweto, July 12.

Marinovich, Greg and Joao Silva (2001). *The Bang-Bang Club: Snapshots from a Hidden War.* London: Arrow Books.

Marschall, Sabine (2010). "Commemorating the 'Trojan Horse' Massacre in Cape Town: The Tension between Vernacular and Official Expressions of Memory." *Visual Studies* 25(2): 135–48.

Newbury, Darren (2009). *Defiant Images: Photography and Apartheid South Africa.* Pretoria: University of South Africa Press.

Newbury, Darren (2011). "Picturing an 'Ordinary Atrocity': Photographs of the Sharpeville Massacre, 21 March, 1960." In Geoffrey Batchen, Mick Gidley, Nancy K. Miller, and Jay Prosser (eds). *Picturing Atrocity: Reading Photographs in Crisis.* London: Reaktion Books.

Nietzsche, Friedrich and Daniel Breazeale (1997 [1874]). *Untimely Meditations.* Translated by Reginald John Hollingdale. Cambridge: Cambridge University Press.

Nieves, Angel Davis and Ali Khangela Hlongwane (2007). "Public History and 'Memorial Architecture' in the 'new' South Africa: The Hector Pieterson Memorial and Museum, Soweto." *Safundi: The Journal of South African and American Studies* 8(3): 351–68.

Noble, Jonathan A. (2008). "Memorialising the Freedom Charter: Contested Imaginations for the Development of Freedom Square at Kliptown, 1991–2006." *South African Journal of Art History* 23(1): 13–32.

Peters, Wonderboy (2004). "Locating and Missing Sisulu: The Paradoxes of the Kliptown Open Air Museum." *Lit Net: Young Voices: South African Online Writers' Conference* [online] Available at http://www.oulitnet.co.za/youngwriters/wonderboy_peters.asp [Accessed October 20, 2009].

Sachs, Albie (2009). "Foreword." In Darren Newbury, *Defiant Images: Photography and Apartheid South Africa.* Pretoria: University of South Africa Press.

Walker, Keith L. (2002). "Art for Life's Sake: Rituals and Rights of Self and Other in the Theatre of Aimé Césaire." In Paul Carter Harrison, Victor Leo Walker, and Gus Edwards (eds). *Black Theatre: Ritual Performance in the African Diaspora.* Philadelphia: Temple University Press.

Weinberg, Eli (1981). *Portrait of a People: A Personal Photographic Record of the South African Liberation Struggle.* London: International Defence and Aid Fund for Southern Africa.

Williams, Paul (2007). *Memorial Museums: The Global Rush to Commemorate Atrocities.* Oxford: Berg.

6
Showing and Telling: Photography Exhibitions in Israeli Discourses of Dissent

Tamar Katriel

The collection and dissemination of testimonies that document routine acts of violence, harassment and intimidation against civilian populations under occupation are part of the agenda of anti-occupation groups in Israel and elsewhere. Indeed, as Givoni (2008) has argued in her study of the French organization "Physicians Without Borders," witnessing has become an intrinsic technique and a shared code of contemporary humanitarian action. As a transnational yet locally embedded cultural configuration, witnessing has become a way of responding to states of emergency, crises and ongoing conditions of human suffering around the globe. It is conceptualized as involving three basic components, which are differently and delicately balanced in every given case: (1) presence in a socially distant scene of suffering, while siding with victimized "others"; (2) documentation and reporting grounded in an empirical epistemology associated with the seeking of evidence; (3) the use of fearless speech, that is, speech that involves risk-taking as it challenges hegemonic positions and power relations by voicing critique, condemnation, or demands for intervention (Foucault, 2001).

Within this framework, I address the testimonial projects of two among many of the dissident groups operating in Israel today in a loosely organized fashion—the veterans' group known as "Breaking the Silence" (*Shovrim Shtika*, here BTS), which was established in 2004 for the purpose of collecting and disseminating soldiers' testimonies about their experiences as part of the Israeli occupation regime in the Palestinian occupied territories (Katriel, 2009),[1] and the women's group known as "Checkpoint Watch" (*Machsom Watch*, here CPW), which was established in 2001 for the purpose of monitoring soldiers' treatment of Palestinian civilians at the many checkpoints dotting these same territories (Ginsburg, 2009; Kaufman, 2008; Kirstein Keshet, 2006; Mansbach, 2007).[2]

Members of both these activist groups construct their activism as a form of witnessing, but each of them manifests its own distinctive configuration of presence, documentation, and fearless speech. Each, in turn, develops its own particular blend of present-oriented activism and future-oriented memory work by combining witnessing practices that are anchored in its members' particular positioning vis-à-vis the occupation regime. Specifically, in this chapter I focus on these groups' use of photography exhibitions as cultural arenas and visual resources in and through which they have chosen to voice their dissent. Defiant of mainstream media coverage and official military parlance, they use their members' witnessing stance to problematize and condemn societal silences and denials concerning the day-to-day reality of the Israeli occupation in the Palestinian territories.

The two groups considered in this study share a basic view that holds the Israeli establishment, especially its military branch, rather than individual soldiers, responsible for the decades-long oppression of the Palestinian population in the occupied territories. They also share the goal of forcing the reluctant Israeli public to confront the nature and the human costs of the Israeli military control over three million Palestinians in the occupied territories of the West Bank and Gaza. The daily reality of life under occupation that remains largely hidden from the Israeli public is witnessed at close range by the soldiers upholding it and by the women activists, who have made it their task to monitor and report human rights violations at the checkpoints. While both these groups of eyewitnesses can claim direct knowledge of the disruptions and suffering the occupation policies and practices bring into the Palestinians' lives, they differ considerably in the nature of their presence at the site of occupation and in their positioning with respect to the reality to which they testify.

Breaking the Silence members perform their witnessing as perpetrator-observers in the scene of occupation. Their presence in this scene is institutionally mandated by their soldiering role, and epitomizes the Israeli matrix of control over the Palestinian population in the territories.[3] These control measures include a labyrinth of ever-changing rules and regulations, ongoing curfews, checkpoints, house searches, street patrols, and so on. The soldier-activists shift from the position of fully enmeshed participants to that of perpetrator-observers as they assume their witnessing role. This shift is often predicated on self-distancing moves resulting from experiences of "moral shock" (Jasper, 1997) in response to incidents of harassment of Palestinian civilians. Being jolted out of their unreflective stance as perpetrators, they turn themselves into self-conscious perpetrator-observers who are able to question their own acts. In some cases, this self-questioning leads soldiers to become conscientious objectors and refuse to continue to serve in the occupied territories when called up for reserve duty (risking military trial, imprisonment, and social censure). Others continue to serve despite their critical stance toward the military policies soldiers are required to uphold as part of the occupation. BTS encompasses a variety of opinions on this highly controversial issue and its members are careful to state that there is no organizationally binding position on it.

The CPW women, by contrast, are self-appointed activist-observers whose explicitly radical left-wing and feminist positions, civilian orientation, older age, observer status, and gendered presence at the checkpoints make them pointedly extrinsic to the functioning of these sites as military installations, whose day-to-day operation is largely invisible to most Israeli citizens. While their presence is tolerated by the army (some high-ranking soldiers even met with the group's representatives to signal their concern over incidents of human rights violations) it is often felt to be burdensome and disruptive by soldiers on checkpoint duty. This is particularly the case when the women attempt to intervene directly in the soldiers' activities to prevent harassment, or intercede with higher military commanders to overrule decisions and practices at the observation site. The reports the women post on their website also irk the military by publicly exposing oppressive arrangements and incidents of cruelty. Thus marking a provocative grassroots intervention that expresses their personal convictions and choices, as well as their willingness to place themselves voluntarily at the very site of others' suffering, they go out in small groups, twice a day, seven days a week, at the peak hours of movement for the Palestinian population, and conduct observations at scores of fixed checkpoints and mobile, so-called "floating" barriers. They collect and record information about the oppressive practices the system has developed over 40 years of occupation, keeping them well out of sight for most Israelis. Not surprisingly, the records of heartless and capricious controlling practices they compile as activist-observers corroborate the accounts of such practices provided by the BTS testimonials.

The testimonies of both the soldiers and the women attest to the plight of the Palestinians living under occupation, whose freedom of movement is severely constrained, endangering their health, economy, and social life. While the women activist-observers are intensely concerned with the human consequences of the checkpoint system, the soldiers, in assuming the perpetrator-observer role, position themselves as victimized-victimizers. Their testimonies foreground their own feelings while attending to, but not foregrounding, the suffering of the local population placed under their control.

The checkpoints—the focus of the activist-observers' female gaze, and the site of some of the soldiers' most severe practices of control—separate villages from towns and other villages, workers from their workplaces, children from their schools, patients and doctors from their health facilities, and family members from one another. They are manned by either young conscripts in their late teens and early twenties, or by reservists who are called up for about a month a year until their early forties. These soldiers come from all corners of Israeli society, including newcomer communities from the former Soviet Union and Ethiopia as well as national-religious settler communities in the West Bank and Gaza (and with the exception of Palestinian citizens of Israel and ultraorthodox Jews who are exempt from military service). Although manning these checkpoints is only part of the soldiers' assignment, these are sites where the coercive power of the occupation regime is both routinely and conspicuously dramatized, and its devastating impact on the Palestinian fabric of life is most keenly felt. It is for this reason, and in response to highly disturbing stories about the checkpoints that occasionally reach the Israeli public through the singular reporting of a few Israeli journalists and activists, that the women observer-activists chose the checkpoints as the target of their monitoring project. By courting media attention, and via development of their own alternative means, the two groups independently launched awareness-raising campaigns, reporting on what they did, saw, heard, and felt to the public at large. While the soldiers' testimonies evidenced their troubled position on what to do and not to do during their tours of duty, the women activist-observers deliberated about ways of intervening in and obstructing the military routines that uphold the occupation regime. While the soldiers testified to their troubled relationship with their own structural power over the Palestinians, as symbolized by gun and uniform, the older, self-assured, and well-connected middle class female members of Checkpoint Watch openly challenged the status quo through their uninvited presence, and reporting of and bringing attention to particular cases of harassment.

The organization of photography exhibitions was an integral part of these two groups' program of activities. In both cases the pictures were taken mainly by amateurs as part of their routine engagement with the scene of occupation, and the exhibitions were curated with the help of professionals who volunteered their services. Both these exhibitions were originally launched in a peripheral venue on the outskirts of Tel Aviv, the Gallery of the Geographic Photography College, and traveled to other, mostly peripheral venues around the country as well as abroad. They played different roles in the organizational history of each of the two activist groups, but in both cases provided a site in and through which the group's concerns and messages were publicly expressed, galvanizing emotions and triggering debate with regard to Israel's occupation and its policies.

In what follows, I will address the social careers of these two photography exhibitions as social arenas, attending to some of the characteristic features of the photographs included in them, but also to the interpretive and viewing practices organized around them. I will then build on these accounts in reflecting on the photography exhibitions as performative sites in which their creators constitute their roles as witnesses through visual display and verbal articulation.

6.1 The "Breaking the Silence" exhibition

The group of discharged soldiers, all in their early twenties, who launched the BTS exhibition in May 2004, had spent a good part of their mandatory military service in the old town of Hebron and its environs and the pictures included in the exhibition represent their experiences in that area. The settlement in Hebron of several hundred orthodox Jewish settlers in the midst of a many-fold larger Palestinian population has made it a site of acute and often bloody daily strife. While for its orthodox Jewish settlers Hebron represents a sacred Jewish site, the City of the Patriarchs, for many Israelis it stands as a potent symbol of the ills of the occupation.[4] The exhibition organizers saw their project as an attempt to bring the reality of Hebron as they had experienced it—with all its complex religious and nationalist struggles—to Tel Aviv, the secular and cosmopolitan heart of the country.

The pictures included in the exhibition were taken by soldiers during their routine military rounds, and were collected in snowball fashion from ex-soldiers' personal albums or boxes where they were kept as military souvenirs. This move shifted the status of the photographs mounted at the exhibition from privately kept personal items to objects of public interest. In addition to the photographs, the exhibition included materials designed for public display such as video segments from interviews with the witnesses (keeping their anonymity by shooting them from the back),[5] and related artifacts such as a striking display of car keys that had been confiscated from Palestinian drivers at the checkpoints (in violation of military regulations).

Despite the fact that it was located in a peripheral venue, the exhibition attracted considerable media attention, which was further kindled when it was raided by the military authorities. Three of its organizers were detained for questioning concerning the self-incriminating evidence included in the display about alleged involvement in human rights violations. The photographs in the exhibition depicted everyday scenes that caught the soldiers' attention as they moved in Hebron's alleyways, and these scenes, in turn, became memorable because of the soldiers' decision to turn them into visual documentation. The amateur photographs showed soldiers' daily interactions with the Palestinian civilian population: scenes such as an elderly man meekly handing an identity card to a young, armed soldier; a blindfolded young detainee slouched on his knees, his head down and hands cuffed behind his back; and Palestinian children playing Israeli soldiers under the watchful eye of an armed soldier.

Indeed, the images depicted in the exhibition's photographs brought difficult scenes of Hebron under occupation into the heart of the largely oblivious Israeli public sphere. Like similarly motivated photographic images that occasionally appear in the press, such as those by the noted photojournalist Miki Kratzman, who acted as curator for the BTS exhibition and whose photographs often accompany the in-depth journalistic reports on the situation in the West Bank and Gaza by journalist Gideon Levy in *Ha'aretz*, these pictures were viewed in conjunction with narrative accounts. In this case, the soldiers offered oral accounts of the exhibition, giving guided tours from the perspective of authentic eyewitnesses grounded in their positioning as perpetrator-observers.

Capturing mundane moments of their military activities and the sights routinely afforded by them—rarely captured by outside witnesses who are more attuned to more starkly dramatic occupation images discussed below—the BTS photographs cumulatively make a strong evidentiary statement. Yet, given what John Berger has called "the innate ambiguity of the photograph" (Berger, 2002), it remains for the accompanying narratives to supply interpretive frames that give the images meaning. The exhibition as a multi-modal display thus exemplified the kind of complementarity that Berger has identified between photographs and words: "In the relation between a photograph and words, the photograph begs for an interpretation, and the words usually supply it. The photograph, irrefutable as evidence but weak in meaning, is given a meaning by the words. And the words, which themselves remain at the level of generalization, are given specific authenticity by the irrefutability of the photograph" (Berger, 2002: 55).

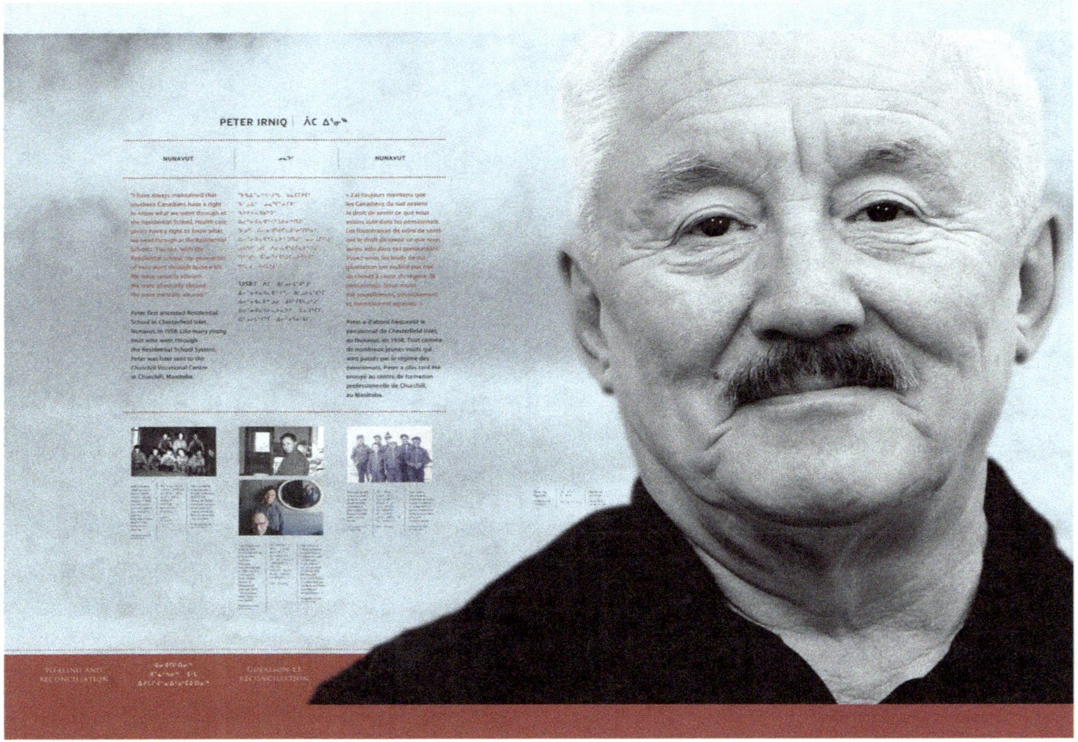

Plate 1.1 Peter Irniq Banner, *"We were so far away": The Inuit Experience of Residential Schools*. (Courtesy of the Legacy of Hope Foundation.)

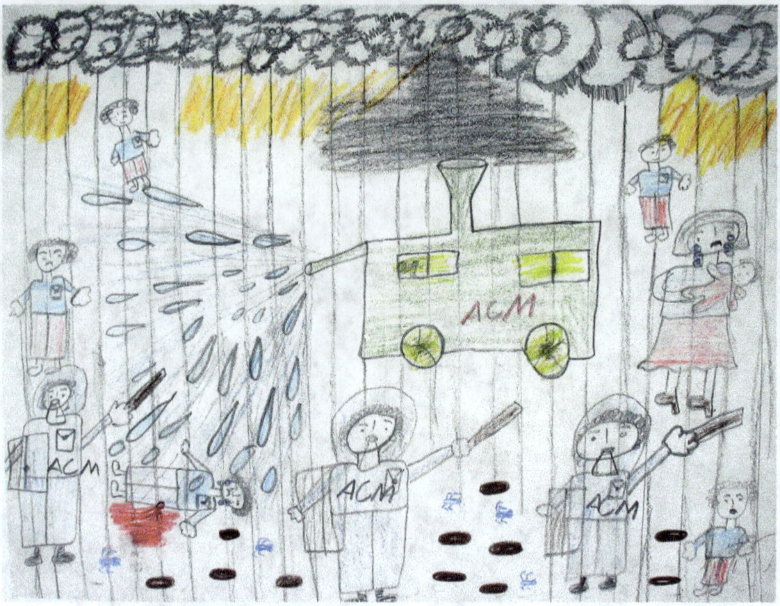

Plate 2.1 "Innocent Victims: Children's Drawings from the Woomera Detention Centre," curated by Serafina Maiorano. (Courtesy of the Migration Museum of Southern Australia.)

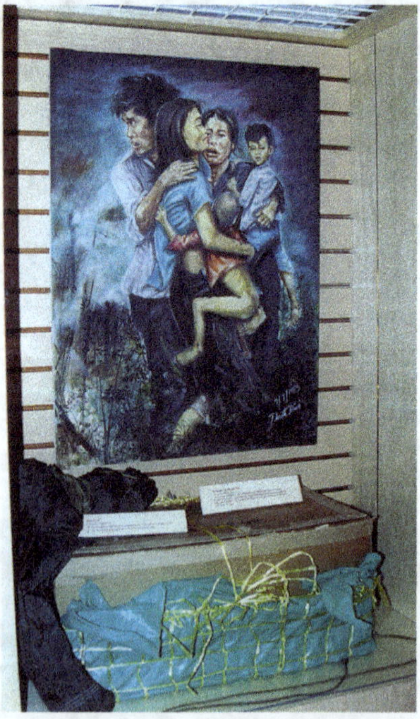

Plate 2.2 "Stories in Cardboard Boxes: The Survival of Cambodian Refugees in South Australia." (Courtesy of the Migration Museum of Southern Australia.)

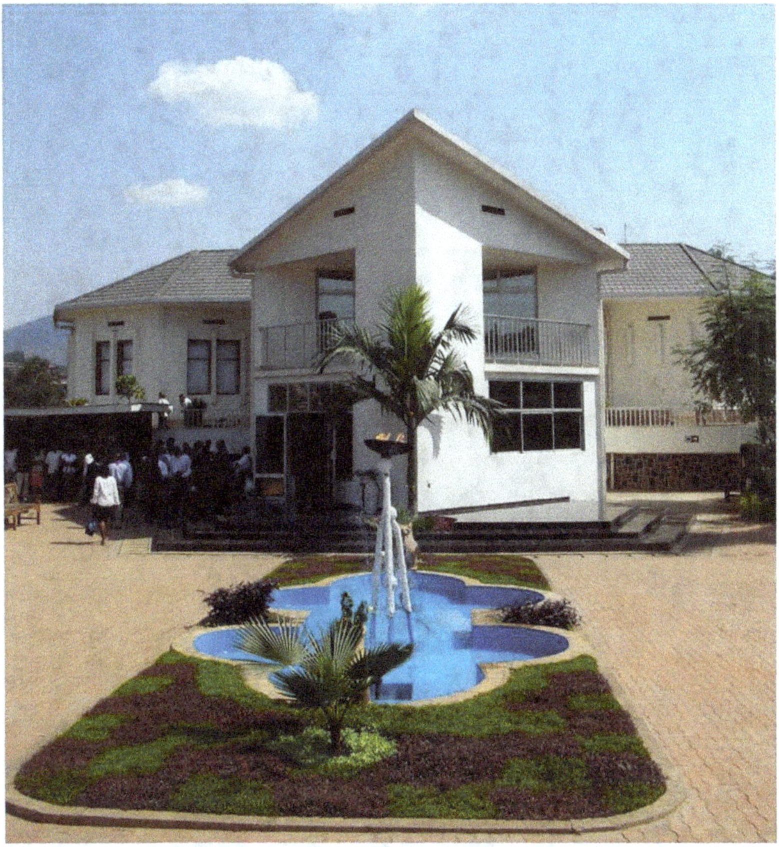

Plate 4.1 Kigali Genocide Memorial Centre, Rwanda. (Photograph by Amy Sodaro.)

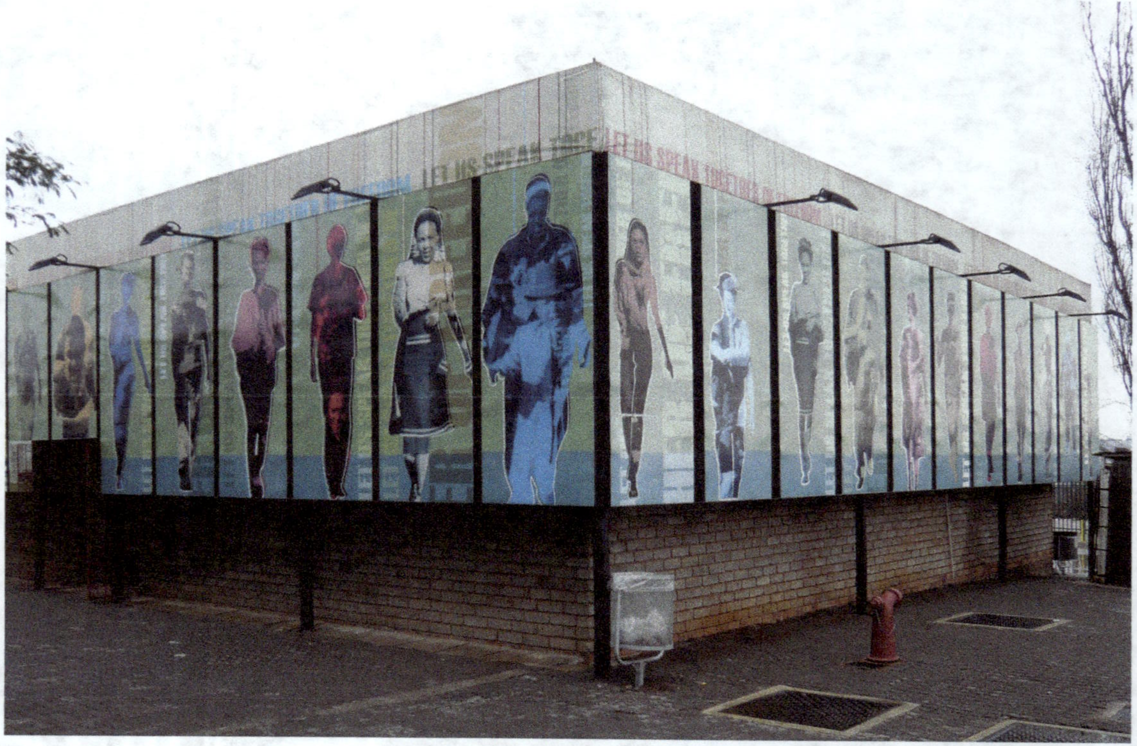

Plate 5.1 Exterior of Kliptown Museum. (Photograph by Darren Newbury.)

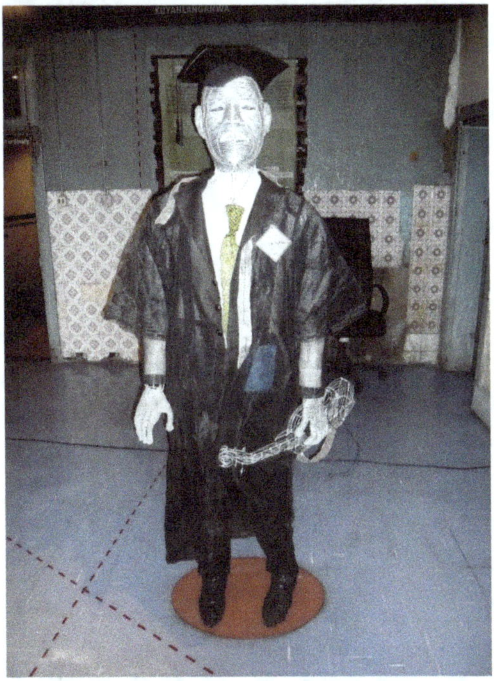

Plate 5.2 Wire sculpture of Z. K. Matthews, Kliptown Museum. (Photograph by Darren Newbury.)

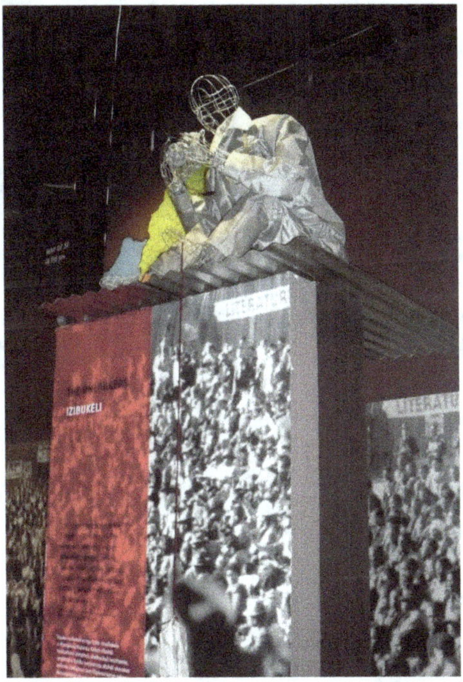

Plate 5.3 Eli Weinberg installation, Kliptown Museum. (Photograph by Darren Newbury.)

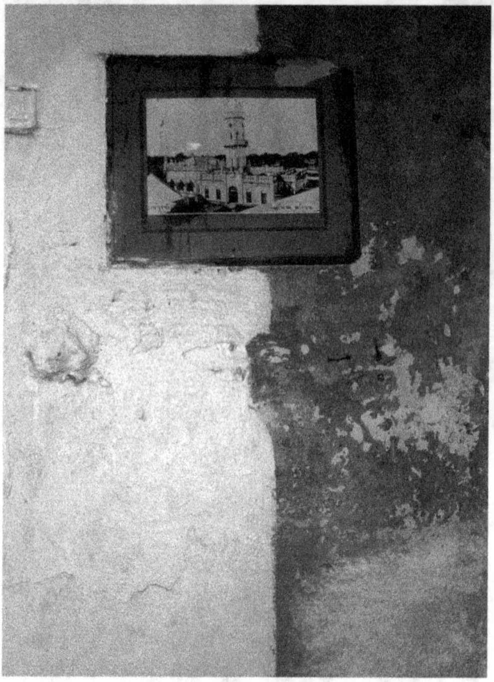

Plate 5.4 Photograph of Jamia Masjid, Lajpur, Kliptown Museum. (Photograph by Darren Newbury.)

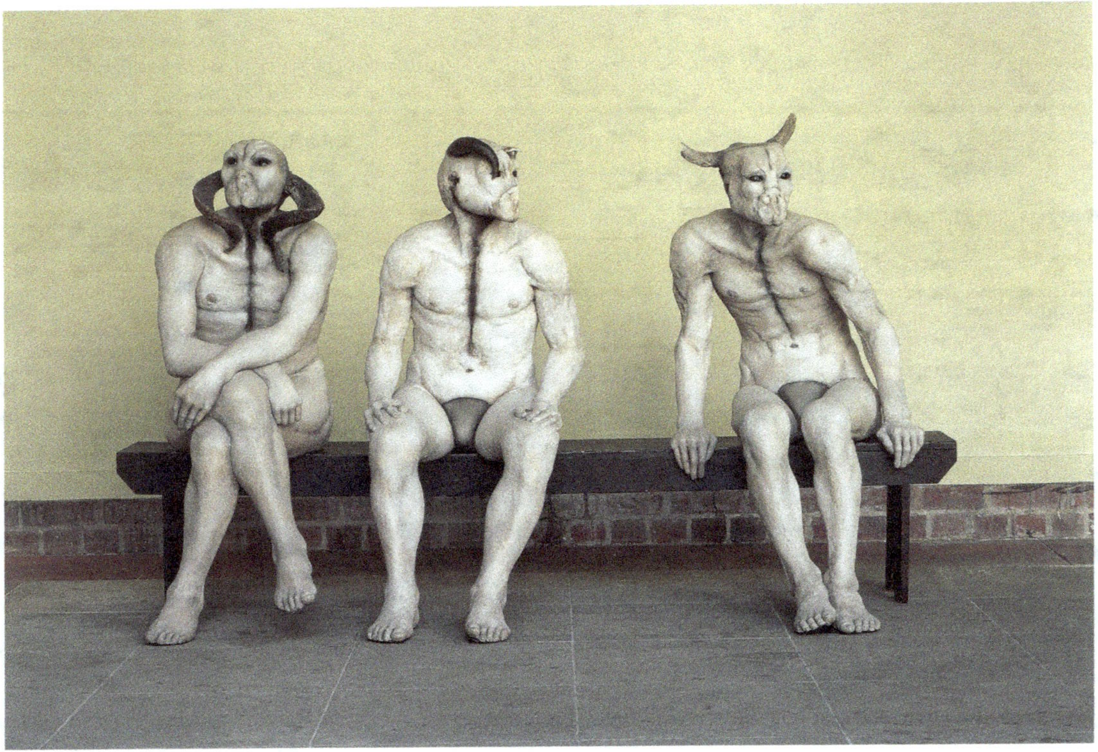

Plate 7.1 *Butcher Boys* (1985–6) by Jane Alexander. (Photograph by Mark Lewis. Courtesy of the artist and Iziko Museums of Cape Town, Iziko South African National Gallery, Permanent Collection.)

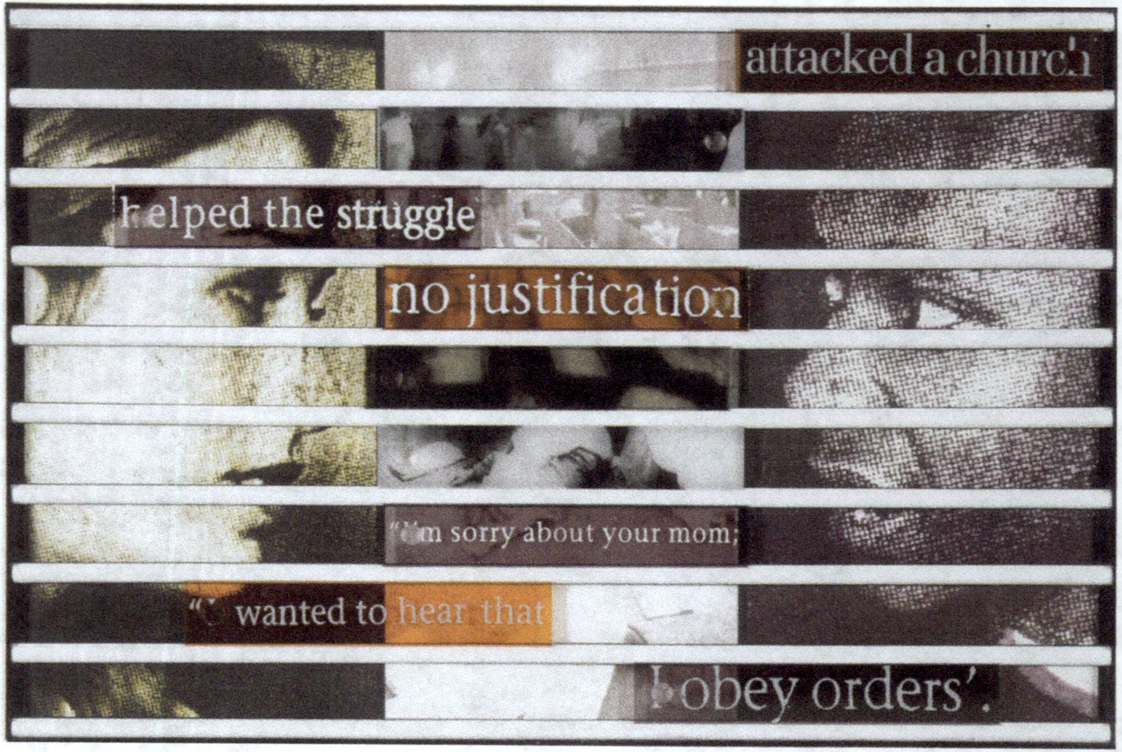

Plate 7.2 *Truth Games series, Liezl Ackerman – not a church – Gcinikhaya Makoma* (1998) by Sue Williamson. (Courtesy of the artist.)

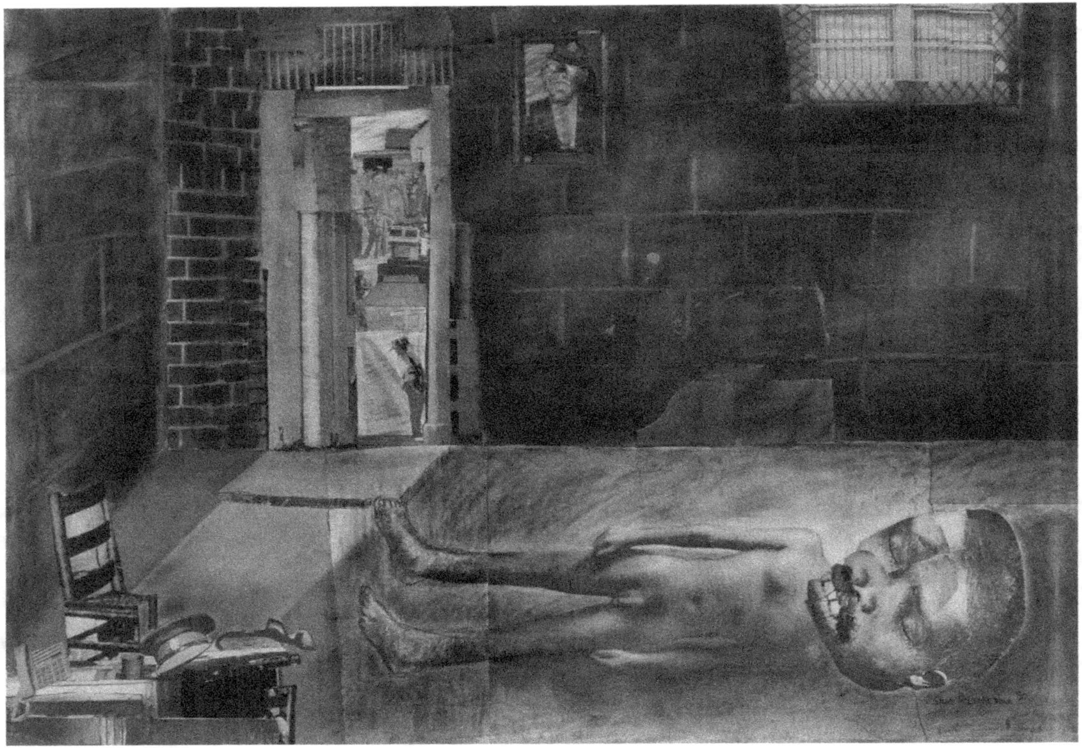

Plate 7.3 It left him cold (the death of Steve Biko) (1990) by Sam Nhlengethwa. (Courtesy of the artist and Wits Art Museum.)

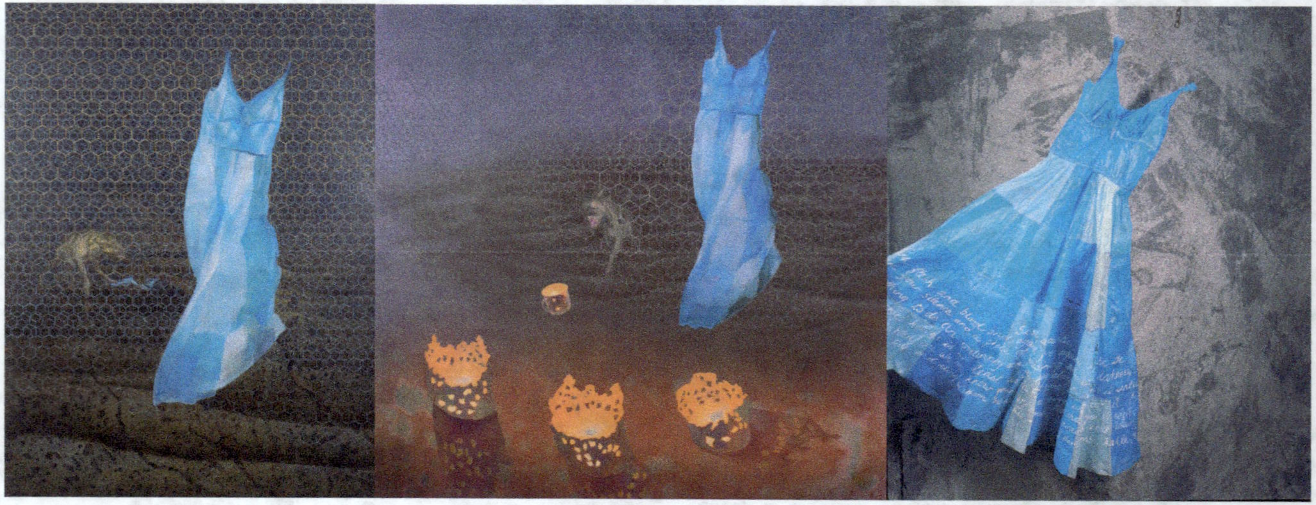

Plate 7.4 *The Man who Sang and the Woman who Kept Silent* (Triptych) (1998) by Judith Mason. (Courtesy of the artist.)

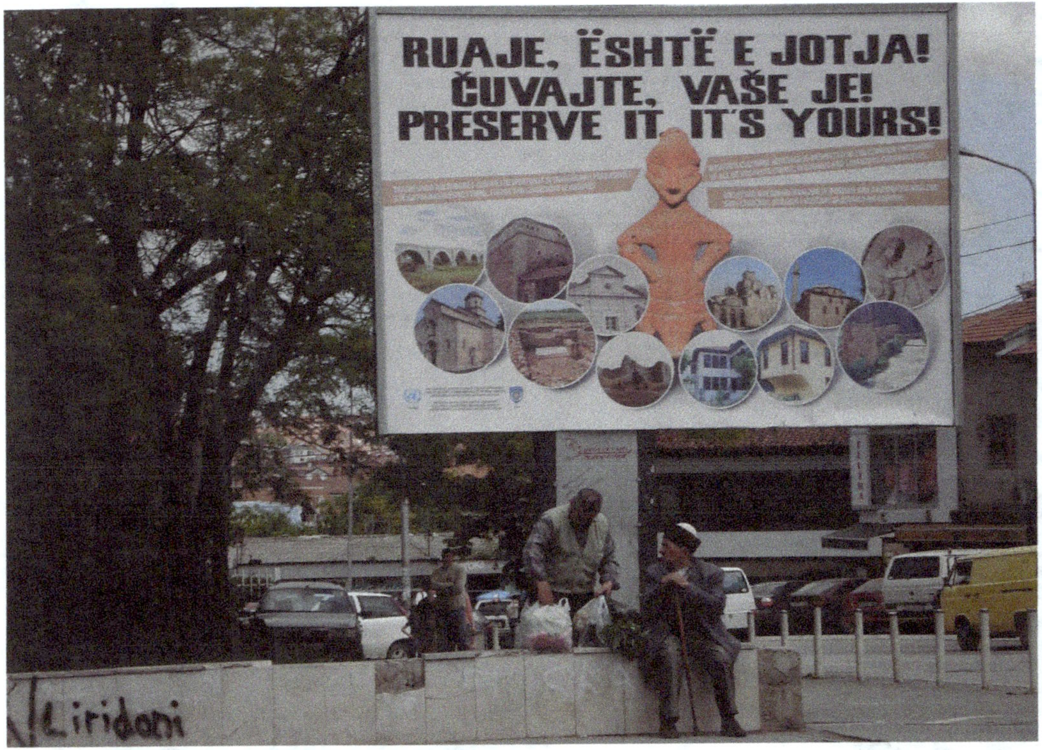

Plate 8.1 Billboard in Prishtina, Kosovo, summer 2004. (Photograph by Andrew Herscher.)

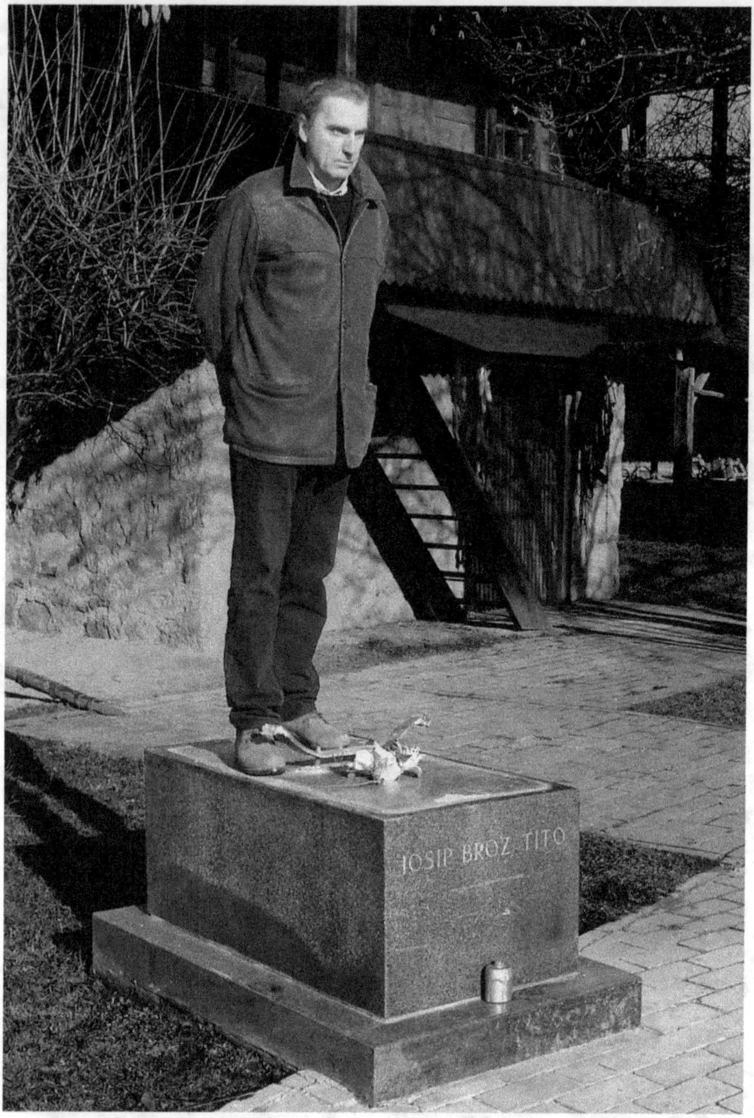

Plate 8.2 Dalibor Martinis, *JBT 27.12.2004*, performance, Kumrovec, Croatia, 2005. (Photograph by Irena Sertić.)

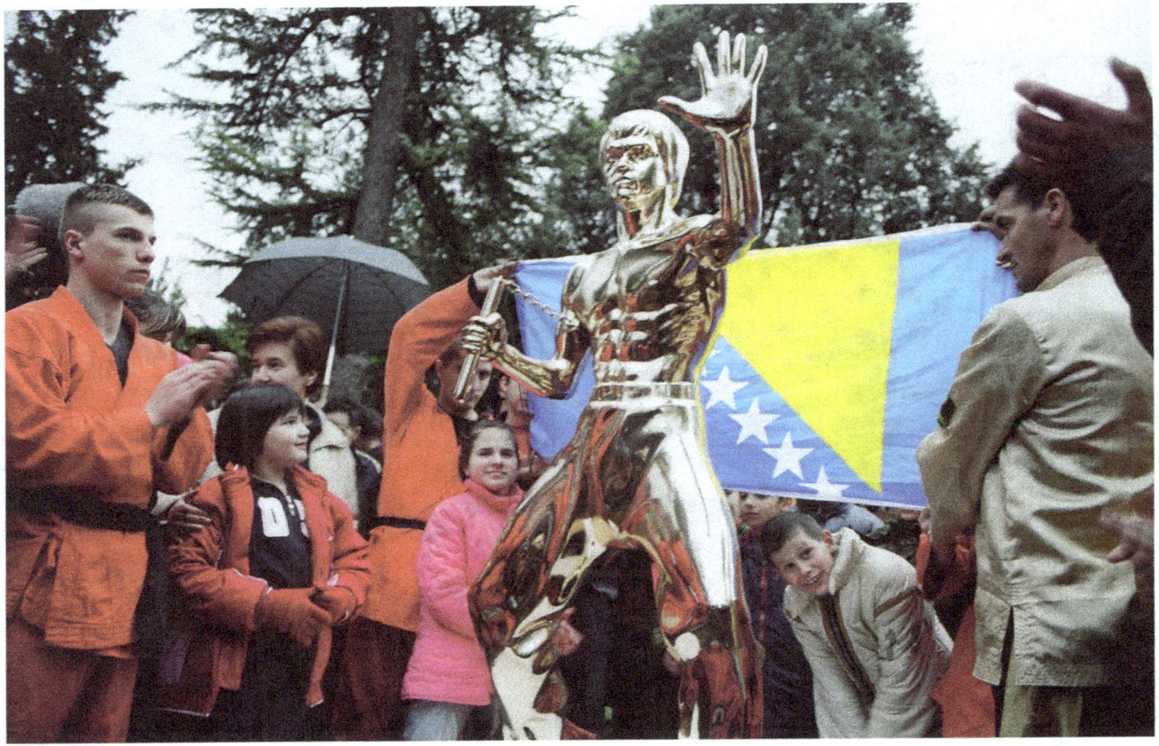

Plate 8.3 Dedication of Monument to Bruce Lee, Mostar, Bosnia-Hercegovina, November 2005. (Courtesy of Sarajevo Center for Contemporary Art.)

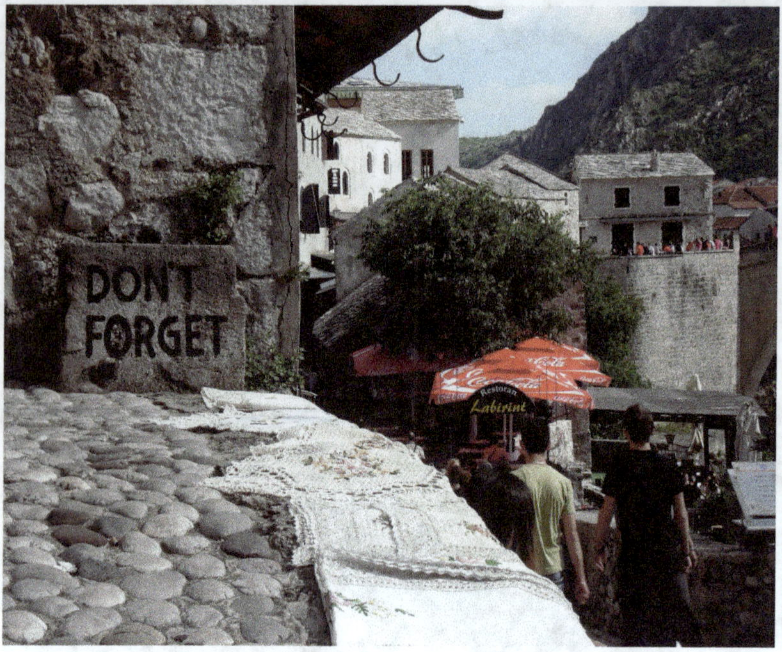

Plate 8.4 "Don't Forget," Mostar, Bosnia-Herzegovina. (Photograph by Andrew Herscher.)

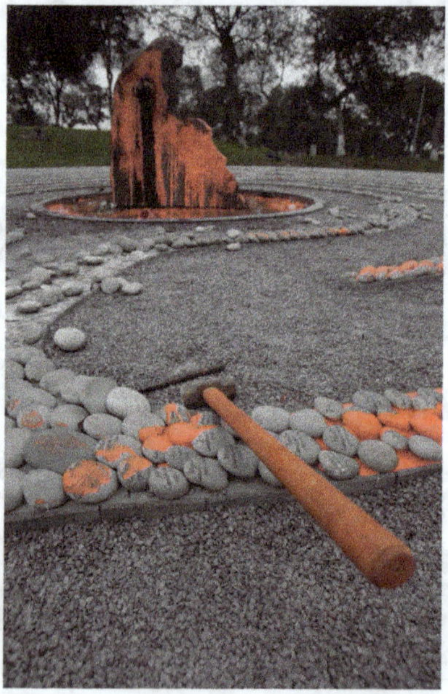

Plate 9.1 The Ojo que llora defaced, Lima, Peru. (Photograph by Yael Rojas.)

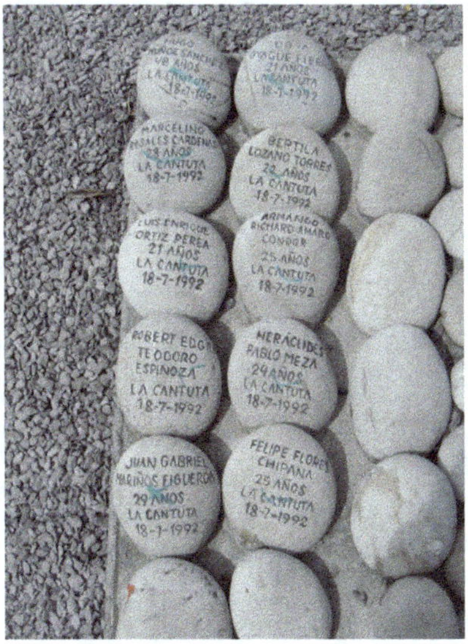

Plate 9.2 The Cantuta victims' names crossed out. The Ojo que llora, Lima, Peru. (Photograph by Cynthia Milton.)

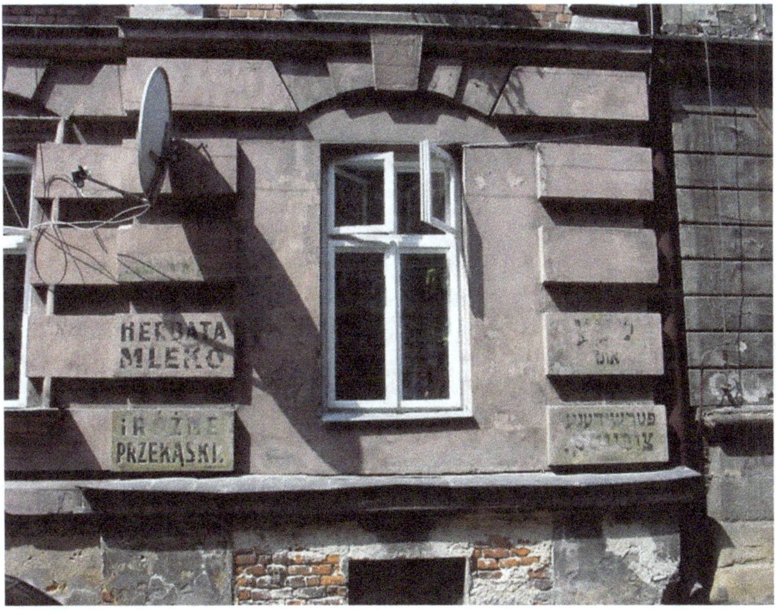

Plate 10.1 Tarnów, Goldhammer Str., 1990s. (Photograph by Sławomir Kapralski.)

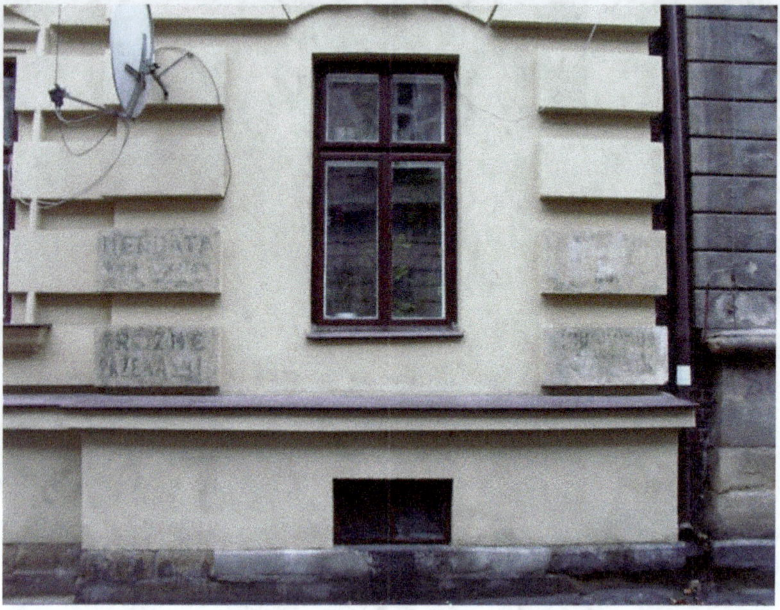

Plate 10.2 Tarnów, Goldhammer Str., 2000s. (Photograph by Sławomir Kapralski.)

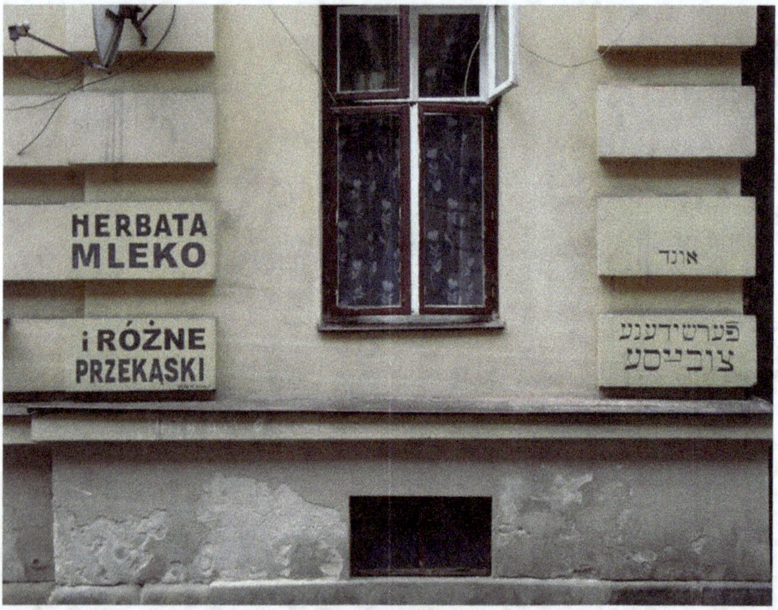

Plate 10.3 Tarnów, Goldhammer Str., June 2008. (Photograph by Mirosław Bieniecki.)

Indeed, the exhibition space became a performative arena in which visual images and verbal interpretations combined to produce a particular version of "difficult knowledge." This knowledge was difficult in different ways for the diverse parties inhabiting the scene of occupation. By allowing it to surface, the soldiers sought to alleviate their own struggle with this knowledge, in the hope of eventually contributing to ending the occupation. By naming this knowledge in the public sphere, group members presented themselves as uniquely positioned to deliver it to society at large through face-to-face performances that authenticated their position as witnesses who "were there." They could speak authoritatively, informatively, and persuasively about what they had seen and done, both pledging and calling for epistemic responsibility, a stance encapsulated in the oft-repeated phrase "Don't say you didn't know." For the soldiers, knowing entails countering denial, speaking out. As they explain in introducing their testimonial project:

> We got out of the army recently. Hebron was the hardest and most confusing place that we served in. Up until now we have all dealt with the shocking things we saw there. Our photo album, a souvenir from our service in Hebron, has remained sealed on a shelf in a room. But as time passed since our discharge, we discovered that those memories were common to all of us who served together. In coping daily with the madness of Hebron, we couldn't remain the same people beneath our uniforms. We saw our friends and ourselves slowly changing. Caught in impossible situations . . . We decided to speak out. We decided to tell. Hebron isn't in outer space. It's one hour from Jerusalem. But Hebron is light years away from Tel Aviv. Now all you have to do is to come. And see. And understand what's happening there.[6]

Thus, the Breaking the Silence exhibition went beyond a simple visual repository to represent the world of the occupation from the soldiers' point of view. It was constructed as a communicative occasion and a performance site that anchored a range of encounters in which occupation images and stories were woven into live exchanges between BTS exhibition guides and viewers, as well as among viewers themselves as they trailed along the exhibition walls. Some viewers encountered the vivid, cumulative documentation of myriad acts of violence and oppression as shocking news; for others they triggered a confrontation with deeply buried memories of a personal past. According to one of the exhibition organizers, the most important contribution of this exhibition was that it provided a space for soldiers to bring their parents and to begin to tell them long-suppressed stories about their experience of military service. Paradoxically, it was only when they were allowed to play out in the public sphere their traumatic experiences that the soldiers could speak with their families. Having overcome the taboo cast upon them by societal denial, the moral dilemmas surrounding military occupation could be inserted into the private, intergenerational dialogue of soldiers and their parents.

In mobilizing the exhibition space to perform their multi-modal soldierly testimonial, the BTS group presented themselves as both perpetrators and culpable witnesses. They consolidated this unusually inflected role in repeated tellings and re-tellings of occupation stories, woven orally around the pictorial display as they spoke. Through their tales they re-fashioned their role as soldiers of the occupation, turning themselves into perpetrator-observers, victimized-victimizers who are trapped in impossible, no-win, morally abhorrent situations of the sort indicated by the pictures lining the exhibition walls. It was only in performing an act of speaking out, in breaking the societal silence in which they and the exhibition's viewers had been enmeshed, that they were able to regain their sense of agency and begin to generate an audience for their protest.

In addition to the mostly peripheral venues in which the soldiers' exhibition was shown around the country, it was also hosted in the Israeli Parliament, the *Knesset*, at the initiative of one of the left-leaning parliamentarians. This combination of marginalization and institutional endorsement signaled the kind of official military policy that was eventually brought to bear in response to the soldiers' challenge. They were commended for their principled stand, and the public was assured that the army opposed human rights violations and was committed to handling all untoward behavior on the part of individual soldiers identified as violators strictly and effectively.

The exhibition received a second, virtual life in the gallery section of the BTS website, and has been available as a virtual resource to viewers for a number of years now. A videotape of the exhibition tour was also edited by the group for public dissemination alongside other materials they produced, notably booklets containing transcribed segments of soldiers' testimonials. Over time, an interesting extension of the group's activities marked an inverted counterpoint to the attempt to bring the sights of occupation in Hebron to Tel Aviv. Through regular organized "alternative" tours of the city of Hebron, Tel Avivians (and others) have also been brought to Hebron to see the tension-filled situation there through the eyes of some of the soldiers who had served there. The checkpoints dotting the landscape, the presence of military patrols, and particularly the sight of the ghostly core of Hebron, with its so-called sterile streets where even Palestinians who live in the area are not allowed to walk, are a striking testimony to the grip of the occupation regime. Photographs of the once-vibrant market area of the city, bustling with people and business—shown on-site by the tour guide to underline the current emptiness of the town's public spaces—and stories of harassment told by Palestinian host guides, whose homes are encircled by local Jewish settlers, provide on-the-ground testimonies that further authenticate the soldiers' personal narratives.

The main outcome of the exhibition, and the cultural conversation it generated, was the establishment of Breaking the Silence as a distinctive voice among other dissenting groups protesting the Israeli occupation of the Palestinian territories. The exhibition was a first step in what became a sustained effort to give voice to Israeli soldiers' predicament; as soldiers of the occupation, for these perpetrator-observers the agony and inhumanity entailed in its procedures and policies constitute a direct and vivid personal memory. The group became a recognized voice and fixture in Israeli civil society, and aligned with other anti-occupation groups. Periodically, the group reasserted its continued work and presence by disseminating new testimonies, offering commentary on published incidents concerning soldiers' conduct in the territories, supporting the staging of a play based on segments of soldiers' testimonies, and the making of documentary films in which such testimonies feature centrally.[7] Occasionally, BTS attempted to reach new audiences that they felt were relevant to their cause—either within Israel, by moving their exhibition to venues around the country, by running weekly installments of soldiers' testimonies in a popular online newspaper, or by organizing lectures by the group's core members for various, especially young, audiences. They even tried to extend the performative reach of their mission beyond Israel by organizing a traveling tour of an upgraded version of their photography exhibition in the US in February 2008, which was mainly targeted to Jewish and campus communities there.[8]

Not surprisingly, the group's activities created a good deal of controversy both in Israel and among Jewish communities in the US. While they commanded a great deal of respect and support from some quarters, articles about the group in the press, as well as the many "talkbacks" appended to articles BTS members themselves wrote in online newspapers, indicate that their activities often met with harsh criticism. They were accused of being soft-hearted and unrealistic, of being traitors who were out to malign the army rather than take responsibility for their own criminal actions, of caring for the Palestinians rather than for their own people, and so on. In addition, criticism coming from the radical left brought out what was considered an inconsistency in their position—their indictment of the immorality of the Israeli occupation regime coupled with their refusal to declare that they will not continue to serve as reservists in the occupied territories as other soldier-critics have done (Handel, 2008).

Over time, the initial belief, or hope, that the distinctive voice of the soldier-witness in the role of perpetrator-observer could directly affect current policies and serve as a wake-up call to Israeli society seemed increasingly untenable. As the freshness of the BTS challenge waned, its core members began to modify their activist goals and to speak the language of collective memory custodians, resigning themselves to the more modest goal of affecting the way the Al Aqsa Intifada and the Israeli occupation would be inscribed in future public memory. In particular, their concern was to include in the annals of Israeli history the voices of the traumatized soldiers who were struggling to reconcile themselves with the memory of what they had experienced and done. The photography exhibition, in its new incarnation in the group's digital archive, provides an ever-accessible reminder of the unsettling sights and experiences that triggered the soldiers' organized protest in the first place. Some of the images were so widely circulated that they became visual signatures of the BTS group and its project. As the reality of the occupation remained as harsh as ever, and the group's efforts were either marginalized or blocked by the military (e.g., their guided tours to Hebron were largely curtailed in the spring of 2008), their project became increasingly archival in its orientation. The soldiers' fearless speech did not provide the intervention they sought and they were left to relegate their hopes to the future, intent on preparing the ground for the change of heart that they hoped the forces of history would bring.

However, in mid-July 2009, the situation changed rather dramatically with the publication of a booklet of testimonies collected by Breaking the Silence group from Israeli soldiers who participated in the Cast Lead Operation in Gaza some six months earlier. All hell broke loose. BTS was virulently attacked by the military authorities, politicians, most media, and a host of public figures (while being more warmly embraced by the radical left than ever before). If their particular claims about human rights violations were not engaged in any substantive manner, their intentions, methods, and loyalty were severely questioned in an establishment-led attack.

The publication of the booklet at a time when the Israeli government was refusing to collaborate with Judge Goldstone's UN commission of inquiry into human rights violations associated with the Gaza incursion probably had a lot to do with the vehemence of the official response.[9] The more vehement the attacks on BTS the clearer it became that even though the public debate the group had wanted to instigate was crushed before it ever began, the group's activities around their Gaza report managed to unsettle officialdom in far-reaching ways.[10] It seemed that BTS had restored its original, activist ambition to affect immediate political change through soldierly voices of dissent, rather than reconciling itself to the more timid and long-term goal of affecting future public memory. Notably, however, in attaining this high public profile—a profile of notoriety—in conjunction with the Gaza invasion, they fell short of their original goal of alerting the public to the *routine* oppression associated with the occupation regime in what are considered to be normal times. Indeed, the extremity of the Gaza case seemed to work further to normalize the ongoing situation of military control in the occupied territories. It is this grinding, relentless reality of the occupation regime that made up the shared concern of both the BTS photography exhibition and that organized by the Checkpoint Watch group, which provides an intriguing case for comparison.

6.2 The "Endless Checkpoints" exhibition

The Checkpoint Watch group coalesced around a humanitarian ideology condensed in the words "No to Checkpoints, Against the Occupation, and For Human Rights" that were inscribed on tags the women wore on their lapels to identify them as members of the group. One way they sought to promote these goals and values was creating the "Endless Checkpoints" exhibition in February—March 2006 to mark the fifth anniversary of CPW. The group is one of a number of feminist women's groups that have been active players in the anti-occupation movement in Israel since the outbreak of the first Intifada in 1987; the most well-known is Women in Black, whose weekly vigils against the occupation have become a fixture in Israel's political landscape. Shortly after the outbreak of the second Intifada in 2000, ten of these groups including CPW sought to compound their effectiveness by forming an umbrella organization named The Coalition of Women for Peace.[11]

Thus, while the exhibition was part of the anti-occupation campaign conducted by CPW, it did not serve as an organizational launching occasion as did the BTS photography exhibition at its time. Rather, it functioned as an interim summary of the group's on-the-ground activities, and a visually anchored "happening" through which the iniquities of the occupation regime—epitomized by the checkpoint system—could be inserted into the Israeli public sphere. The CPW photography exhibition focused on images and stories designed to bring the grim reality of the occupation alive to Israeli audiences who had neither the occasion nor the will to familiarize themselves with its details. The CPW women rejected the prevalent "out of sight—out of mind" orientation that they considered responsible for the normalization of the occupation in the Israel/Palestine political landscape. The very fact that these pictures were taken by women activists who voluntarily and deliberately placed themselves in the zone of occupation in an attempt to monitor and constrain the army's activities in it was of particular significance. This usually unsung witnessing activity pointed to the possibility of non-violent dissident action. The exhibition and the publicity surrounding it were designed to demonstrate and legitimize this kind of witnessing as a concrete activist strategy.

In both BTS and CPW testimonials, "being there" was a condition for the constitution of the role of witness, but the process of becoming witnesses in each of these cases was quite a different proposition. The starting-point for BTS witnesses was total enmeshment and complicity with the scene of occupation, requiring a movement of self-estrangement and a reflexive stance. Their authority as narrators of soldiers' occupation experiences was not in question, but their claims concerning the representativeness of their personal points of view needed to be substantiated again and again. This was the case not only in establishing the factuality of their accounts, but also in their self-positioning as helpless victims of the chaotic situation in which soldiers consistently found themselves.

The Checkpoint Watchers—most of them older, educated, middle-class Jewish women—initially had no direct familiarity with the scene of occupation. In fact, some of their narratives echoed the soldiers' troubled stories of moral shock on their first encounters with the occupation scene. The women's explicit point of departure, however, was a generalized identification with a humanitarian ethos that led them to take the unpopular step of positioning themselves at the checkpoints in full sight of the Palestinians' daily scenes of suffering and humiliation. Their empathy with the plight of the Palestinians under occupation and their critical attitude toward its outrages clearly placed them in opposition to the military forces controlling the checkpoints and, not surprisingly, their attempts to mediate between the Palestinians and the soldiers in individual cases often triggered the army's anger and disapproval.

In audaciously inserting themselves into the checkpoint scene, the Checkpoint Watchers sought to familiarize themselves with what had previously been to them a socially and emotionally distant reality. They did not content themselves with displays of emotional solidarity, but educated themselves about the arrangements and procedures that made possible the scenes they recorded in word and image. They closely followed individual cases and stories of abuse in real time, and, more often than not, under duress. They thus gradually gained some recognition by high-level military commanders on the one hand and the Israeli left on the other, and used it to promote an alternative to the highly militarized checkpoint narrative; in their version, it was Palestinian civilian suffering, rather than Palestinians as a potential threat to Jewish security, that took center stage. The commentary accompanying the CPW exhibition indicates that the pictures included in it "document the unbearably harsh life to which the Palestinian population is subjected" and expresses the hope that "glancing into this reality may bring this nightmare closer to its end."[12]

The women's point of view remained external and highly gendered, yet it was a many-layered one, simultaneously encompassing a recognition of the Palestinian civilians' suffering and humiliation, a recognition of the Israeli soldiers' exasperation at the tasks assigned to them, and the ways in which fulfilling those tasks often led to their own brutalization. The women were keenly aware of the wider society's concern about the moral degradation associated with the occupation regime, but also understood that this concern was coupled with a widespread inability truly to confront the occupation's roots or consequences. Traces of this complex stance could be found in the kinds of visual images included among the 80 photographs that made up the exhibition, and the commentary attending them. They contained memorable images of anguish and humiliation—as inscribed, for example, in the postures and faces of Palestinians crowded at checkpoints, scrambling over a barrier, crouched under the towering Separation Wall. There was also a picture of a forlorn soldier facing overwhelming crowds.

A recurrent feature in both the soldiers' and the women's pictures involves the juxtaposition of the soldier figure with Palestinian individuals or crowds, in postures of domination and instances of direct contact. Notably, however, in the Breaking the Silence case the soldiers' documentation of their own and their peers' presence at the site of occupation cannot help but address the core problematic of their complex positioning; their credibility rests on their presence and visibility as perpetrators as well as observers. The Checkpoint Watchers, by contrast, are not visible within the picture frames. They are mere observers, apparent outsiders to the scene of occupation they meticulously document.

Alongside poignant and disturbing scenes of occupation, the CPW exhibition also contained information in the form of texts and maps that shared with visitors the group's extensive knowledge of the occupation machinery. The information was attractively packaged and disseminated by CPW members on wall panels, as well as in leaflets and brochures used in other protest meetings. Using both words and images, the Checkpoint Watchers' sought metaphorically to bring the checkpoints to Tel Aviv as part of their humanitarian campaign.

Bringing the checkpoints to Tel Aviv, however, turned out to be a difficult venture. Not only did the group find it hard to locate a venue for the exhibition in the Tel Aviv area, they also had difficulties moving it to other locations when the Tel Aviv exhibition ended. Most notably, plans to bring it to the southern city of Beer-Sheva were aborted by the city's Mayor, Yaacov Turner, a former Air-Force General who, following some citizens' complaints, cancelled a previously granted permit to use a municipally-operated Teachers' Center as an exhibition venue. CPW's protest against the violation of their freedom of speech was overruled in the interest of "not hurting public feelings." As in the case of the BTS exhibition, the CPW version had a second life on the group's website as well as in printed publications disseminated by the group. Also in this case, the visual experience provided by the exhibition was later complemented by an invitation to take an unmediated look at the reality of the checkpoints in actual tours organized by the Watchers as part of their campaign to educate the public about the arrangements and practices of containment and control the checkpoints epitomize.

The CPW exhibition was more an educational and public relations effort based on a strongly visual representational strategy, than a self-constituting, performative organizational tool. By inviting the public to actual and virtual tours of the lived reality of the checkpoints as captured by the activist-observer gaze, CPW sought to mobilize public opinion in the struggle against the normalization and routinization of the Israeli matrix of control in the occupied territories. They did so by dramatizing its effect on both the Palestinian population and on a young generation of Israeli soldiers. Their photographic project, which was an extension of their provocative witnessing and interventionist strategies, was grounded in the assumption that seeing is believing, and that knowledge of visually communicated truths carries with it epistemic responsibility. It was mainly through their actual, real-time, practices of physical presence that they performed their dissenting role.

These on-the-ground practices—in which the women were *present* within the frames of oppressive occupation activity—remained the heart and soul of their project, rather than the mediated truths of their subsequent exhibitions.

6.3 Concluding remarks

The overall goal of the two dissident groups discussed in this chapter is to help end the Israeli occupation of the Palestinians' territories. Both see ending the occupation as a first step in alleviating the Palestinian plight, doing justice to their demands for national sovereignty as well as ridding young Israeli soldiers of the burden of participating in the daily control of the Palestinian population. Both groups, too, respond to what they consider to be the self-imposed silence that prevents Israelis—as individuals and as a nation—from facing the consequences of the ongoing occupation regime.

The Breaking the Silence testimonial project—while anchored in the recognition of the human rights violations associated with the daily military measures—foregrounds the soldiers' predicament in their role as upholders of the occupation regime. The Checkpoint Watch project, on the other hand, while recognizing this soldierly predicament, promotes its dissident claims mainly by foregrounding the plight of the Palestinians under occupation. In so doing, they insist on the need for military policies that can be better reconciled with Israel's core humanistic values and its commitments as signatory to international agreements designed to preserve the human dignity of all.

The two groups disseminate their messages through a combined strategy of showing and telling, constructing their campaigns by weaving together words and images in a range of genres and media. In each case, and in similar ways, they mobilize the public to become part of the message's trajectory of circulation. Viewers are not just invited to act as audiences to the visual and verbal testimonies produced by the group, but asked to incorporate these into their everyday lifeworlds through self-examination and social interaction in family groups and public settings. As indicated earlier, the display strategy and viewing experience of these exhibitions involve notable performative dimensions; the sense of participation, though, is more clearly marked in the BTS exhibition, as it galvanized soldiers and their families and opened new avenues for long-suppressed intergenerational conversations.

The difference, I suggest, lies in the different relations between the photographic images and the verbal texts in these two exhibitions.

Building on a distinction drawn by Barthes (1977), we could say that in the BTS exhibition the relation is one of *anchorage*, that is, the soldiers' accompanying (oral) verbal texts are mainly used to fixate the meanings of the highly ambiguous images the photographs present. In the case of the CPW exhibition, the (mainly written) verbal accounts integrated into the exhibition text as captions, maps and associated data function as what Barthes terms *relays, positioning* the verbal and the visual in complementary relations, as amplifications of each other rather than as meaning-making, interpretive tools.

This analysis resonates with Nathanson's (2007) study of the banalization of photographic representations of the Occupation in the Israeli press, which he contrasts with photographic images found in private albums of some BTS soldiers. It may shed some light on the particular "transgressive" nature of the BTS project of visual testimony as discussed by Nathanson. He argues that the BTS soldiers' photographs are transgressive in that they do not follow the implicit norms that govern journalists' published photographic images of the occupation. Their pictures do not follow the normative photojournalistic code that mandates that the power relations between occupier and occupied be visually dramatized in a clear-cut, binary fashion.

The Breaking the Silence pictures include a range of ambiguous images, inscribing border-zones where power relations are blurred and social categories unsettled. Rather than unthinkingly reproducing the assumptions underlying the occupation scene through the use of familiar tropes, they entice viewers to realign their visual expectations in ways that lead toward questioning the social arrangements underpinning them. These uncoded images, which capture the human face of the occupation in its small, unexpected moments, are ideologically under-determined. Unlike the moral shock produced by the dramatic photographs of the occupation found in the mainstream media and in part of the CPW exhibition, BTS's transgressive images seem to contain the performative seeds for viewers' interpretations, appropriations, and dissemination of the group's call to re-moralize the Israeli public sphere in response to the invitation extended from the perpetrator-observers' unsettled and unsettling position.

The Checkpoint Watch exhibition invites viewers to join the Watchers as unlikely humanitarian witnesses in the scene of military occupation. As self-appointed observers, not backed by any institutional endorsement, their very presence disturbs the gendered military logic that dominates the checkpoint scene. Exhibition viewers are called upon to share the women's sense of shock and dismay triggered by the stark images that dramatize the power differential between occupier and occupied as binary categories and thereby make a strong claim on viewers' empathy and sense of "truth."

Along somewhat different lines, the BTS exhibition invites viewers to share in the soldiers' self-reflexive move, to relate what they see to their deeply buried personal experiences, or to re-examine their position as secondary, background participants in the occupation scene. Through back-and-forth talk between guides and viewers that punctuate the guided tour of the exhibition—exchanges that seem to encourage further spontaneous conversation among groups of viewers themselves—visitors to the BTS exhibition are enticed into a socially oriented viewing experience: they can be seen huddled in small groups in front of images that have caught their attention, exchanging hushed commentaries, providing additional layers of meaning and affect to the images through emotional displays and the performance of personal anecdotes. The exhibition's ability to provide the impetus for a new kind of encounter between soldiers and their parents created ripples of dialogue that penetrated viewers' intimate circles and innermost lives.

Presence is the condition of possibility for the construction of the witnessing role by the BTS and CPW groups. It is through "being there" that they can document the scene of occupation that unfolds before their eyes. Yet their different ways of being there—as post-factum reflective perpetrator-observers in the BTS case, or as unlikely, yet ultimately transparent intruders in the occupation scene in the CPW case—have yielded different sorts of truth-telling occasions. In Foucault's (2001) terms, both groups—each in their own way—engaged in "fearless speech": choosing to speak the truth when silence is the norm. Both placed themselves squarely outside the consensus, relinquishing their preferential position as *bona fide* soldiers in the first case and as respectable, educated middle-class women in the second. Taking advantage of the freedom of speech that dissident groups in Israeli society enjoy, they promoted discourses that counter hegemonic speech and give voice to silenced realities.

It is difficult to assess what impact, if any, the critical voices of these two groups have had. The vehemence with which their campaigns have been attacked by detractors suggests they have touched a raw nerve in Israeli society. The groups themselves seem to vacillate between two goals—a maximalist, activist desire to effect real change in the world around them, and a more subdued recognition that all they can currently do is to expand the nature and reach of public "sayables." In so doing, they inscribe the present as the future's imagined past, ensuring that the lessons of the occupation become part of the historical record.

Notes

1. The BTS veterans' group, which is comprised of some 15 core members, has collected over 700 testimonies from soldier-witnesses to date. Further information about it, including a photography archive, can be found on the group's website, available at http://www.shovrimshtika.org/index_e.asp [Accessed September 26, 2010].
2. Further information about the CPW group, which is comprised of some 400 members, can be found in the group's website, available at http://www.machsomwatch.org/en [Accessed September 26, 2010].
3. These on-the-ground measures, which are formulated within a discourse of "security," can be seen as materializing what Yosefa Loshitzky has called Israel's "fantasy of absolute power" that she considers to be a response to the "memory of powerlessness" associated with Diaspora Jewish experience (Loshitzky, 2006). The centrality of the power/powerlessness theme in the making of Israeli ethos has been discussed in my earlier work in conjunction with the emergence of Israeli style of "straight talk," or *dugri* speech (Katriel, 1986).
4. The 1994 massacre by the Jewish orthodox settler-physician, Dr. Baruch Goldstein, of 29 Palestinians who were praying in the Cave of the Patriarchs, a site holy to both Jews and Muslims, marks the peak of what has become an ongoing struggle over control of Hebron involving the Palestinians, Jewish settlers, activist groups, and the military. For Jewish Hebron see Hebron, City of the Patriarchs, available at http://www.hebron.com/english/ [Accessed September 26, 2010].
5. Anonymity was needed for fear that the soldiers whose testimonies incriminated them would be prosecuted by the military police. The detention of some of the BTS core activists when the exhibition initially opened indicated that this fear was not unfounded.
6. BTS booklet, *Soldiers Speak out about their Service in Hebron*, excerpts from "The Soldiers' Letter," Hebron, February 2004. Printed in Jerusalem, March 2004.
7. Notably, BTS are credited in an award-winning documentary made up of testimonies of women-soldiers who had served in the territories. Tamar Yarom (2007) *To See If I'm Smiling*. Available at http://2nd-ops.com/editors/?p=5370 [Accessed September 26, 2010].
8. The exhibition was shown in Philadelphia and at the Harvard Hillel House. My former students, Oren Livio and Keren Tennenboim, conducted interviews and ethnographic fieldwork related to the tour in Philadelphia, and we hope to address these events in a future publication.
9. In a journalistic interview he gave to a local Haifa weekly following the publication of the report issued by the committee he headed, Judge Goldstone explicitly mentioned the BTS booklet on the Cast Lead Operation as one of the sources they consulted (Matan, 2009).
10. The attacks on BTS were so virulent that the Tel Aviv and Jerusalem weeklies, *Ha'Ir* and *Kol Ha'Ir*, jointly devoted an extensive article to the army spokesperson's institutionalized effort to delegitimize and silence the group and to his success with the Israeli media in this endeavor (Grossman and Matan, 2009). Also, a critical report of the media's treatment of the BTS intervention in the Gaza case was disseminated by a civic media-monitoring organization (in Hebrew). *Keshev*: The Center for the Protection of Democracy in Israel

(2009). Available at http://www.keshev.org.il/site/FullNews.asp?NewsID=182 &CategoryID=9 [Accessed September 26, 2010].

11. Information about the Coalition and its member organizations is available at http://coalitionofwomen.org/home/english [Accessed September 27, 2010].
12. *Endless Checkpoints*, "Galleries" section of CPW website, available at http://www.ziv-p.com/MW/ [Accessed September 26, 2010].

Works cited

Barthes, Roland (1977). *Image, Music, Text*. New York: The Noonday Press.

Berger, John (2002). "The Ambiguity of the Photograph." In Kelly Askew and Richard R. Wilk (eds). *The Anthropology of Media Reader*. Oxford: Blackwell.

Foucault, Michel (2001). *Fearless Speech*. Los Angeles, CA: Semiotext(e).

Ginsburg, Ruthie (2009). "Framing, Misframing, and Reframing: 'The Fiddler at Beit-Iba Checkpoint.'" In Elisabeth Marteu (ed.). *Civil Organizations and Protest Movements in Israel*. New York: Palgrave Macmillan.

Givoni, Michal (2008). *Edut Bif'ula: Etika Upolitika Be'olam Lelo Gvulot*. [Witnessing in Action: Ethics and Politics in a World without Borders]. PhD. Dissertation, Tel Aviv University.

Grossman, Lital and Matan, Ofer (2009). "Hatzenzor Harashi." [The Head Censor] *Ha'Ir*, July 24, pp. 38–42.

Handel, Ariel (2008). "Me'ever Latov Velaro'a—Hatismonet: Busha Ve'achrajut Ba'edujot." [Beyond Good and Evil: Shame and Responsibility in Soldiers' Testimonies] *Theory & Criticism* 32: 45–69.

Jasper, James M. (1997). *The Art of Moral Protest: Culture, Biography, and Creativity in Social Movements*. Chicago: The University of Chicago Press.

Katriel, Tamar (1986). *Talking Straight: Dugri Speech in Israeli Sabra Culture*. Cambridge: Cambridge University Press.

Katriel, Tamar (2009). "Inscribing Narratives of Occupation in Israeli Popular Memory." In Michael Keren and Holger H. Herwig (eds). *War Memory and Popular Culture: Essays on Modes of Remembrance and Commemoration*. Jefferson, NC: McFarland Publishers.

Kaufman, Ilana (2008). "Resisting Occupation or Institutionalizing Control? Israeli Women and Protest in West Bank Checkpoints." *International Journal of Peace Studies* 13(1): 43–62.

Kirstein Keshet, Yehudit (2006). *Checkpoint Watch: Testimonies from Occupied Palestine*. London: Zed Books.

Loshitzky, Yosefa (2006). "Pathologizing Memory: From the Holocaust to the *Intifada*." *Third Text* 20(3/4): 327–35.

Mansbach, Daniela (2007). "*Mecha'a al Hagvul: Kocha shel Hadu'alijut Bepraktikot Hamecha'a shel Tnu'at Machsom Watch*." [The Power of the Duality: The Protest of the "Checkpoint Watch" Movement] *Theory and Criticism* (31): 77–99.

Matan, Ofer (2009). "Lema'ase, Kol Hamivtza Be'Aza Jachol Lehechashev Pesha Neged Ha'enoshut." [Actually, the Whole Operation in Gaza Can be Considered a Crime against Humanity] *Kolbo*, September 25, p. 46.

Nathanson, Regev (2007). "Metzalmim Kibush: Soziologia shel Jiizug Chazuti." [Shooting Occupation: Sociology of Visual Representation] *Theory & Criticism* (31): 127–54.

7
Visualizing Apartheid: Re-Framing Truth and Reconciliation through Contemporary South African Art

Erin Mosely

Amid the South African government's 1985 declaration of a state of emergency, as violent struggle against the system of racial oppression known as apartheid was intensifying, artist Jane Alexander made a statement—a chilling, perverse, and unforgettable statement in the form of three, life-size sculptures. Aptly titled *Butcher Boys* and permanently housed in the South African National Gallery, this assemblage of creatures elicits a visceral sensation of fear and repulsion. They were men, but have transformed into demons; they are human, but simultaneously not human, or at least not anymore. Evoking the larger societal context in which apartheid flourished—a racist, overly militarized, and masculinized regime sustained by authoritarianism and the routine use of violence—Alexander's piece lends stark visualization to the insidious ways in which the apartheid system distorted the humanity of its perpetrators. (See Plate 7.1.)

Encountering *Butcher Boys* in the gallery space, which allows observers fully to apprehend the eerie details of their diseased state—horns and snouts, knotted spines, those vacuous, soulless eyes—one cannot avoid being struck by the corrosive effects of apartheid on its white practitioners. Alexander's piece stands as a testament to darker days, a time in which boys grew into butchers, and as such it makes an important insight into South Africa's transition to democracy. Provocative, frightening, and uncomfortable to witness, this sculpture functions as a powerful visual reminder of what the country has left behind and, along with many other contemporary art pieces and installations, contributes to a growing archive of visual culture that seeks to make sense of the violence and complexity of the former regime.

This chapter aims to connect the activities of contemporary artists in South Africa to the country's larger project of national reconciliation, specifically with regard to memorialization. How have artists contributed to and shaped the construction of collective memory about apartheid? In particular, how have they engaged and/or re-imagined the Truth and Reconciliation Commission (TRC), which served as the country's official public mechanism for excavating the past?[1] Through a visual overview and analysis, I hope to demonstrate that South African artists have acted as skillful agents of change during the transition and as important "curators" of difficult knowledge, undertaking projects which not only grapple with the varied legacies of apartheid but which contest the narrow ways that those legacies have been framed through the dominant TRC process.

The larger argument conveyed in this chapter—based on a selection of representative artwork and exhibits—is that contemporary art and visual culture can act as an insightful prism through which to understand the highly nuanced and sometimes contradictory experiences generated by conflict and authoritarianism. Furthermore, it is imperative that we recognize the diverse ways in which people seek to reckon with and represent violent events of the past. Periods of transition do not simply end with the publication of an official truth commission report or with the judgment of former dictators and war criminals. On the contrary, the politics of memory continue; in fact, it is often in the wake of these moments of national closure that some of the most provocative and meaningful responses to former atrocities materialize. Building on Gómez-Barris's work on "memory symbolics," which she claims "can be mobilized to selectively manage history in ways that reproduce state hegemony," I position my discussion of South African art within her framework of an "alternative memory symbolics," which both "challenge[s] and cast[s] doubt on these limited renditions by suggesting that memory-making is complex, fluid, unending, and incomplete" (2008: 5–6).

7.1 The truth about apartheid: a critical appraisal of the TRC

Societies undergoing political transitions have come to rely heavily on memory as an indispensable tool within larger processes of transitional justice and reconciliation. Whether by way of war crimes trials, truth commissions, or the creation of monuments and museums (or some combination of these approaches), the public articulation of memory, specifically with regard to trauma, has come to occupy a privileged position within efforts to deal with and make sense of the past.

Since the early 1990s, truth commissions in particular have emerged as one of the most popular mechanisms for investigating past periods of violence, and because of this they have assumed a powerful role in the creation of both national and international collective memories about former conflicts.[2] During South Africa's transition this was certainly the case, for the TRC operated as the central framing device through which individual memories about apartheid circulated. The entire process has had a demonstrable effect in shaping the country's collective understanding of its own modern history. And yet, popular criticism of the TRC suggests that it resulted in an incomplete picture of the past. Overlooking the issue of structural violence, imposing what many considered to be a confining "reconciliation" framework, and reducing the highly gendered experiences of living during the apartheid era to a series of civil and political rights violations, the TRC ultimately functioned as a hegemonic enterprise, one which restricted, and on a certain level predetermined, the overall story that would be told about the past. In the end, despite its notable achievements, the Commission was heavily faulted, both for its overemphasis on symbolic redress and for its perceived failure to convey a meaningful "truth" about apartheid.[3]

Given these limitations, the TRC might best be considered as merely the prelude to the story. And, as Edkins usefully observes, "The story is never finished: the scripting of memory by those in power can always be challenged, and such challenges are very often found at moments and in places where the very foundations of the imagined community are laid out" (2003: 18–19). Gómez-Barris echoes this point, commenting that while official mechanisms such as truth commissions attempt to bring finality to past political violence, "from below the heterogeneous effects of violence constantly threaten to rupture and disarticulate the transitional national project" (2008: 26). Ultimately, then, we must situate the TRC in its appropriate context, recognizing that in addition to (or in spite of) the work it completed, it has served as a valuable springboard for the continued negotiation of memories relating to apartheid.

7.2 Alternative memory makers: South African artists as public citizens

The contemporary art world in South Africa has served as a veritable hotbed for re-articulating the past, and as an important counterweight to the dominant narrative imposed by the TRC. As Enwezor writes:

> They had a passion for it. Throughout the 1990s artists in South Africa took on enunciating the relationship between memory and history. As if in one paroxysm of recollection a flood of artistic works—profound and prosaic—began entering the public domain. (2004: 33)

Just surveying a list of exhibits that have taken place since the early 1990s—*Fault Lines, Setting Apart, Liberated Voices, Digging Deeper, Truth Veils, Facing the Past: Seeking the Future*—reveals that exploring the complexity of South Africa's past and engaging its transition to democracy have been of high priority for both artists and curators. According to a press release for the 1996 exhibition *Fault Lines: Inquiries into Truth and Reconciliation*, "Betrayal, sadism, mourning, loss, confession, memory, reparation, longing, these are the persistent themes of the arts . . . Through the arts we can explore who we are, and why we do what we do to one another" (cited in Marlin-Curiel, 1999: 1). What this statement suggests is that the artistic realm may serve as a particularly appropriate forum in which to address painful histories of trauma, owing to its unique capacity to navigate the emotional dimensions of such experiences.

South African artists have also maintained a relative amount of autonomy, remaining independent from national political projects such as reconciliation, nation building or, as was the case in South Africa, legitimizing the post-apartheid government. And yet, in many interesting ways, South African artists have contributed to the nation building process. As Stremlau comments about Sam Nhlengethwa, whose work innovatively fuses remembrance and aspiration:

> He is in essence a 'Mandela man', who forgives but does not forget, looking to the future with hope and exuding joy in our progress thus far without minimizing our shortcomings or the problems just ahead. Sam Nhlengethwa is at heart a nation builder, trying to locate and amplify the chords within us, which with enough goodwill and empathy could be improvised into the social harmonies required to develop a truly democratic nation.
>
> (2006: 143)

Given that many of South Africa's esteemed contemporary artists were deeply involved in the struggle against apartheid, engaging in various forms of protest art and other activism, one can argue that it was somewhat of a foregone conclusion that they would remain tuned in during apartheid's unraveling and continue to be active during the period following its demise.[4] As Becker explains, in South Africa during the early 1990s this did not even prompt much discussion—it was just "assumed that all cultural workers would have a significant role in the long-awaited transition and in future decision making" (1994: xvi).

Underpinning Becker's comment is the idea that artists serve a civic function in society, especially in times of political and social upheaval. In the context of transitional South Africa, many artists agreed with this perspective, articulating in interviews and other statements that they felt they must be involved, to propel the transition forward by probing the complicated layers of the past. As Penny Siopis explained in the late 1990s:

> [O]ur very sense of the present, the very idea of being a "new South African" is predicated not only on a shared, politically-charged history, but also on the imperative to look back, unpick and unpack that history, to understand not only what happened . . . but also, more importantly, the psychic and affective dimension of that experience.
>
> (Cited in Neke, 1999: 8)

Fernando Alvim, Carlos Garaicoa, and Gavin Younge, in their 1997 artists' statement for the exhibit *Memorias Intimas Marcas*, attested to a similar feeling of civic duty, declaring:

> [W]e cannot afford to invest in placebo cures to the past. We need to explore our consciences and our complicity with recent history, deconstructing the legacies of apartheid. This cannot only happen "officially" as it is currently through the Truth and Reconciliation Commission; it is an invested process which involves the individual and needs to be enacted on many levels.
>
> (Cited in Marlin-Curiel, 1999: 1)

Reflecting on these two statements in the historical context of South African art practice, we can begin to understand the subtle shifts in perception that have occurred among artists regarding their roles as public citizens. What emerged as a radical opposition movement dedicated to exposing the racism and brutality of apartheid and actively combating the state has evolved into a more self-reflexive set of practices grounded in reflection and memorialization.[5]

7.3 Building blocks: artistic engagement with the TRC archive

The TRC has served as a vibrant source of creative inspiration for South African artists. As Richards describes, "The proliferation of publications, literary, and artistic responses to the TRC and what it represented (good and ill) bear testimony to what a fundamentally generative, creative phenomenon it was, and remains" (2004: 17). A number of artists have readily borrowed from the TRC, especially its archival documents and photographic images, as a way to reassemble these materials within new interpretive frameworks for understanding the past.

Sue Williamson is one of the most notable artists in this regard. In describing her interest in building on the TRC process, she has said: "To think we would finally hear the truth, which was beyond what could have been imagined, beyond the veil of secrecy and absolute blatant lies. I knew I would do something with it. I cut out newspaper articles and kept files and finally had the idea to do something case by case" (*Art Throb*, Art Bios). One result was Williamson's series *Truth Games* (1998), which has appeared in multiple exhibits throughout South Africa and abroad. (See Plate 7.2.) An assortment of interactive art pieces, *Truth Games* consists of "fragmented and dissected text from the TRC hearings arranged on sliding panels with photographic images that viewers can manipulate themselves" (Marlin-Curiel, 1999: 5). Dawes describes the spatial setup of each piece as follows:

> On the left is the victim or accuser; on the right, the perpetrator or defendant. The central panel is an image that stands in for the unrepresentable event: a photograph of the dead person, a gravestone, a shattered vehicle, a weeping crowd. These images in turn are cut across by . . . phrases excerpted from transcripts of the hearings: "Can't forget," "That is ludicrous," "I'm sorry about your mom," "Reduced the bodies to ash," and so on in a terrible rhythm of banality and trauma, tort and confessional.
>
> (2003: 10)

Viewers are invited to move the sliding panels in order to create their own set of textual juxtapositions. To explain her choice of wanting to have the audience participate in the piece, Williamson says:

> I like to make work people feel ready to get engaged with, so they don't just walk past. Lots of images are quite familiar images so I re-present them so viewers are seeing something quite familiar to them in a new or different context. In many ways, I am acting as an archivist. I am presenting material in a serious way.
>
> (*Art Throb*, Art Bios)

In addition to acting as an archivist, however, Williamson manages to subtly question the TRC's authority. By creating a space in which observers become the authors of the truth and by referring to truth telling as a game, this piece complicates the very notion of collective truth, suggesting instead that the TRC produced multiple, and sometimes incompatible or incommensurable truths.[6] As Dawes insightfully concludes, when the viewer walks away from *Truth Games*, "There are no winners, only a concealing-revealing slippage between phrases in dispute" (2003: 10).

7.3.1 Creative acts of solidarity: art and the amnesty hearings

Another way that artists have engaged the TRC is through work that interacts directly with the Commission's controversial amnesty hearings.[7] Sam Nhlengethwa's *It left him cold (the death of Steve Biko)* (1990), for example, depicts the torture and murder of one of South Africa's most beloved figures, Black Consciousness leader Steve Biko.[8] (See Plate 7.3.) According to the artist:

> Biko's piece reflects my emotions at the time of his death. I was very angry at the Apartheid system, its injustices and human rights abuses. When the news of Biko's death broke, there was turmoil throughout the country; there was anger that seemed to rub off instantly. His death flew right into the face of his hope when he said, "In time, we shall be in a position to bestow on South Africa the greatest possible gift—a more human face."
>
> (Cited in Dodd, 2006: 70)

The result was both haunting and elegiac. As Oliphant describes the piece:

> Nhlengethwa presents the vulnerability of the body and its decimation through torture. The multiple perspectives are more than the mere formalities of the cut, paste, draw and paint techniques of assemblage. They are the inscriptions of torture and dismemberment. The twisted figure lies naked on the floor of what can only be described as an interrogation chamber. The torso, resting rigidly on its side, is turned to the viewer. The feet, severed from the lower parts of the legs, are twisted upward to conform to a body lying on its back. The large head is fractured and bruised. The dark interior is filled with icons of a police world. Beyond this, a universe in tumult looms.
>
> (1995: 258)

It left him cold—which eventually was chosen as one of the century's most powerful images in Phaidon's 1996 publication *The 20th*

Century Art Book—evokes an immediate response on the part of the viewer. As Dodd explains, "There is a great tenderness at the heart of Nhlengethwa's work . . . You've got to be willing to give yourself over to the image, but in doing so, you may well discover that through aesthetic associations . . . this kind of communicative gesture is also a healing one" (2006: 87). Undoubtedly, the piece provides a sharp juxtaposition to former Minister of Justice James Kruger's statement immediately following the murder (reflected in Nhlengethwa's choice of title) in which he said, "I am not glad and I am not sorry about Mr. Biko. It leaves me cold" (cited in Peffer, 2009: 178). It also serves as a poignant supplement to the later amnesty hearings in which Biko's murderers "confessed" to his torture. Through its subtle and provocative rendering of what Gómez-Barris describes as the "terror imaginary," *It left him cold* delivers a powerful visual indictment of Biko's murderers, providing a much-needed counterbalance to the amnesty hearings in which they refused to take responsibility for their crimes, insisting that Biko's death was accidental (2008).[9]

Such artistic solidarity can also be seen in Judith Mason's series *The Man who Sang and the Woman who Kept Silent* (1998), which hangs proudly in the foyer leading up to the Constitutional Court in Johannesburg.[10] The catalyst for Mason's piece, which consists of three related parts, was a story that emerged in one of the TRC's amnesty hearings about the torture, degradation, and eventual murder of activist Phila Ndwande, whom the security personnel forced to strip naked for the duration of her detention and interrogations. At a certain point, Ndwande found a discarded blue plastic grocery sack, and proceeded to fashion it into an undergarment—it was to be her last defiant attempt at restoring her own dignity. When her body was later exhumed, remnants of the blue plastic bag remained.

Mason was deeply affected by Ndwande's story, but felt frustrated that she had to hear about it through the callous, unapologetic voices of her killers at the amnesty hearings. "I wept when I heard Phila's story, saying to myself, 'I wish I could make you a *dress*'" (cited in Sachs, 2009: vii). Deciding to act on this impulse, the artist re-imagined the legendary blue undergarment as a series of blue dresses, one of which is actually sewn from blue plastic grocery sacks. (See Plate 7.4.) Painted onto the skirt of the sewn dress, she includes the following message:

> Sister, a plastic bag may not be the armour of God, but you were wrestling with flesh and blood, and against powers, against the

> rulers of darkness, against spiritual wickedness in sordid places. Your weapons were your silence and a piece of rubbish. Finding that bag and weaving it until you were disinterred is such a frugal, common-sensical, house-wifely thing to do, an ordinary act . . . At some level you shamed your capturers, and they did not compound their abuse of you by stripping you a second time. Yet they killed you. We only know your story because a sniggering man remembered how brave you were. Memorials to your courage are everywhere; they blow about in the streets and drift on the tide and cling to the bushes. This dress is made from some of them.

Mason's imaginative commemoration of Ndwande's struggle represents an act of "repersonalization" that, as Marlin-Curiel notes, "is a necessary step in the process of the societal transformation . . . the TRC aim[ed] to achieve" (1999: 3). I would also argue that pieces like *The Blue Dress* and *It left him cold,* which situate themselves within and yet beyond the limits of the TRC, manage to free themselves from its confining reconciliation framework, if only in that they permit a greater range of emotional reactions and critique—in this case to the often unsatisfactory amnesty confessions.

7.4 Filling the gaps: artistic examinations of structural violence

In addition to artwork that has complemented the work of the TRC—albeit in imaginative and subversive ways—there has also been art that has worked well beyond its narrow purview, underscoring how certain dimensions of the past were completely excluded from the TRC process. In particular, projects focusing on structural violations, such as racially-coded spatial planning and forced removals, have been among the most compelling in South Africa during the transition, bearing witness to what many consider to be apartheid's most destructive crimes.

The installation *Setting Apart,* for example, undertaken by architect Hilton Judin and exhibited at the Cape Town Castle in 1995, focused on the official language of racial separation during the apartheid years, presenting archival documents such as maps, city plans, and official communications.

> The aim was to display and dissect the syntaxes of official apartheid discourse, and the way its language conferred power by naming, ranking, and classifying by race, gender, and class. In particular it laid bare the repetitive exclusionary grammar that justified spatial zoning

on racial lines, demonstrating the controlling practice of regulatory syntax itself.

(de Kok, 1998: 68–9)

Setting Apart also incorporated an aural dimension, or a "speaking back" as de Kok describes it, in the form of audio projected interviews in which "elderly black people spoke of the consequences of removal on individual and community life, on social trust, on consequent activism." The combination was forlornly powerful. In de Kok's words, "The narrative of destruction, in voice and document, was a mutually soliloquized text" (1998: 67). Another reviewer came away with a more extreme reaction, feeling disturbed and distressed. To him, *Setting Apart* "[read] like a brain scan of South African power and madness . . . a narrow, mean, brutal, colonial place [with] detailed procedures through which black people were turned into objects of disgust and dread, and expelled . . . beyond the limits of the city" (cited in Neke, 1999: 8).

The location of Judin's exhibit in the Cape Town Castle only amplified its symbolic impact, given the Castle's longstanding associations with "military power, apartheid control, and secrecy" (de Kok, 1998: 67). Through its layered exposé of the cold logic and brutal ramifications of apartheid's spatial planning policies, *Setting Apart* functioned as a powerful companion to the narrative being constructed by the TRC, which was just beginning its work when the exhibit launched. As a cautionary tale, it also urged viewers to contemplate the ways in which South Africa's social categories of the past—ascribed and entrenched through the lexicon of colonial and apartheid policy—may persist beyond the formal end of apartheid. As de Kok concludes, "The question Judin implicitly grappled with is: 'How does one develop a new civic language? Is it even possible'" (1998: 70)?

The District Six Public Sculpture Exhibit, which took place in Cape Town in 1997, is another example of artistic efforts to work beyond the limited scope of the TRC. Ninety-six artists participated in this event, whose purpose was to commemorate both the community and the landscape of District Six—an originally diverse and vibrant neighborhood that was cleared of its residents and razed to the ground after being declared a "whites only" area in 1966. Given the particular history of District Six, and the fact that it represents, along with many other lost communities in South Africa, "apartheid's savage attack on family life and its ruthless destruction of the fabric of functioning societies," this sculpture exhibit garnered considerable attention, especially in light of the TRC's relative neglect of forced removals (de Kok, 1998: 64).

In many artists' views, it would present a valuable opportunity to publicly conjure the individual memories of District Six, which in many respects are all that remain of this place.[11]

Among the various outdoor sculptures that marked the occasion, there were a number of significant pieces. An untitled work by James Mader, for example, consisted of 20 pedestals, each presenting a black and white photograph of the old District Six (see Figure 7.1). The procession of images led observers in the direction of the Cape Flats, the peripheral area where most of District Six's residents were forcibly relocated. As Morphet describes the piece:

> The pictures were all facing one way and to view them one had to walk down the line, the city at one's back, the Flats out in the distance ahead . . . It was clear from the clothes and the cars that the pictures of the District were all from the 70s. Passing from one to another, framed in the air, there was a sense of the past hanging over and haunting the place where we were standing.
>
> (1997: 8)

Mader's choice not to title his piece may have been symbolically intentional. At the very least, the anonymity seemed to underscore the principles of community erasure that the apartheid government put into practice in District Six between 1966 and 1981. As de Kok explains, "What happens in the register is chillingly logical: first the occupations of residents are deleted, so that there is no sense of economic activity at all. Then the names of residents become fewer and fewer and then, as the houses are demolished, even street names are no longer recorded. By the end it is as if nobody ever lived in District Six" (1998: 65).

Though officially only exhibited for one day, the sculptures created for the District Six project were intended to stay on site as long as possible, until either weather, vandalism, or theft managed to break them down. According to Meyer:

> This process was interesting as it showed how differently sculpture could relate to the everyday world; it allowed the public to reuse the material as they saw fit . . . but it also allowed the public to mark its own presence . . . Some artists expressed the view that to have their work destroyed was not a new concept considering the history of the District Six landscape, where so many people's lives and homes were destroyed.
>
> (1997: 1)

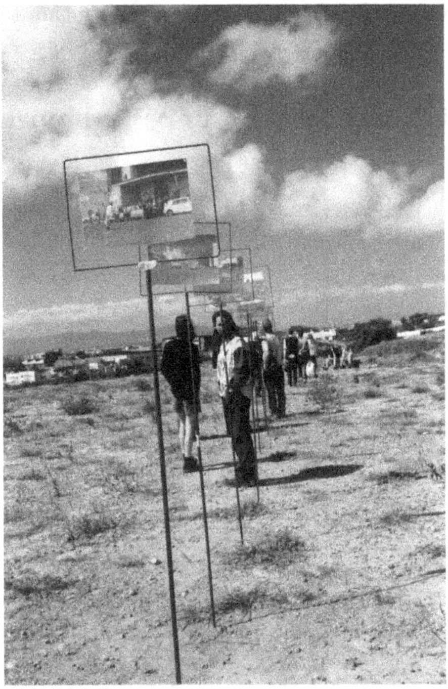

Figure 7.1 *Untitled*, by James Mader, 1997. (Photograph courtesy of the artist and the District Six Museum.)

In Mader's case, this happened almost immediately, for "the work was destroyed by the first evening of wind, leaving bent useless metal behind" (Soudien and Meyer, 1997: 41). In his view, this came as "an unexpected parody," and the sculpture's demise ended up further enhancing its symbolic power as a representation of the arbitrary demolition of District Six.

Resurrecting individual memories as a means to reconstitute community, the District Six Public Sculpture Exhibit helped initiate what Gómez-Barris refers to as "a meaningful reinstatement of the microhistories of political repression, resistance, and its memory" (2008: 42). Here I am drawing on her discussion of the importance of community spaces in the "afterlife" of Chile's Pinochet dictatorship. According to her argument, which resonates well in the context of South Africa, these spaces ultimately "[enable] the exercise of cultural citizenship" and "[enliven] the practices of democracy" (2008: 154–5). In similar ways to their gallery counterparts, then, informal public projects such as the one in District Six lend support to the nation building enterprise, while at the same time producing "forms of cultural memory that complicate the uneven story the nation has told through its institutional processes" (2008: 30).

7.5 Conclusion: curating violent pasts through art and visual culture

Reinterpreting the legacies of apartheid through a direct engagement with the TRC, South African artists have contributed to a revisionary history of South Africa's transition to democracy. While the TRC played an invaluable role in providing a space and a procedure through which both victims and perpetrators could come together and begin the difficult work of mining their individual and collective histories, the official "truth" it constructed about the country's experience with apartheid was inevitably compromised and thus failed to resonate with key sectors of South Africa's population. Given these limitations, it becomes imperative to examine other modes of memorialization in South Africa, especially those whose activities can be placed in direct conversation with the TRC, such as contemporary art making. To return to Jane Alexander's *Butcher Boys* for a moment, it has been observed that "After nearly two decades, [the work] has lost none of its disquieting effect of threatening potentiality, as if at any moment the monsters of apartheid's past might again waken in the dusk of reason's termination" (Enwezor, 2004: 42). Thus, in a similar and yet perhaps more enduring manner than was accomplished during the TRC, Alexander's sculpture functions as a stark and ominous reminder—both of the dark era of the past, but also of the social vigilance required to keep moving forward.

Contemporary art in South Africa has in many ways culturally legitimized the work of the TRC, despite raising provocative questions about its goals and methodology. In addition to this, however, many artists have felt the need to critically re-imagine the TRC process, creating work that speaks to the many untold stories of apartheid that were rendered invisible as a result of the Commission's limited scope. Through their careful and sustained examination of the past, these artists have succeeded in broaching difficult but essential conversations—about the subjective nature of truth, about the largely unfulfilled expectations for justice, and about the genuine impediments to reconciliation that exist in South Africa, even today. With the support of public galleries and museums, which have been reconfigured to present a new set of discourses, South African artists have served as essential "curators" of difficult knowledge in the post-apartheid years, providing reflections not only on South Africa's past, but also on the way the new South African nation has chosen to remember it.

Notes

This chapter builds upon an article of a similar title published in *Antípoda*, vol. 5, 2007. The author wishes to thank the respective artists for allowing images of their work to be included as part of this analysis.

1. Enacted into law in 1995, the South African TRC remains one of the most high-profile examples of how a society might effectively make amends with a violent past. As a mechanism for investigating apartheid, the TRC was tasked to assemble "as complete a picture as possible of the nature, causes, and extent of gross violations of human rights committed between 1 March 1960 and 5 December 1993" (TRC Mandate). Its final report was published in 1998.
2. See Gibson (2004) and Gillis (1994) for discussions of the strategic process of collective memory construction. For useful explanations of how truth commissions fit into this process of memory making, see Wilson (2001) and Bilbija et al. (2005).
3. See Mamdani (1996), Wilson (2001), Ross (2003), and Moon (2006) for critical assessments of the TRC's limitations.
4. On protest art during the apartheid era, see Williamson (1989), Peffer (2009), Seidman (2007), and Wylie (2008).
5. For more on the move away from the "resistance aesthetic" in South African art, see D'Amato (1999).
6. Another example of this kind of work is Williamson's interactive video installation *Can't Forget, Can't Remember* (1999) which, according to the artist, highlights "the gap between the recollections of victim and perpetrator, and the flawed nature of memory" (cited in Dawes, 2003: 36).
7. See Wilson for a critique of the TRC's amnesty policy.
8. Given its deep impact, a number of artists have created work in response to the murder of Steve Biko. Examples include Willie Bester's *Homage to Steve Biko* (1992) and Paul Stopforth's *The Interrogators* (1979).
9. Biko's murderers were later denied amnesty on these very grounds. In addition to their repeated refusal to divulge the "full truth" about Biko's detention (amnesty condition no. 1), the Commission ruled that an "accidental killing" could not be viewed as having a political motivation (amnesty condition no. 2). As Hayner writes: "because none of the applicants was admitting to a crime, logic would hold that they could not receive amnesty for it" (2002: 44).
10. Constitution Hill, which officially opened in March 2004, is the site of South Africa's Constitutional Court; it is also home to a substantial collection of contemporary art, of which Mason's piece is a crowning achievement.
11. In 1994 a permanent institution was established, the District Six Museum, to honor the memories of those displaced from District Six and highlight the issue of forced removals more generally.

Works cited

Art Throb: Contemporary Art in South Africa, 1998–2003: The Archive (CD-Rom)

Becker, Carol (1994). *The Subversive Imagination: Artists, Society, and Social Responsibility*. New York: Routledge.

Bilbija, Ksenija, Jo Ellen Fair, Cynthia E. Milton, and Leigh A. Payne (eds.) (2005). *The Art of Truth-telling about Authoritarian Rule*. Madison: The University of Wisconsin Press.

D'Amato, Mark (1999). "Beyond the Trauma: The Transition of the Resistance Aesthetic in Contemporary South African Art." In Frank Herreman (ed.). *Liberated Voices: Contemporary Art from South Africa*. New York: The Museum for African Art.

Dawes, Nicholas (2003). "Sue Williamson and the Trauma of History." In *Sue Williamson: Selected Works*. Cape Town: Double Storey Books.

de Kok, Ingrid (1998). "Cracked Heirlooms: Memory on Exhibition." In Sarah Nuttall and Carli Coetzee (eds.). *Negotiating the Past: The Making of Memory in South Africa*. Oxford: Oxford University Press.

Dodd, Alex (2006). "Jazz and the Retrieval of Lost Histories." In Kathryn Smith (ed.). *Sam Nhlengethwa*. Johannesburg: Goodman Gallery Editions.

Edkins, Jenny (2003). *Trauma and the Memory of Politics*. Cambridge: Cambridge University Press.

Enwezor, Okwui (2004). "Contemporary South African Art at the Crossroads of History." In Sophie Perryer (ed.). *Personal Affects: Power and Poetics in Contemporary South African Art*. Cape Town: Spier.

Gibson, James L. (2004). "Does Truth Lead to Reconciliation? Testing the Causal Assumptions of the South African Truth and Reconciliation Process." *American Journal of Political Science* 48(2): 201–17.

Gillis, John R. (1994). *Commemorations: The Politics of National Identity*. Princeton: Princeton University Press.

Gómez-Barris, Macarena (2008). *Where Memory Dwells: Culture and State Violence in Chile*. Berkeley: University of California Press.

Hayner, Priscilla (2002). *Unspeakable Truths: Facing the Challenge of Truth Commissions*. New York: Routledge.

Mamdani, Mahmood (1996). "Reconciliation Without Justice." *South African Review of Books* (46): 3–5.

Marlin-Curiel, Stephanie (1999). "Art in Response to the TRC." Conference Paper. *TRC: Commissioning the Past*. University of the Witwatersrand.

Moon, Claire (2006). "Narrating Political Reconciliation: Truth and Reconciliation in South Africa." *Social and Legal Studies* 15(2): 257–75.

Morphet, Tony (1997). "Sculpture in the Elements at District Six." In Crain Soudien and Renate Meyer (eds.). *The District Six Public Sculpture Project*. Cape Town: The District Six Museum Foundation.

Neke, Gael (1999). "(Re)Forming the Past: South African Art Bound to Apartheid." Conference Paper. *TRC: Commissioning the Past*. University of the Witwatersrand.

Oliphant, Andries Walter (1995). "A Human Face: The Death of Biko and South African Art." In *Seven Stories about Modern Art in Africa*. London: White Chapel Art Gallery.

Peffer, John (2009). *Art and the End of Apartheid*. Minneapolis: University of Minnesota Press.

Richards, Colin (2004). "Our Giftedness." In Gary Van Wyk (ed.). *A Decade of Democracy: Witnessing South Africa*. New York: Distributed by Axis Gallery and Sondela.

Ross, Fiona (2003). *Bearing Witness: Women and the Truth and Reconciliation Commission in South Africa*. London: Pluto Press.
Sachs, Albie (2009). *The Strange Alchemy of Life and Law*. Oxford: Oxford University Press.
Seidman, Judy (2007). *Red on Black: The Story of the South African Poster Movement*. Johannesburg: STE Publishers.
Soudien, Crain and Renate Meyer (eds.) (1997). *The District Six Public Sculpture Project*. Cape Town: The District Six Museum Foundation.
Truth and Reconciliation Commission of South Africa Report (TRC Report) (1998). Cape Town: Truth and Reconciliation Commission.
Williamson, Sue (1989). *Resistance Art in South Africa*. Cape Town: David Philip.
Wilson, Richard A. (2001). *The Politics of Truth and Reconciliation in South Africa: Legitimizing the Post-Apartheid State*. Cambridge: Cambridge University Press.
Wylie, Diana (2008). *Art and Revolution: The Life and Death of Thami Mnyele, South African Artist*. Charlottesville: University of Virginia Press.

Part III
Materiality and Memorial Challenges

Introduction

Monica Eileen Patterson

This section speaks to the spatiality and materiality of memory and pushes us to take seriously the physical world, its attributes, possibilities, and limitations: What are the agencies of the inanimate? Objects and buildings also have lives, and exert influence and control over the people who engage around and with them. Things and traces, architecture and places, landscapes and spaces constrain and promote particular memories. As societal palimpsests, they bear not only the marks of the dominant players and their intended interpretations of the past, but also subtler signs of the dispossessed, the destroyed, and the disappeared. Reading these physical memoryscapes, and engaging with the material world as a witness to and source of evidence of past conflict requires certain literacies and perspectives.

As a framing device used to define a collective, time can be easily manipulated to unite or to divide. Whether through a sanctioned attempt to preserve or restore, or a prohibited act of vandalism, no intervention in time or historical representation is ever innocent. What is included and forgotten, emphasized and minimized, centered and marginalized all reflect inequalities steeped in history and grounded in the present. But in engaging past conflicts, the weighty choice of when to start or stop the clock of history is challenged by the materiality in which these multiple histories are embedded. Even as buildings are bulldozed, streets are renamed, and fresh coats of paint are applied to a range of materials for official and illicit ends, physical objects record and retain traces of the past and its meaning in ever-unfolding presents.

Each of the authors in this section explores the unruly ways that the past perseveres despite concerted efforts to domesticate or obliterate it. In these contexts, ordering frames are recast and conflated, monuments transformed through recontextualization or defacement, texts erased, replaced, or altered—but never quite as their original designers intended. The material world seems to possess its own unique kinds of agency—and a resilience that has been too often underestimated or overlooked.

8

Points of No Return: Cultural Heritage and Counter-Memory in Post-Yugoslavia

Andrew Herscher

"Preserve it: it's yours!" In Albanian, Serbian, and English, this message—or, more precisely, this command—appeared on billboards throughout Prishtina, the capital of Kosovo, in the summer of 2004. (See Plate 8.1.) The billboards displayed what the people of Kosovo ought to preserve in a series of twelve images. Each image showed a historical site: the Dečani and Gračanica monasteries, the Sinan Pasha mosque, an Ottoman-era *konak* (mansion), the Prizren League building, traditional stone tower houses, the Roman-era Ulpiana archaeological excavations, and so on. These sites comprised an exemplary set. Including Byzantine and Ottoman heritage, Christian and Islamic patrimony, Serb and Albanian monuments, and high and vernacular culture, this set represented nothing less than the United Colors of Kosovo, a multi-cultural and multi-ethnic Kosovo of vivid and complementary differences. Looming above all other images on the billboards was the form of a Neolithic figurine, among the oldest products of human culture discovered in the territory that is now known as Kosovo. The figurine's size and position on the billboard were easy to understand; as a *pre-ethnic* artifact, it was the only heritage object whose *multi-ethnic* credentials were truly impeccable.

Sponsored by the Ministry of Culture, Youth, and Sports, the billboards were a response to what Kosovo's government, as well as many international institutions, delicately termed the "March events." In these "events," which took place some months earlier that same year, Kosovar Albanian demonstrators expelled many of the few remaining Serbs in Kosovo and destroyed 35 Serbian Orthodox churches and monasteries, as well. This was the destruction of the property of a despised ethnic other, an other judged responsible for prior acts of violence, including violence against heritage that Albanians identified with. At least according to the Ministry, however, all this heritage actually belonged to *all* ethnicities in Kosovo, hence the injunction to preserve it—not because it was the other's, it is important to note, but because it was everyone's. The Ministry's preservation campaign thus attempted to enlist Kosovo's citizenry in what may be regarded as a state-sponsored curatorship of cultural heritage. The Ministry posed the "memory" of a common multi-ethnic heritage as an antidote to what is usually understood as "ethnic violence." Heritage was thereby recruited as a medium of interpellation: an instrument to produce the subjects and subjectivities deemed appropriate to a post-violence regime of order, stability, and reconciliation.

On one level, however, this new curatorial project merely extended the prior project it was designed to overcome—the wartime enlistment of heritage as the patrimony of a violent ethnic other. In the case of this enlistment, heritage was also a medium of interpellation, connecting individuals to ideologies of ethnic identity that were appropriate to and supportive of communal violence (Herscher, 2010). Postwar preservation fixed on the same heritage sites and objects, but merely transformed their significations from narrowly ethnic to broadly multi-ethnic—"the common patrimony of all of Kosovo's ethnic, religious and linguistic communities," in the academically inflected words of the preservation campaign. In the campaign, then, the difficult knowledge of Kosovo's recent history of ethnicizing violence was not only curated but disappeared, its material remainders reinscribed into the seemingly kinder, gentler context of postwar multi-ethnic brotherhood and unity.[1]

There were a number of different responses to the state's curatorial project. As theorists have described, analysis of interpellation must account for the diverse and often contradictory reactions that interpellation provokes—"the multitude of heterogeneous resistances and revolts," in the words of Michel Pecheux (1982: 26), "which smolder beneath dominant ideology, threatening it constantly." It is these "resistances" and "revolts" that establish interpellation as a fraught, contested interface between the institutions of government and the governed; interpellation thus becomes enmeshed in what Michel Foucault termed the "strategic reversibility" of power relations—the ways in which practices of governing can be reformulated as objects of resistance, or "counter-politics," on the part of the governed (Burchell et al., 1991).

In the context of memory studies, such counter-politics have typically been considered in terms of what James E. Young (2002) has termed the "counter-monument." Young's notion of counter-monumentality is itself indebted to Pierre Nora's formative historicization of collective memory. Nora (1996: 1) posited a primordial time in which memory was "a real part of everyday existence." This was a time, according to Nora, when communities existed in "ethnographical slumbers," when "ideologies based on memory . . . smoothed the transition from past to future," when "memory without a past . . . eternally recycles a heritage"; a time, that is, without history (1996: 2). For Nora, history—as change, dispersal or alterity—"eradicated" memory and *milieux de mémoire*. "[A]t the heart of history," he wrote, "is a criticism destructive of spontaneous memory" (1996: 3). To live in history, for Nora, is to be able to access memory only from a distance, through mediation, in a virtual, incomplete, or inauthentic form: "the less memory is experienced from within, the greater its need for external props and tangible reminders" (1996: 8). Nora's supposition is that authentic memory, "experienced from within," does not rely on non-human or inhuman sites, forms or objects; the latter, which Nora calls *lieux de mémoire*, are "exterior" to memory, substituting for human memory work, and so historically subsequent to the pre-historical time when such memory work proceeded unimpeded, unrepresented, in sublime ignorance of itself. For Nora, the time of memory was not only a time without history, but also a time without monuments.

By posing "memory" as temporally prior to and conceptually independent of "history," Nora is compelled to regard contemporary sites of memory and other forms of historical inscription as compensatory at best and inadequate at worst, mere substitutes for memory work undertaken in the fullness of time, without need for material prostheses, by human consciousness itself. For Nora, the contemporary monument assumes "the responsibility of remembering," an assumption that involves a loss for the human subject, who is divested of remembrance as a fundamental and proper mode of existence (1996: 13). Here, Kosovo's heritage preservation campaign could be posed as symptomatic, with Kosovo's citizens enlisted *not* to remember anything of the past, but merely to preserve the objects and sites that seemingly perform that memory work in their stead—a transformation from memory to history, in Nora's terms.

James Young fully assimilates Nora's distinction between memory and history in his formulation of the counter-monument. For Young, as for Nora, monuments, "in shouldering the memory work . . . may relieve viewers of their memory burdens" (Young, 1993: 5). The critical task for a monument, according to Young, is to work against this relief and deliver this burden back to the human subject, to whom it properly belongs. Young (2002: 118) uses the term "counter-monument" to describe those monuments that fulfill this task, that "return the burden of memory to visitors themselves by forcing visitors into an active role." The effect of a counter-monument, he therefore writes, should be to leave "nothing but the visitors themselves standing in remembrance, left to look inward for memory"—a temporary return to what Nora described as the pre-historical *milieu de mémoire* (Young, 2002: 96).

Young understands the counter-monument as a device for recuperating memory as human praxis, the praxis it supposedly once was, the praxis that Nora poses as displaced by history. From this position, Young has discovered counter-monumentality in projects whose physical form is somehow negated, elusive, transient, or nondescript. In these projects, the humanist narrative of living memory becoming displaced by the dead forms of history is played out in reverse; the undead forms of the counter-monument bring memory back to life. This revival of memory is valorized on its own terms, as if the preservation of memory was valuable in and of itself. Thus, Young (2002: 92) privileges the "perpetual irresolution" of memory questions because only this guarantees the "life of memory." "The counter-monument reminds us that the best German memorial to the fascist era and its victims may not be a single memorial at all—but simply the never-to-be-resolved debate over which kind of memory to preserve, how to do it, in whose name, and to what end" (Young, 2002: 119). At stake in the counter-monument, then, is the perpetuation of memory—a substitution for the inadequate *lieu de mémoire* and a recuperation of the lost *milieu de mémoire*.

For Young, the "never-to-be-resolved debate" about the past that the counter-monument should initiate and maintain is opposed to sheer forgetting. At the same time, however, Young's investment in unresolvable memory can also be understood as an investment in the psychic state that Sigmund Freud defined as "melancholia." In a now-famous distinction, Freud (1984) compared mourning, in which a subject works through the loss of a love object and comes to accept that loss, to melancholia, in which the subject, unconscious of loss, withdraws its attachment to the lost object into itself. In Freud's words (1984: 258), "the shadow of the object (falls) upon the ego" of the melancholic subject, who then obsessively acts out its identification with the lost object. Thus, if mourning involves a coming-to-terms with what may be regarded as the "difficult knowledge" of loss, then melancholia involves acting-out this difficulty instead. Young's stake in the sheer perpetuation of memory represents a rehabilitation of melancholia as critical practice—a gesture, moreover, that has been rehearsed and reprised in many other contemporaneous contexts and discourses (Žižek, 2000a). His idealization of unresolvable debates about memory, of endless discussions of how and what to remember—in short, of remembrance as an end in and of itself—testify to a melancholic attachment, an attachment that should not be worked through and overcome but that should be acted out, over and over, without hope of or even desire for release. As theorists of melancholy have pointed out, the focus of the melancholic attachment is not so much a *lost object* as an *unobtainable one*.[2] In this sense, Young's reading of the counter-monument can be seen not so much as a response to the loss of Holocaust memory, as the counter-monument poses itself, but to the epistemic absence of memory in the historical era as described by Nora. This absence is irrecuperable. *How to remember the loss of memory?* A perfect question for melancholic reverie.

But could more be at stake in the question of memory than merely the perpetuation of memory itself? What if memory could provide not only such a perpetuation, a reflection of a time before history *à la* Nora, but also an intervention into history, an intervention with unique possibilities and agencies? What if the difficult knowledge of past violence offers itself up for more than simply remembering or forgetting? What if counter-memories of such difficult knowledge provide not only representations of the past but also intimations of the future, of ways to propel memory into politics? What if the possibility of counter-memory, of "memory as it flashes up in a moment of danger," is to bring about *change*—a "real state of emergency"—which is to say, history? (Benjamin, 1969: 255–7). What if a self-reflexive curatorship of the knowledge of loss would be one that could acknowledge its own historical contingency, its own passage into something different—its own loss?

In raising these questions, I would like to explore the counter-politics of memory without fixing on the counter-monument as the decisive instrument of those politics and without positing memory-as-such as their only possible outcome. Rather, in what follows, I will examine some of the multifarious forms that resistance to historic preservation has assumed in Kosovo and throughout post-Yugoslavia. In particular, my interest is in how memory is not simply "perpetuated" in this resistance, but actively displaced, distorted, parodied, exaggerated, or otherwise transformed. My examination will be organized according to what Pecheux calls "counter-identifications" and "disidentifications" with interpellation (1982). These other forms of identification yield alternatives to the preservation of heritage that states, post-conflict and otherwise, typically seek; they also comprise attempts to enlist heritage in the acknowledgment and political mobilization of the difficult knowledge of the past, rather than in the disappearance of this knowledge in the name of post-conflict reconciliation. What follows, then, is not organized around the opposing poles of "remembering" and "forgetting"; rather, I am interested in the many forms that remembrance can take, some of which may even appear as forgetting and all of which comprise, in relation to state-sponsored memory, *remembering otherwise.* Attention to these alternative forms of memory suggests not only, as Young (2002: 119) has already argued, that "the monument has increasingly become the site of contested and competing meanings," but also that the monument has become a medium by which individuals and collectives enter into and participate in political discourse and action.

Counter-identifications have contested the status of cultural objects as heritage deserving of respect, as patrimony of specified communities, and as artifacts necessary to preserve. More generally, counter-identifications also contest the seemingly inevitable nature of identification; they pose identification with heritage as a necessity only in a context where this identification is a means of assuming and maintaining order. Counter-identifications with heritage can take the form of either under-or over-identification, each embodying a refusal of the affective response, social action, or political effects that cultural heritage conventionally solicits. These refusals, however, are not symmetrical.

Under-identification is the explicit opposite of identification; withholding, protesting or contradicting the "proper" respect for heritage that identification engenders, under-identification comprises what Slavoj Žižek has termed an "inherent transgression." As such, under-identification is structured into heritage ideology insofar as that ideology presumes resistance as part of its very operation. A critical refusal of this ideology, then, does not take the form of its explicit refusal, or *under-identification,* but rather its obsessive acceptance, or *over-identification.* As Žižek (2000b: 220) has argued,

> In so far as power relies on its "inherent transgression," then, sometimes, at least, overidentifying with the explicit power discourse—ignoring this inherent obscene underside and simply taking the power discourse at its (public) word, acting as if it really means what it explicitly says (and promises) can be the most effective way of disturbing its smooth functioning.

Whether a particular intervention comprises under-identification, over-identification, or identification, however, is itself a matter of interpretation. Consider, for example, vandalism, which aims not at the preservation of heritage but rather at its deformation or destruction. The vandalism of the cultural heritage of ethnic others during the wars of

Yugoslav succession can easily be regarded as under-identifications with that heritage, withholding and even contradicting the respect that heritage conventionally demands. And yet, in the context of postwar reconstruction, vandalism is a highly charged aesthetic practice mediating multiple forms of identification. In an example from 1998, the project Black Peristyle (Crni peristil), the artist Igor Grubič clandestinely painted a large black circle on the stone floor of the peristyle of Diocletian's Palace in Split, Croatia (see Figure 8.1).[3] The peristyle was the center of the palace, a UNESCO World Heritage Site and one of the most historically significant cultural heritage sites and tourist destinations in Croatia. The painting of a black circle inside the peristyle was thus classified by public authorities in Split as an act of vandalism against a monument of cultural heritage—an act of under-identification.

Yet a note left on the door of a nearby tourist agency signed "Black Peristyle," read: "In honor of the group Red Peristyle (Crveni peristil), 30 years later the Peristyle, as a magic mirror, reflects the state of society's conscience" (Marjanić, 2007). This note referred to a project, completed 30 years earlier to the day, when the floor of the peristyle was painted red—an artistic project that had also been classified as vandalism. Under-identification with the peristyle as one kind of heritage—the heritage of antiquity—thus involved identification with the peristyle as another kind of heritage—the heritage of modern art as represented by Red Peristyle. The invocation of modernist heritage extended beyond Red Peristyle: the black circle painted on the palace's floor, potentially reminiscent of Kazimir Malevich's black circles, was later termed by Grubič "a legacy of Suprematism and Constructivism" (Marjanić, 2007).

At stake in Black Peristyle, then, is not simply whether or not to remember cultural heritage; rather, the project suggests a modernist alternative to a classical genealogy of heritage. At the same time, this alternative was not posed in the spirit of liberal politics as simply the object of a "choice"; it was, rather, an active and even violent displacement, with the proposition of a modernist heritage disturbing the sanctity of its classical counterpart. The under-identification with Diocletian's Palace as cultural heritage in its given form thus mediated an identification with another formulation of heritage, the heritage of modernism.

The status of under-identification with one heritage object as simultaneously an identification with other heritage objects is revealed not only in vandalism, but also in protests over the definition of cultural objects as heritage. For example, in May 2007, the Kosovar Albanian NGO, Vetëvendosje (Self-Determination) protested the building of a protective wall around the Byzantine-era Patriarchate in Peć, Kosovo,

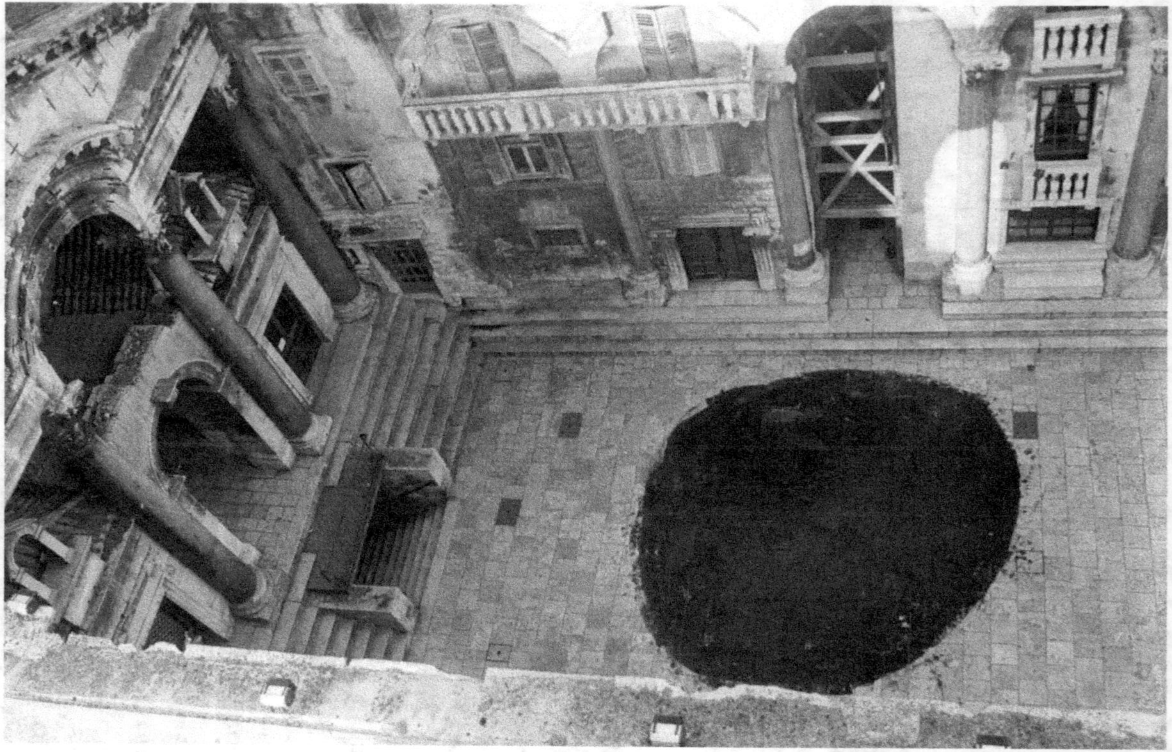

Figure 8.1 Igor Grubić, *Black Peristyle*, intervention at Diocletian's Palace, Split, Croatia, 1998. (Photograph courtesy of Igor Grubić.)

seat of the Serbian Orthodox Church and a focal point of Kosovo's Serb cultural identity. For the Serbian Orthodox Church, the wall was an objectively necessary instrument of protection, especially important after the destruction inflicted on Serbian Orthodox churches and monuments in the "March events." After those events, the low wall surrounding the Patriarchate appeared wholly inadequate to block hostile actions against its buildings and grounds.

For Vetëvendosje, however, the wall was a symbolic expression of the Patriarchate's status as exclusively Serb property, unavailable to both the predominantly Albanian city of Peć (Peja in Albanian) and the predominantly Albanian state of Kosovo. In a demonstration outside the Patriarchate, Vetëvendosje members built a section of a barbed-wire barricade and displayed posters proclaiming "No New Walls," "Kosovo Will Not Be Palestine," and "Peja is Not Mitrovice," seemingly speaking on behalf of Kosovo Albanians excluded from the Patriarchate.[4] Vetëvendosje's protest did not refuse the status of the Patriarchate as heritage as such; rather, it refused its presumed status as specifically Serb heritage, managed not by the Kosovar state but by the Serbian Orthodox Church. Yet Vetëvendosje's refusal was not made in the name of secularism or the state, but of Kosovar Albanian nationalism. Thus, the organization conjoined protests against the Patriarchate's new wall with the publication of historical narratives documenting the Orthodox Church's supposedly Albanian roots and political narratives asserting exclusive Albanian sovereignty in Kosovo (Vetëvendosje, 2007). The protest thus comprised both under-identification with the Patriarchate's status as Serb patrimonial heritage and identification with the Patriarchate's supposedly former status as Albanian heritage—the replacement of one form of exclusion, of Serbs against Albanians, by another, of Albanians against Serbs.

If the preceding examples are typical, then under-identification with one heritage object or genealogy becomes a means for identifying with yet another object or genealogy. This slippage between under-identification and identification might be understood to testify to the status of under-identification as implicitly included in dominant systems of heritage management and historic preservation. Under-identification, in this sense, would be a kind of oppositional identification, explicitly positioned against an existing or dominant alternative. Yet if under-identifications are thereby inscribed in ideological systems of heritage management and preservation, over-identifications present such systems with a more profound challenge by presuming to take their claims and imperatives more rigorously than such systems are capable of doing themselves.

One example of such an over-identification is the piece, "JBT 27.12.2004," in which the artist Dalibor Martinis photographed himself standing on a plinth formerly occupied by a bronze statue of Josip Brož Tito, founder of socialist Yugoslavia. (See Plate 8.2.) The statue, in Tito's birthplace of Kumrovec, Croatia, was destroyed—a performance of under-identification with socialist heritage—on December 27, 2004, a date commemorated in the title of Martinis' piece. Mere identification with the statue would yield either a project to reconstruct it or, perhaps, preserve its empty plinth. But Martinis over-identified with the preservationist agenda by collapsing the distinction between the preserving subject and the preserved object; on the plinth, he became both subject and object, both preserving and preserved. In so doing, Martinis' work makes manifest the distance that is maintained in "normal" identification with heritage and raises questions about just what sort of effects such identification can have. When human beings preserve "their" heritage in conventional ways, in other words, how might this preservation actually shape or alter them? Narrating his experience in an interview, Martinis said, "when I stood on the marble pedestal with the inscription 'Josip Brož Tito,' I realized that I was at a place where it is not possible—neither physically, politically, or symbolically—for anyone to stand except Tito himself" (Kalčić, 2005). His realization frames identification, in the form that states typically solicit it, as inherently incomplete, founded on unacknowledged gaps—physical, political, and symbolic—between subject and object, between public and monument.

A similar registration of such gaps was accomplished by the "Monument to Bruce Lee" erected in Mostar, Bosnia and Herzegovina, in November 2005 by the Bosnian NGO Urban Movement. Mostar was heavily damaged during the Bosnian war, with both Serb and Croat forces laying siege to the city, divided as a result between Bosniaks, in East Mostar, and Croats, in West Mostar. According to Nino Raspudić (2004), Urban Movement's co-founder and director, Mostar's division was only amplified in postwar reconstruction: "each one of the two constituent parts of the city is trying to give "their own" space "their own" characteristics, to "possess" it even more by constructing their religious and cultural objects and symbols." The sectarian instrumentalization of heritage produces the possibility for the contrasting instrumentalization of heritage as multi-ethnic or universal. But instead of reframing local cultural objects as unifying works of heritage, as post-ethnic national governments have tended to do, Urban Movement posed the hero of 1970s kung-fu movies, Bruce Lee, as this object. Lee, according to

Raspudić (2004), "was dear to all, no matter our political or ideological convictions . . . (he) was, above all, a symbolic bridge between the East and the West." Thus, Raspudić concluded, it was quite appropriate to memorialize Bruce Lee in between the divided Eastern and Western parts of Mostar, with the citizens of both parts able to agree on Bruce Lee's significance, if on little or nothing else besides. (See Plate 8.3.)

Bruce Lee, a product of late capitalist global culture, was presented as an object of cosmopolitan and post-ethnic identification that revealed other objects of such identification as merely ideological. The universality of the cultural heritage that served as the object of "normal" identification becomes a fantasy when compared to the universality of an object of global culture such as Bruce Lee; by over-identifying with the universality of cultural heritage, the Monument to Bruce Lee radicalizes and literalizes universality. In Mostar, the Monument thus stands in sharp contrast to the city's most renowned work of heritage, the Stari Most (Old Bridge), an Ottoman-era bridge over the Neretva River. In 1993, while held by Bosniaks in East Mostar, the bridge was destroyed by Croat army artillery. This destruction provided a symbol of sectarian conflict in Mostar, while the bridge's reconstruction (completed in 2004) was framed by its sponsors and by state officials as a sign of that conflict's overcoming (Makaš, 2005). The Monument to Bruce Lee foregrounds the artifice of such a framing by memorializing a cultural object whose heritage was shared in a far more profound fashion between East and West Mostar. It also raises the question of what counts as heritage and who arrogates responsibility for defining heritage. To see the Monument to Bruce Lee as merely ironic, a parody of "authentic" heritage or an expression of fatigue with heritage politics, is to hold onto conventional notions of authentic heritage and of the state as the arbiter of heritage politics. The radical proposition that the Monument to Bruce Lee advances is that 1970s kung-fu movies are just as much cultural heritage as Ottoman bridges for the population of Mostar, whether Bosniak or Croat.

In Pecheux's theorization of the positions that are possible to assume in response to ideological interpellation, both identification and counter-identification confirm ideology, the former by passively accepting it and the latter by contesting it. In what Pecheux (1982: 156–8) terms "disidentification," by contrast, ideology is neither accepted nor contested as such; rather, according to Pecheux, ideology is problematized, or disidentified with, with the act of disidentification thrusting the subject into new forms of subjectivity. Disidentification, in other words, comprises a transformation in ideology *from within.*

I see this sort of transformation as staged in a final intervention situated on either side of the reconstructed Old Bridge in Mostar. The intervention comprises two small stone blocks on which are painted the words, in English, "Don't Forget." (See Plate 8.4.) The stones frame views of the bridge from a distance and precede and follow passages over the bridge. Thus, the injunction against forgetting is connected both visually and experientially to the bridge, whose reconstruction was framed as a crucial recovery of cultural memory. But the message on the stones neither accepts nor rejects this recovery. Indeed, the message accommodates both acceptance and rejection: the injunction to remember could be read as a confirmation of the reconstruction of the bridge as a recovery of memory or as a contestation of this recovery.

What, precisely, should not be forgotten? That an Ottoman bridge once spanned the Neretva River in Mostar? That this bridge was destroyed in war and is now reconstructed? That this reconstruction involved the destruction of the traces of destruction: a loss of loss, a loss of the memorialization of war? Or that what should not be forgotten in Mostar is just like what should not be forgotten according to platitudinous invocations of "never again"? The memory that "Don't Forget" enjoins is reducible to *all* of these memories and thus irreducible to *any one* of them in particular. The intervention raises similar questions about its author and the audience whom that author addresses. Written in English, the message on the stones is available to both Bosniaks and Croats, as well as to both residents of Mostar and visitors to the city. Who is authorized to ask for memory? And who is required to remember? These questions, too, are posed but not answered.

What ideology typically does is provide answers to these sorts of questions, answers that, in the context of cultural heritage, define subjects in terms of their relationship to historical objects. Here, however, a definition is gestured toward but left incomplete. Subjects are implored not to forget, but not told *what* not to forget. Historical objects are confirmed as repositories of memory in general, but not a specified memory in particular. History is situated not in one collection of heritage or another, but in the agencies that endow that heritage with meaning. These small stones around the Old Bridge, then, comprise neither a strategic intervention in the existing order, an identification with heritage, nor the destructive negation of such an intervention by a counter-identification, but rather provide a miniature yet decisive opening onto a "trans-strategic intervention which redefines the roles and contours of the existing order" (Žižek, 2004: 81). According to Pecheux, that is, the command "Don't Forget" poses questions without answers, but these are not unanswerable questions doomed to be rehearsed again and again in melancholic pain/pleasure. Instead, *answering* is cast as *acting*, as taking a position, as making a claim that can change something of "the existing order."

While identification with heritage is sponsored by post-conflict states as a way to manage difficult knowledge of the past and thereby overcome conflicts and their legacies, counter-identifications and disidentifications with heritage involve the initiation of new conflicts—conflicts over the nature, interpretation and functions of heritage. If identification with heritage promotes order and stability through return to a putatively ordered and stable past, then counter-identifications and disidentifications promote change premised not on *returns* but *turns*.

Figured as a return, identification suppresses historicity: the possibility of transformation and alterity. To suppress these possibilities is to manage temporality, to render the present not as an actively produced reality but a mere reflection of the past. The present is interred in the past as its inevitable legacy. Temporal linearity, continuity and repetition figured as "history" allows for the mimetic representation of the past and, thus, for the suppression of historicity. This kind of representation poses itself as a "recovery" of the past, a mimesis of the past in the present. History becomes, then, a site of recoveries and a destination of revisits, always out there, waiting for us to rediscover it.

Counter-identifications and disidentifications with heritage are, by contrast, potential openings onto historicity, onto the generation of difference. They contest the seemingly natural status of heritage as a representation of an objective, neutral past and they explore the capacity of heritage to embody or engender different pasts or even novel pasts. In so doing, they invoke not only counter-histories, alternative pasts to those produced according to a mimetic model of inheritance, but also a counter-concept of history: history as an intervention or eruption of alterity. The object of counter-identifications and disidentifications, heritage becomes not a site of actual or even contested pasts, but a generator of new pasts for new futures: points of no return.

Notes

1. On the institution of multi-ethnicity in post-Yugoslavia, see Hayden, 2002.
2. "Melancholy would not be so much the regressive reaction to the loss of the love object as the imaginative capacity to make an unobtainable object appear as if lost." See Agamben, 1993: 20.
3. Grubić eventually claimed responsibility for his role in the project. See Marjanić, 2007.

4. Mitrovice is a city that was divided between Serbs and Albanians in the aftermath of the 1998–9 war.

Works cited

Agamben, Giorgio (1993). *Word and Phantasm in Western Culture*, trans. Ronald I. Martinez. Minneapolis: University of Minnesota Press.

Benjamin, Walter (1969). "Theses on the Philosophy of History." In *Illuminations*, trans. Harry Zohn. New York: Schocken, pp. 253–64.

Burchell, Graham, Colin Gordon, and Peter Miller (eds) (1991). *The Foucault Effect: Studies in Governmentality*. Chicago: University of Chicago Press.

Freud, Sigmund (1984). "Mourning and Melancholia." In Richards Angela (ed.). *On Metapsychology*. Harmondsworth: Penguin.

Hayden, Robert M. (2002). "Intolerant Sovereignties and 'Multi-Multi' Protectorates: Competition Over Religious Sites and (In)tolerance in the Balkans." In Chris M. Hann (ed.). *Postsocialism: Ideologies and Practices in Eurasia*. New York: Routledge.

Herscher, Andrew (2010). *Violence Taking Place: The Architecture of the Kosovo Conflict*. Stanford: Stanford University Press.

Kalčić, Silva (2005). "*Strategija kušača vina.*" *Zarez* (147), January 27. Available at http://www.zarez.hr/147/zariste3.htm. Accessed May 16, 2010.

Makaš, Emily Gunzburger (2005). "Interpreting Multivalent Sites: New Meanings for Mostar's Old Bridge." *Centropa* 5(1): 59–69.

Marjanić, Suzana (2007). "*Aktivizmom protiv crne mrlje na duši: razgovor s Igorom Grubićem.*" *Zarez* (219), November 29. Available at http://www.zarez.hr/219/kazaliste3.html. Accessed April 5, 2010.

Nora, Pierre (1996). *The Realms of Memory: Rethinking the French Past*, vol. 1, trans. Arthur Goldhammer. New York: Columbia University Press.

Pecheux, Michel (1982). *Language, Semantics, Ideology: Stating the Obvious*, trans. Harbans Nagpal. London: Macmillan.

Raspudić, Nino (2004). "The Monument to Bruce Lee—Yes and Why?" Available at http://www.projekt-relations.de/en/get/pressematerial/de_construction.php. Accessed February 21, 2010.

Vetëvendosje (2007). "Action in Pejë, *Vetëvendosje!*" (43), May 23, 2007. Available at http://www.vetevendosje.org. Accessed March 13, 2010.

Young, James E. (1993). *The Texture of Memory: Holocaust Memorials and Meaning*. New Haven: Yale University Press.

Young, James E. (2002). *At Memory's Edge: After-Images of the Holocaust in Contemporary Art and Architecture*. New Haven: Yale University Press.

Žižek, Slavoj (2000a). "Melancholy and the Act." *Critical Inquiry* 26(4): 657–81.

Žižek, Slavoj (2000b). "Da Capo senza Fine." In Judith Butler, Ernesto Laclau, and Slavoj Žižek (eds). *Contingency, Hegemony and Universality: Contemporary Dialogues on the Left*. New York: Verso.

Žižek, Slavoj (2004). *Organs without Bodies: On Deleuze and Consequences*. London: Routledge.

9
Defacing Memory: (Un)tying Peru's Memory Knots

Cynthia E. Milton

Lika Mutal, the artist behind one of Peru's only monuments that attempts an encompassing homage to the victims of their internal war (1980–2000), invited me to walk through the Ojo que llora (The Eye that Cries) (see Figure 9.1) in Lima in March 2008. Some 32,000 stones collected from the Chancay sea on Peru's central coastline—of which 26,000 bear the name, age, and year of death or date of disappearance of a victim—mark a river-like pathway that spirals in toward an obelisk-shaped rock with an embedded smaller sacred stone (the "eye") that continuously sheds "tears." This central rock—intended to represent "the core inside of each person"—holds special significance: it represents "Mother Earth (*Pachamama* or *Madre Tierra*) who cries for what has happened to her children" (Cárdenas, 2006). The serpentine paths are meant to resemble the meanderings of rivers; in particular, the artist had in mind the River Huallaga in the Amazon basin and the thousands of victims disappeared in it (ibid.). The quietness of the monument in the otherwise bustling city and the solemnity of the names and ages of victims weighs heavily. Reflection is paramount. To leave, one must wind one's way back through the paths of names, and thus continue contemplation. The design forces one to walk slowly; one cannot rush through this memorial site.

The Ojo que llora had made international news the previous year because of attacks against the site: in response to the recent extradition of the former president Alberto Fujimori to stand trial in Peru for charges of corruption, abuse of power, and human rights violations (for which he was later found guilty), presumed Fujimori sympathizers gagged and bound the night watchman, splashed bright orange paint over the center piece, and took a sledge hammer to some of the stones and to the eye itself. While Mutal and I walked through the vandalized site, discussing the potential

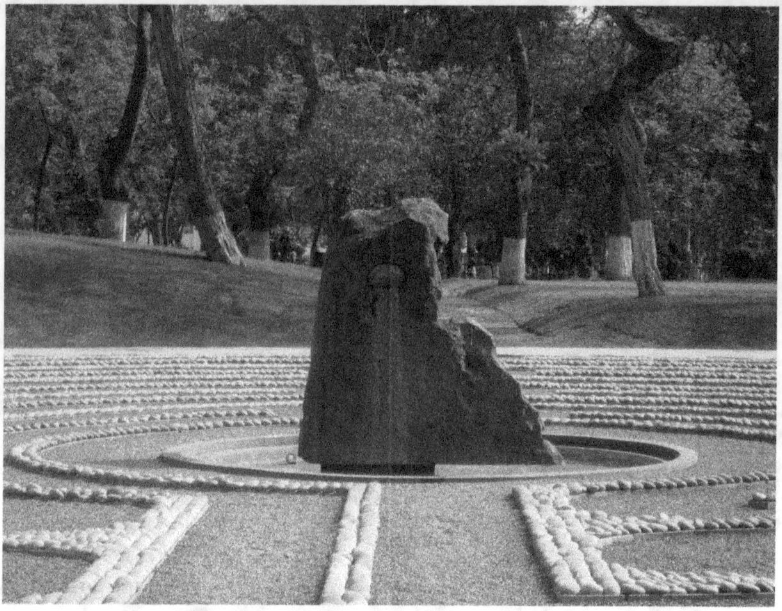

Figure 9.1 The Ojo que llora, Lima, Peru in March 2008. (Photograph by Cynthia Milton.)

meanings of such defacement, my eyes were caught by the names of the victims of the Cantuta massacre—the nine students and one professor who had been taken out of their university classroom by an elite squad of the military and disappeared in July 1992 (their partial remains were found a year later). In what must have happened just the day before, someone had taken a green marker (as though dug out from the bottom of a backpack) and crossed out their names, a protest most likely to the claims (later substantiated by Peruvian courts) of Fujimori's involvement in their deaths. Lifting my gaze, I saw a young man walking quietly through the memorial site, looking at the many names. The only other visitor, I asked him why he was here. He had stumbled across the site by accident, he said. I asked what he was thinking. He replied, "these are things we need to know . . ."

As a historian of Latin America, I am struck by these counter-currents of Peru's past: the continued violence exercised against victims through attacks on this memorial, and the spontaneous homage paid to these same victims as expressed by the accidental visitor. This chapter is a reflection upon the efforts and challenges in Peru to create a public space for remembering their past, and the modes by which Peruvians engage this difficult history. Other scholars have studied the Ojo que llora within the polemics of Peru's memory debates: Katherine Hite (2007) addresses the vexed issue of defining "victim" and Paulo Drinot (2009) has eloquently parsed out the entangled ontologies of violence and interpretations of Peru's conflict. This chapter takes a slightly different approach, while building upon other scholars' contributions. Here, I argue that the Ojo que llora, as a performative memorial site, is a tangible working out of conflicting memories: that is, through the swinging pendulum of (re)inscription and defacement, Peruvians perform contrasting narratives of their past in order to push forward their narrative as the dominant one. In the back and forth of inscribing different pasts onto the Ojo que llora, we see subtle changes taking place within each memory narrative.

Recently, a commission was set up to discuss the creation of a memorial museum (a long-standing project since the publication of the Peruvian Truth and Reconciliation Commission's *Final Report*), so questions of what kind of memory, for whom, and how best to represent the past are in the forefront of Peru's memory debates. These debates are staged at many levels: among groups of memory workers, between human rights organizations and the state, and within communities. Through an analysis of the multiple and often conflicting uses of this memorial space—ranging from choreographed homage to victims of the internal conflict to assailing (metaphorically) these same victims through "vandalism," I wish to understand the currents of memory that seemingly run counter to each other—attempts at dialog and at closing down conversation. While the Ojo que llora makes visible past violence in the inscription of names of the dead and disappeared of Peru's recent past, the continued disfigurement of this memorial site bears witness to the violent past's ongoing legacies, and indeed Peru's present situation in the process of reckoning with its past.

I try in this chapter to understand the meanings of the attacks on the Ojo que llora not simply as "vandalism," a term that implies a lack of political intent, nor as "iconoclasm," a term that connotes the willful destruction of art.[1] Furthermore, there is an inherent moral weight attributed to these terms: that "vandalism" reflects bad aggression and "iconoclasm" recalls revolutionary ideals. Either term, I argue, obscures our ability to interpret the meanings of the attacks on the Ojo que llora in Peru's ongoing memory puzzle. Rather, from the angle of reading the physical uses of this memorial site, we see contrasting endeavors to rewrite the past. That is, rather than "vandals" or "iconoclasts," agents are writing (though violently) a narrative of the past that stands in contrast to that of individuals and groups who use this space for remembering Peru's war and the victims of it. That is, various groups are "exhibiting" their own interpretation of the past upon the Ojo que llora. Ultimately, such writings/exhibitions are resulting in a melding of narratives, one that has the effect of limiting the category of "victim."

9.1 Peru's recent past

The Dutch-born artist, Lika Mutal has resided in Peru since 1968, scouring the country for stones and rocks that are the foundation of her métier. As Mario Vargas Llosa has written of her relationship with the stones of Peru, they "owe as much to her as she does to them," and "when they pass through the strong and willful hands of Lika Mutal, the stones become sculptures without ceasing to be nature" (2008). Inspired by an exhibition called *Yuyanapaq: Para Recordar* (in Quechua meaning "In order to remember") that documented through personal and professional photographs the violence inflicted upon Peruvians by Peruvians, Mutal wished to use her skills as an artist to remember and render homage to the nearly 70,000 victims of Peru's internal war (1980–2000), of which three-fourths were rural Quechua speakers from the Peruvian highlands.[2] The Peruvian Truth and Reconciliation Commission (Comisión de la Verdad y Reconciliación, or CVR), who sponsored the *Yuyanapaq* exhibition, made public their *Final Report* in August 2003; indeed, *Yuyanapaq* was the *Final Report's* visual accompaniment. The *Final Report* highlighted Peru's deeply embedded racism against indigenous and rural peoples of the highlands and Amazon regions, the long-standing centralism of power in the mestizo, Spanish-speaking coast, and the heavily gendered nature of the violence. While the CVR condemned the armed group *Sendero Luminoso* (Shining Path) as the main perpetrators of violence (in 54 percent of documented cases) and to a much lesser extent the urban-based Revolutionary Movement of Túpac Amaru or MRTA (1.5 percent), the CVR also placed responsibility in the hands of successive governments (including former president Alan García during his first term from 1985–90) and political parties who abdicated authority to the armed forces (found responsible for 29 percent of the documented violence), and police (6.6 percent) (CVR 2003, vol. 2 "Los actores del conflito"). The CVR dated the beginning of the armed conflict to when Shining Path burned ballot boxes in a center-south highland town in May 1980 in rejection of Peru's return to democracy after a prolonged military rule, thus launching a "people's war" against the nation state; yet, ultimately, the CVR saw the root causes of the violence in Peru's endemic socio-economic, regional, and ethnic inequalities.

In his address at the submission of their *Final Report* to the then President of the Republic, Alejandro Toledo, truth commission president Salomón Lerner called these years of violence a "double scandal": the first scandal was the large-scale assassination, disappearance, and torture; the second was the indolence, ineptitude, and indifference among those in authority and positions of socio-economic well-being who could have prevented this humanitarian catastrophe from happening.[3] The latter scandal endures in public forums: indifference to past violence continues in the form of quasi-denial mixed with a rewriting of the past. The result is a narrative that describes human rights violations as "excesses" committed by a few rogue elements within the armed forces, casts Fujimori's heavy-handed authoritarianism and disregard for human rights as the price that had to be paid to quash Shining Path, and maintains that "we" in Lima did not really know the extent of what was going on (and because of this lack of knowledge deserve absolution). The Ojo que llora—and the memory workers associated with it and other similar memory projects in Peru—acts as a countervailing force against this quasi-denialist narrative: the memory workers repeat the findings of the CVR over and over through various forums (public gatherings, conferences, media presentations, Internet blogs, etc.) to a largely indifferent, if not actively obtuse, general public in Lima and current government. One way to repeat the message of "Never Again," a phrase widely used by Peruvian human rights groups, is to inscribe it in the very landscape of the nation in memorial spaces such as the Ojo que llora. But, as the repeated defacement of the Ojo que llora demonstrates, counter-memory projects also seek to inscribe their own narratives on the same site; that is, defacement is a form of writing.

Steve Stern's notion of "memory knots," presented in his study on memory struggles in post-Pinochet Chile, is useful in thinking through the public conflicts in Peru over its past (2004: esp. 120–4). The image of knots invokes the pain inflicted on bodies by traumatic events (and more quotidian knots in the stomach or the throat), and the potential limitations this pain poses to language in the aftermath of violence (Scarry, 1985). The image of the knot also points to processes: social actors with competing memorial frameworks tie knots (survivor and family groups, NGOs, politicians, and the military), and thus memory work that aims for encompasing, democratic narratives entails a process of working out (untying) knots in the social body. In this metaphor, the tying of a knot might foment social discord, yet the untying of knots necessitates agreement upon a collective narrative to which various social actors contribute their competing memories. Finally, the memory knot in the Peruvian context has strong historical connotations: the Incaic *quipus* (*khipus*) or cords consisted of mnemonic knots which were read by the *khipukamayuq*, or specially trained "cord reader or master." The destruction of this tradition due to Spanish colonialism meant the loss of an important memory tool and form of writing (Salomon, 2004). Yet the *quipu* remains socially relevant today: a key symbolic performance of national reconciliation called the "Walk for Peace and Solidarity" ("Caminata por la paz y la solidaridad") was the collective creation of a new national *quipu* whereby four runners (named after the Incaic predecessors, *chasquis*) ran over 2000 km to some 142 towns where mainly school children had woven 1005 knotted cords of different textures and colors to add to the central "national" cord. The knotted cords were meant to recall the victims of the war, and the action of tying the various communal cords onto the central cord, an act of bringing together a fragmented nation.[4] In this use, tying the knots meant binding the nation and writing the victims' presence into the nation's history.

The problem of the "memory knot" in Peru is distinct from that in Chile or other South American countries for its specific historical context. Peru was a democracy facing a real subversive threat while the other cases of "dirty war" took place under dictatorships that largely exaggerated and fabricated threats to the state. As such, the use of now commonplace narratives in transitional justice literature—"dictatorship to democracy" and "dirty war"—in the Peruvian context are misleading. Other deceptive narratives also circulate. There is the heroic myth of Fujimori: as economic savior of Peru (from García's hyperinflation), captor of Abimael Guzmán (effectively decapitating Shining Path), and later the crusher of the much smaller armed group, the MRTA. These narratives efface what Fujimori did not do (including seriously addressing the root causes animating Shining Path such as endemic poverty, racism, and unequal access to resources and nation-state) and elide the significant participation of civil society in eradicating Shining Path. Yet, while much of the national debate seems to circulate around these competing narratives (Fujimori's heroism and the government's necessarily brutal response versus civil society's defense of human rights), and they are the units that make up a social knot, they are not in themselves clear and complete narratives.[5]

What we see in Peru today is *not* a "culture of impasse," or stalemate (Stern, 2004: 138). That is, memory work in Peru is advancing in fits and starts, and there have been major breakthroughs in promoting public discussion of the past: the sentencing of Alberto Fujimori to 25 years in prison for crimes against humanity, the Berlin Golden Bear award for the film *The Milk of Sorrow* (*La teta asustada*) about the legacies of the violence, and the reluctant acceptance by the García government of the German government's donation of funds to build a memory museum. The next generation of Peruvians is active in the creation of cultural and intellectual forums for the discussion of the past, such as international conferences and Internet blogs. And there is a boom in cultural production, ranging from graphic novels that recount the war to the creation of a map listing memory sites in Peru. Yet Peruvians remain in a heated debate about the past. The recently failed bid to pass a legislative decree that would have granted *de facto* amnesty to individuals being processed in Peruvian courts for human rights violations is but just a recent example of continued maneuvers to "erase" the past (Burt, 2010; *El Comercio*, 2010). Furthermore, in Peru, memory is no longer synonymous with human rights. "Memory" has become the trope for those individuals and groups who wish to promote a heroic narrative for the armed forces, and culture the battlefield: the armed forces have called for their own "museum of memory," and film screenings promoted in international film festivals cast the military as the untarnished heroes defending the vulnerable highlands people (Milton, 2011). The conflict over memory and its representation is made visible at the Ojo que llora in the different ways this site has become a stage for performing various claims about the past, inscribing not only the names of victims but the history of the conflict in which they died.

9.2 The Ojo que llora as symbolic reparations

The truth commission's mandate focused on truth-seeking/telling as a form of justice and reconciliation, whereby an integral model brought together both retributive and restorative justice (González, 2006). Retributive justice is what recently landed Fujimori and others in prison for human rights violations. For restorative justice, the "peace and agreement" sought by the CVR entailed both civil and symbolic reparations (*El Peruano*, 2001). The Ojo que llora monument is one component in the plan for symbolic reparations.

The Ojo que llora differs from many memorial sites elsewhere in that it has no *physical* connection to the violence it seeks to commemorate, as would a prison, a massacre site, or a mass grave. So far in Peru, the only memory site connected to the internal war that is thus-structured is the "general prison number 51," known as "Los Cabitos," where hundreds of supposed Shining Path members and sympathizers were imprisoned, tortured, killed, or disappeared. Family members of the victims wish to have the training grounds of Los Cabitos—where many remains have been found—turned into a "Sanctuary for Memory," a place where they can remember and pay tribute to the victims and give a new meaning to this place that took the lives of their loved ones.[6] Thus, on a spectrum from physical contiguity with the actual events to symbolic construction, the Ojo que llora is closer to the latter, an entirely newly created esthetic site. But with time and use, the site has become more entwined with the past to which it refers, endowing it with a sacred connection to the events remembered, despite lacking an original physical connection. Furthermore, as a site of performance of memory and human rights claims, *and especially as the target of continued defacement*, the Ojo que llora has become a stage on which the perduring presence of the past—in its still-conflictual strains—is made visible for national and international publics. It thus refuses the very closure that government narratives would impose, and thereby keeps open public engagement with the past.

In Peru, state-level discourse remains deeply conflicted over how to interpret (or even whether to interpret) the internal war. There are no national monuments to the victims, with the exception of a small plaque placed in the central square of Ayacucho at the time of the formal public presentation of the CVR's *Final Report*. This is a far cry from the self-reflexive monuments by states acknowledging the violence against their own citizens in the style of The Memorial to the Murdered Jews of Europe in Germany or the Parque de la Memoria (Memory Park) in Argentina, both countries that are several decades removed from these difficult pasts (Sion, 2008). The Ojo que llora is a private iniative by the sculptor Lika Mutal, supported by citizens and non-governmental organizations. While not a state-sponsored monument, it did receive initial support from the mayor of the tranquil, residential, middle-class neighborhood of Jesús María, who granted permission to erect the memorial in the Campo de Marte (Champs de Mars) park (he later repealed this permission after a controversy, described below), and it has at times received some encouragement from various government figures in the form of supportive statements in favor of symbolic reparations.

The location of the site itself suggests the uncomfortable position of the government in relation to the past: while the government has stated the need to memorialize the victims of the internal war, they do not want such a memorial to attract much attention. The memorial is placed toward a quiet end of the Campo de Marte, a short distance from the staging of military parades (such as that on "National Day," 28 July), training, and headquarters. It is in a barred-off triangle with few points of entry and few signs indicating where a visitor might find it. The site is hard to get to, with the most direct access—via a major road—blocked. Next to the unmarked pathway to the memorial, one has to traverse training grounds for police dogs. Depending on the weather, the approach may be muddy. Once there, a guard is present. Access is almost always granted to foreigners, but Peruvians might have to convince the guard to let them pass.[7] These are hardly inviting conditions by which to visit the site.

9.3 The Ojo que llora as a Performative Memorial Site

In concept and design, the Ojo que llora is intended as a performative memorial site that engages visitors at the level of emotion rather than intellect. There is no explanation or explicit plan to educate the visitor about what happened. As one moves toward the central "crying" obelisk, one must wind one's way through the names. The site has become a place not only to mourn, but also to *perform remembrance*, as well as to gather and discuss a plethora of societal concerns. Since its unveiling at the second anniversary of the CVR's *Final Report*, visitors (both Peruvian and foreign), civic groups, and school children have come to the Ojo que llora. The site has served for several activities and commemorative performances: an annual remembrance ceremony on the Day of the Dead (November 2), a rally for International Women's Day (March 8), the location of Buddhist prayer ceremonies, the stage for theater troupes, the gathering site for family members to knit pieces for a kilometer long "Scarf of Hope" ("La Chalina de la Esperanza") in memory of lost loved ones, and other uses of the space. It is an important place for remembering lost lives, especially for those families who do not have the remains of their loved ones and thus do not have traditional sites of morning, such as a tombstone in a cemetery. Furthermore, this memorial is one that renews Peruvians' commitment to remember by calling for volunteers to repaint the stones when the names begin to fade, a kind of "defacement through time"—or a natural erasure.[8] As Drinot powerfully notes, this memorial site "re-member[s] (in an embodied sense) those bodies [that] were dis-membered by the violence." Indeed, by inscribing the names of the victims, many of whom were denied the basic rights of citizenship (such as birth certificates or identity cards), these individuals became part of the nation. Thus, the stones of the Ojo que llora "should be seen not as a recording of their death but as their coming into being as actually existing, if dead, Peruvians" (2009: 17–18).

As a performative memorial site, the Ojo que llora has elicited varying responses, capturing the attention of admirers and detractors, and suggesting that the site has successfully engaged Peru's memorial debates and processes. The Ojo que llora has had a "trickle down effect" in other regions. Among its admirers are community members in Llinque, Apurimac who built a scaled-down re-creation of the original, inaugurated on July 4, 2008. Subsequent "ojitos," or "little eyes," have emerged in other highland communities to remember their local dead, tortured, and disappeared.[9] But beyond the achievements of Mutal's Ojo que llora as a space for remembering and gathering, and its inspiration for other communities' expressions of remembrance, the Ojo que llora has also sparked violent reactions. Despite its status as an imaginative artistic creation in a hard-to-reach spot in Lima, groups and individuals have gone out of their way to come and desecrate this site.

Such acts of defacement are powerful statements against indifference both to the site and to the past. The Ojo que llora is public art, and as James Young has stated "in the absence of shared beliefs or common interests, art in public spaces may force an otherwise fragmented populace to frame diverse values and ideals in common spaces. By creating common spaces for memory, monuments propogate the illusion of common memory" (1993: 6). Yet, what happens when art in public spaces *does not* create "the illusion of common memory," but instead highlights its fragmentation? How are we to read the "vandalism" of memorial sites?[10]

9.4 The crying eye bleeds: contestation over public space and public memories

Conflict over the interpretation of the past can be dramatic. Monuments and memory sites invite such contestation; indeed some "countermemorial" artists solicit dispute as integral to remembering (Young, 1993). In his essay "Memoryscapes," Louis Bickford, like Young, states that public commemoration and sites have the ability to shape the physical landscape of collective memory: "memoryscapes recapture public spaces and transform them into sites of memory and alternative truth-telling about the authoritarian past" (2005: 96). The Ojo que llora is one such memoryscape that "captures" public space and converts it into a space for "truth telling," and concomitant contestation, even though the artist's original intention had been to reconcile Peruvians rather than to provoke debate.

Mutal designed the space as a public homage to the victims as well as a place for contemplation and remembering in the hope of healing, reconciliation, and fostering a more just and democratic future (Cárdenas, 2006). Yet the very fragility of Peru's democracy is apparent in the violent uses of the Ojo que llora as distinct memory camps promote their competing memories and interpretations of Peru's recent past.

Though the site originated as a location at which to pay homage to victims and historical remembrance, it became the "ojo de la tormenta," or the eye of a storm, at the end of 2006, and again in September 2007 (Drinot, 2009; Hite, 2007; Milton, 2007). The first time the Ojo que llora hit the news was in response to the ruling by the Inter-American Court of Human Rights (CIDH) recommending that the inmates of the Castro Castro prison (largely interned as Shining Path members or *senderistas*) killed by the Fujimori government should have their names inscribed at the Ojo que llora. Not only was it strange that a court ruled on how a private memorial should be structured, the ruling itself was nonsensical. In an odd twist, this international court ruled that perpetrators of violence (*senderistas*) were also "victims," and as such should appear along with the victims of their own violent acts (CIDH, 2007).

As a result of bringing to light and to public debate the painful problem of defining "victim," the Inter-American Human Rights Court's ruling ignited a series of condemnations of the Ojo que llora: newspapers such as *El Diario* and *Expreso* called the site "a monument to terrorists" because among the thousands of rocks the names of *senderistas* could already be found (*Expreso*, 2007).[11] The presence of these *senderista* names sparked a heated controversy, one that did not allow for a complicated notion of "victim." Opponents of the Ojo que llora called for the abolition of the monument (though the mayor of Jesús María stopped short of this). Those who came to the defense of the monument (in a "march to save the Ojo que llora") were accused of participating in "a pro-terrorist march" (Wiener, 2007). Using humor and creativity to defend themselves against these accusations—a throw-back to the Fujimori era when anyone who spoke in the defense of human rights was accused of sympathizing with or being a "terrorist" (Burt, 2007)—the Asociación Paz y Esperanza (Association of Peace and Hope) and the citizens' movement Para que no se repita (In Order that It Not Happen Again) organized a public activity, "Origami for Peace," on January 12, 2007. On this day, participants took sheets from the newspapers "that had begun a campaign of disinformation" by calling the Ojo que llora "a monument to terrorists"; through the ancient Asian art of folding paper, they transformed these newspapers sheets into doves of peace.[12]

The Ojo que llora had become a stage for Peruvian politics. Alan García and others used the Inter-American Human Rights Court's ruling to criticize the preceding Paniagua and Toledo governments for having returned Peru to the jurisdiction of the Inter-American Court and for having allowed the Castro Castro case to be heard by an international court. García called for Peru's immediate removal from the Inter-American Court. He also took this opportunity to seek popular support for the introduction of the death penalty for terrorists into the Peruvian legislation. In an opinion piece published in Spain's *El País* and reproduced in Peru's *El Comercio* after the CIDH's ruling, Peruvian Nobel laureate in literature, Mario Vargas Llosa, encouraged Peruvians and tourists to come and see the monument soon. "Hurry," he wrote, "because it is not impossible—Peru is a country of all possibilities—that a peculiar plot of ignorance, stupidity, and political fanaticism could do away with it" (2007).

Vargas Llosa's words proved prescient. On September 22, 2007 Chilean courts extradited Alberto Fujimori to Peru to face charges of human rights violations and corruption. The next day, Peruvians discovered a severely marred memorial: the central stone or "eye" had been crudely hammered off, several other stones broken, and the central obelisk and other parts of the monument drenched in neon orange paint, the color of the political movement "Sí, Cumple" ("Yes, he delivers") that had kept Fujimori in the Peruvian political scene despite his absence. (See Plate 9.1.) Rather than clear "tears" flowing from the "eye," a pool of paint floated below. According to an email that circulated among well-wishers a few days after the assault, Lika Mutal wrote that the monument now looked like "Pachamama, the Mother Earth, is crying blood and this calls for reflection. This wound—impossible to restore—represents the wound which in Peru throughout its history was never healed and which during the years of terrorism became infested with evermore violence, intolerance and a dirty power game."[13] It is difficult to state with certainty that the group who assaulted the Ojo que llora intended a message of wanting to "re-attack and re-murder the victims" of the preceding 20 years. Perhaps, more simply, they chose this site to make a specific political statement: they contested Fujimori's extradition to face charges for his involvement in the murders at La Cantuta and Barrios Altos, the victims whose names are among those inscribed in the stones of the Ojo que llora, and whose family members had gathered to celebrate the news of Fujimori's extradition.

This very public defacement of the Ojo que llora—where memory of the past in general was assailed—stands in contrast to a later, smaller disfigurement of individual stones by drawing green lines across the names of the victims of La Cantuta massacre. (See Plate 9.2.) The effort of tracking down specific names in a small section of the memorial site and crossing them each out speaks of a more targeted message. By comparison, the splashing of orange paint and breaking of stones reads as a more generalized attack on a human rights narrative that remembers and pays homage to victims of the internal war. The crossing out of the Cantuta victims' names was a quieter, more private, aggression: it did not draw any media attention that I am aware of. It was as though whoever did it had a personal axe to grind with these individuals and what they symbolized as agents in the possible (and later actual) downfall of Fujimori. The smaller act seems meant to erase specific victims and event, while the larger one is part of an ongoing polemical conversation.

These two acts of defacement present a particular kind of "silencing": that of intimidation, and an implicit threat against those who speak in favor of remembering those who suffered during the internal war. The disfiguring of the Ojo que llora, while trying to suppress dialog about the past, ends up paradoxically generating more public discussion about it. Indeed such acts continually reactivate public memory. Family members of victims of the internal war, human rights groups, and concerned citizens have returned to the Ojo que llora to clean the stones in the wake of their defacement. Most recently, on March 12, 2010, family members of the victims of Uchurraccay, the Cantuta, the Frontón, and Accomarca massacres, among others, re-inscribed the names of their loved ones – names erased not by vandalism, but faded by sun and rain—in order to keep present the name and memory of each of the victims of the internal conflict in this space of memory.[14] Not only will the names be renewed and thus be continually visible, but also the actions of re-inscribing the names form new "sites" and processes of enlivening memory. The act of re-inscription creates a new memorial ritual, perhaps a new way to bind the living and the dead. Recently acquired funding to engrave permanently these stones might, unfortunately, curtail this ceremonial renewal.

The defacement of the Ojo que llora is different from making a site invisible—demolishing it—such as the military government dynamiting the ovens of Lonquén in Chile, where the bodies of supposed subversives had been incinerated.[15] Rather, by targeting the Ojo que llora, "vandals" are unwittingly reinvigorating it, indeed endowing it with cultural capital as a place of memory and as a place for remembering. That is, the Ojo que llora has become more than an artist's homage to victims of the internal war; it has become a "memory knot" in itself and thus a place where Peruvians can mark the "contentious processes" by which emblematic memories are made and unmade, where "people build bridges between personal knowledge or experience, and the imagined national community of experience" (Stern, 2004: 124). The defacement of the Ojo que llora, ironically, is an important element in the ongoing memorial process.

9.5 A consensual memory? The counter-currents of Peru's collective memory in the present

The present socio-political climate in Peru poses unique challenges to the memorialization of the preceding decades (1980–2000). In the aftermath of violence, where blame is spread widely and few social groups are willing to acknowledge the CVR's findings, competing narratives and memories jockey for primacy as "truth." The CVR report was one exercise to create a public forum for discussion of the past and to establish a complex national narrative. The Ojo que llora is another such site that seeks to bring private and collective memories into the public sphere, and in so doing create more inclusive national narratives. Spheres of representation are prominent in memory negotiation precisely because of the little political weight of the CVR and the official history that the CVR wished to pass as Peru's collective memory (Drinot, 2009: 20).

One of the thorny "truths" initially told by the CVR and mirrored in the Ojo que llora was that that the victims of Peru's war were many, from many different social groups, and that the boundary between victim and perpetrator is, at times, far from clear. Yet, with the different memory camps competing for establishing their narrative as *the* national narrative, the very notion of "victim" has changed. We see this in the Ojo que llora: initially intended as a global homage to the victims of Peru's internal conflict, Lika Mutal originally painted the names of all the victims listed by the CVR (no matter whether they were members of subversive groups or the armed forces); after the controversy over *senderista* names among the victims named at the Ojo que llora, Mutal has turned to the much more narrowly defined Single Victim Registry ("Regsitro Único de Víctimas") composed by the National Reparations Council created in 2006, which excludes members of Shining Path and MRTA. This decision (by both the National Reparations Council and Mutal) to change the list of victims suggests a subtle melding of competing memory groups' narratives: the result is a narrative that maintains the armed forces as potential victims (while evading their abuses), and through the *senderistas'* absence from the Ojo que llora highlights their violence, but effaces the structural inequities that gave rise to their movement.

The repeated defacement of the Ojo que llora suggests that there is limited public space in contemporary Peru in which to talk peacefully about the past. In reference to those who denied the findings of the CVR, former commissioner Carlos Iván Degregori (2004: 84) wrote that Peru suffers from a "long period of forgetting, or, better said, [a] custom of repressing subaltern memories." The conflict over the Ojo que llora seems to confirm this tradition of suppressing memories. According to the artist Natalia Iguíñiz, calling the Ojo que llora a monument to terrorism "is to continue to generate confusion over what happened, attempting to make a blank slate about everything and our [Lima's and the coastal residents'] complicity in the conflict that we have lived through" (Bayly, 2007). In response to the attacks on the Ojo que llora, Gisela Ortiz Perea, sister to one of the student victims of La Cantuta, said, "not only did they end the lives of our family members, now they try to end our memory" (*Prensa Libre*, 2007). Ortiz Perea echoes Holocaust survivor Elie Wiesel's statement that "the executioner always kills twice, the second time with silence."[16]

Yet the violence waged against the Ojo que llora is not silencing. Rather, such acts provoke debate, dialog, and remembering. Perhaps, indeed, it might be more productive to think of defacement as a form of curation—a kind of re-ordering of the past (though a violent one) according to one group's desire for a single, authoritative interpretation of the past. This form of exhibiting a strongly held interpretation stands in stark contrast to another form of curation of Peru's difficult past, one that endeavors to "care for" the past through inclusive remembering and memorialization of the experiences painfully documented by the CVR or the names carefully engraved, painted, cleaned, and repainted on the stones of the Ojo que llora. "Vandals" contest a human rights narrative in Peru, and work to tighten Peru's memory knot of the past decades, thus making public discussion difficult. Human rights groups and others work to loosen the knot. Despite their differences, what both memory camps seem to agree upon is the very presence of a knot.

Notes

Acknowledgments: I wish to thank Jo-Marie Burt, Paulo Drinot, Katherine Hite, Erica Lehrer, Lika Mutal, Monica E. Patterson, Anna Sheftel, and Maria Eugenia Ulfe for their comments on earlier versions of this chapter, and to Yael Rojas for her photographs. My research has received generous support from the Social Sciences and Research Council of Canada, the Canada Research Chair program, and the Fonds québécois de la recherche sur la société et la culture. I also thank *Memory Studies* (Sage Publications) for permission to publish here my article of the same title.

1. I have found Gamboni's *The Destruction of Art* (1997) useful in thinking through the different historical meanings of attacking art and objects. Because vandalism is usually associated with gratuitous destruction, without intent or motive, it strips the instigators of political agency. Nevertheless, as this is the predominant interpretation within Peru of the attacks on the Ojo que llora I use the term here, though in quotation marks. One could also consider vandalized sites as ruins. On ruins as memory sites for politically engaged presents and futures see Lazzara and Unruh (2009).
2. "Conversación con Lika Mutal," by Roxana Chirinos. Available at http://www.agenciaperu.com/cultural/portada/cvr3/mutal.html#arriba. Accessed March 15, 2007. Mutal built the Ojo que llora with the help of architect Luis Longhi.
3. Announcement for "Ceremonia de presentación de la Alameda de la Memoria," email correspondence from organization Para que no se repita, August 28, 2005.
4. "Logros de la Caminata por la Paz"; available at http://devocionalescristianos.org/2005/09/ce-peru-logros-de-la-caminata-por-la.html. Accessed April 19, 2010.
5. Paulo Drinot's (2009: 24–7) article does the hard labor of untangling the competing interpretations over Peru's past, narrowing them to two key versions of why the violence occurred: one camp who sees Shining Path as singly responsible for the violence because *senderistas* are inherently violent; and the other camp who sees the most recent eruption of violence as an extension of the structural violence inherent in Peruvian society, hence the emergence of Shining Path and the poorly discriminating response of the authorities, elite, and middle-class citizens.
6. Available at http://www.aprodeh.org.pe/casos2007/campanacabitos/index.html. Accessed February 2, 2010.
7. Lika Mutal, personal communication, March 7, 2008.
8. For example, The Pro-Human Rights Association (Acociación Pro Derechos Humanos, APRODEH) sent out an invitation on December 6, 2006 to come and help restore the names on the International Human Rights Day. Email correspondence, Para que no se repita, December 7, 2006.
9. Available at http://www.aprodeh.org.pe/sitiomemoria/apurimac.html. Accessed April 19, 2010.
10. Andrew Herscher's analysis of the vandalism of an UNESCO World Heritage site, the peristyle of Diocletian's Palace in Split, Croatia in 1998 (discussed in his chapter here) suggests that such attacks represent an "under-identification" with this heritage site. In the case of the attacks on the Ojo que llora, which is not a heritage site, my interpretation differs somewhat: it is because the assailants are *not* indifferent to the past and to what the Ojo que llora signifies that they have chosen to deface the signifier.
11. The cover of *Expreso* on January 3, 2007 has a picture of the Ojo que llora with the lead article heading "there exists a monument to terrorists!"
12. Email announcement received January 11, 2007 from Rosa Villarán de la Puente.
13. Email correspondence of Lika Mutal, September 26, 2007.
14. Rosario Narváez, representative of Asociación Pro Derechos Humanos (APRODEH); available at http://www.aprodeh.org.pe. Accessed April 19, 2010.

15. Despite having destroyed the ovens, the site has become a "pilgrimage" destination. Similar paradoxical processes are at work as in the Ojo que llora. Stern writes on Chile, "whatever the process and its mix of physical descent and cultural creation, once a place becomes endowed with sacred connection to a traumatic and still polemical past, it can unleash ferocious ongoing memory struggles. As with charged events and anniversary dates, motivated human groups can feel a 'call' to recognize or create physical sites connected to their sense of collective remembrance, or alternatively, to shun or render culturally invisible those sites that lend credibility and organizing energy to rival memories" (2004: 123–4).
16. Cited in William Logan and Kier Reeves (2009: 2).

Works cited

Bayly, Doris (2007). "En el Ojo de la tormenta." *El Comercio*, January 5.

Bickford, Louis (2005). "Memoryscapes." In Ksenija Bilbija, Jo Ellen Fair, Leigh A. Payne and Cynthia E. Milton (eds). *The Art of Truth-telling about Authoritarian Rule*. Madison: University of Wisconsin Press, 96–102.

Burt, Jo-Marie (2007). *Political Violence and the Authoritarian State in Peru*. New York: Palgrave Macmillan.

Burt, Jo-Marie (2010). "1097: la nueva cara de impunidad." In *NoticiasSER.pe*. Available at http://www.noticiasser.pe/08/09/2010/contracorriente/en-edicion. Accessed September 15, 2010.

Cárdenas, Miguel Ángel (2006). "En el Ojo de la memoria." *El Comercio*, 10 December.

Chirinos, Roxana (2007). "*Conversación con Lika Mutal*." Available at http://www.agenciaperu.com/cultural/portada/cvr3/mutal.html#arriba. Accessed March 15, 2010.

Comisión de la Verdad y Reconciliación (2003). *Informe Final*. Available at http://www.cverdad.org.pe/ifinal/index.php. Accessed December 11, 2005.

Inter-American Court of Human Rights (CIDH) (2007). "Caso del Penal Miguel Castro Castro *vs*. Perú"; available at http://www.corteidh.or.cr/casos.cfm?idCaso=258. Accessed March 22, 2007.

Degregori, Carlos Iván (2004). "*Heridas abiertas, derechos esquivos: Reflexiones sobre la Comisión de la Verdad y Reconciliación*." In Raynald Belay, Jorge Bracamonte, Carlos Iván Degregori and Jean Joinville Vacher (eds). *Memorias en conflicto: Aspectos de la violencia política contemporánea*. Lima: Embajada de Francia en el Perú, IEP, IFEA, Red para el Desarrollo de las Ciencias Sociales en el Perú, 75–85.

Drinot, Paulo (2009). "For Whom the Eye Cries: Memory, Monumentality, and the Ontologies of Violence in Peru." *Journal of Latin American Cultural Studies* 18(1): 15–32.

El Comercio (2010). "La ONU advirtió que el DL 1097 tiende a que violadores de derechos humanos queden impunes." September 8.

El Peruano (2001). Article 1 of Decreto Supremo n.065-2001-PCM. June 4.

Expreso (2007). "Existe un monumento a terroristas!" January 3.

Gamboni, Dario (1997). *The Destruction of Art: Iconoclasm and Vandalism since the French Revolution*. London: Reaktion Books.

González, Eduardo (2006). "The Peruvian Truth and Reconciliation Commission and the Challenge of Impunity." In Naomi Roht-Arriaza and Javier Mariezcurrena (eds). *Beyond Truth versus Justice: Transitional Justice in the Twenty-First Century*. New York: Cambridge University Press, 70–93.

Hite, Katherine (2007). "The Eye that Cries: The Politics of Representing Victims in Contemporary Peru." *Contracorriente* 5(1): 108–34.

Lazzara, Michael J. and Vicky Unruh (eds) (2009). *Telling Ruins in Latin America*. London: Routledge.

Llosa, Claudia (dir.) (2009). *La teta asustada*. Spain and Peru: Olive Films.

Logan, William and Keir Reeves (eds) (2009). *Places of Pain and Shame: Dealing with "Difficult Heritage"*. London: Routledge Press.

Milton, Cynthia (2007). "Public Spaces for the Discussion of Past Violence: The Case of Peru." *Antipoda—Revista de Antropologia y Arqueologia* (July–December): 143–68.

Milton, Cynthia (2011). "Parallel Lies? Peru's Cultural Memory Battles Go International." *e-misférica* 7(2). Available at http://hemisphericinstitute.org/hemi/en/e-misferica-72/milton. Accessed February 22, 2011.

Prensa Libre (2007). Interview with Gisela Ortiz Perea. September 21. Available at http://www.youtube.com/watch?v=YBRgYVQkFOY. Accessed November 15, 2007.

Salomon, Frank (2004). *The Cord Keepers: Khipus and Cultural Life in a Peruvian Village*. Durham: Duke University Press.

Scarry, Elaine (1985). *The Body in Pain: The Making and Unmaking of the World*. New York: Oxford University Press.

Sion, Brigitte (2008). "Absent Bodies, Uncertain Memorials: Performing Memory in Berlin and in Buenos Aires." Unpublished doctoral thesis, New York University, New York.

Stern, Steve, J. (2004). *Remembering Pinochet's Chile*. Durham: Duke University Press.

Vargas, Llosa Mario (2007). "The Ojo que llora." *El País*. 14 January. Available at http://www.elpais.com/articulo/opinion/ojo/llora/elpepuint/20070114elpepiopi_5/Tes. Accessed February 28, 2010.

Vargas, Llosa Mario (2008). "Lika Mutal o la tentacion de la piedra." In *Lika Mutal o la tentacion de la piedra*. Santiago, Chile: Patricia Ready Galeria.

Wiener, Raúl (2007). "*El Ojo que Llora y el que mata*." Available at http://alainet.org/active/15205&lang=es. Accessed March 21, 2010.

Young, James E. (1993). *The Texture of Memory: Holocaust Memorials and Meaning*. New Haven: Yale University Press.

10
(Mis)representations of the Jewish Past in Poland's Memoryscapes: Nationalism, Religion, and Political Economies of Commemoration

Sławomir Kapralski

10.1 Memory and space

In contemporary culture and society, space is privileged over time as the main frame by which we orient ourselves in our lifeworlds. Even if this claim exaggerates a trend, the trend nevertheless exists: the growing role of space in late modernity marks this period as different from classical modernity with its emphasis on linear time and narrative.[1] Likewise, if classical modernity was the age of history, late modernity is the age of memory: the capricious, non-linear work of remembrance, jumping from one image of the past to another, buffeted by the feelings evoked by the particular space in which we are located, or the communication networks in which we participate (Delanty, 1999: 71).

It is amid such "flows of space and communication" (Delanty, 1999: 71) that we form and express our attitudes to and perceptions of the past, and through them construct a rough sense of who we are. To capture this complex relation of intertwined processes with a single word, I refer to the concept of "memoryscape," a sort of "memorial landscape" with a certain material and symbolic shape, through which "collective memory is commonly spatialized" (Muzaini and Yeoh, 2005: 345). The suffix -*scape* here suggests, as in Appadurai's work (1996: 33), the fluidity of the terrain and its multifaceted nature: despite material qualities that give the impression of stability and immutability, the landscape of memory is constituted in and through the imagination of those who refer to it.

While fluid, perspectival, and imagined, the spatialization of memory also implicates power, in the sense of creating a hegemonic narrative about the past. This process often involves various practices of sanitizing history, highlighting similarities, eliding differences, and establishing a dominant, privileged way of seeing (Muzaini and Yeoh, 2005: 345). A memoryscape can be thus defined as a "site of concentrated cultural practice," the main cultural function of which is to impose order and coherence on the meanings attributed to the past–present relationship, including the domestication of difference so that it is not subversive. Memoryscapes contain an array of memories, some of them at times in symbolic conflict, just as the bearers of these memories may themselves be in reality. Consequently, memoryscapes as sites of cultural practice are frequently enlisted "in efforts not only to normalize or homogenize but also to hierarchize, encapsulate, exclude, criminalize, hegemonize, or marginalize practices and populations that diverge from the sanctioned ideal" (Sewell, 2005: 56).

Thus memoryscapes do not simply express and convey memories; just as often they erase the memories of those lacking sufficient resources to support a public presence, or silence uncomfortable memories that may haunt those who control the landscape. Even those memories "sanctioned" in a given landscape are not simply conveyed from the past or "copied" from the memories of a particular group. They are often distorted memories that offer a convenient vision of the past that legitimizes a group's claim of control over a territory, its meaning and its history. A memoryscape is thus simultaneously a product of power relations and a powerful producer of both consciousness and amnesia about the past (Yoneyama, 1994: 103). In this sense, memoryscapes play a role within larger "frames of memory"—complex structures of time-perceptions, chronologies, visions of history, discourses, symbols, concepts, narratives, material objects, and places, which by simply "being there" act together to organize our thoughts and unconscious emotions related to the past (Irwin-Zarecka, 1994).

10.2 Jews in Poland's memoryscapes

The Holocaust wiped out a Jewish world that for centuries formed a substantial part of Poland's landscape. The post-Holocaust exodus of survivors left Poland with only traces of Jewish memory; those few who decided to stay against all odds were unable to make a significant mark on the landscape. As a result, Poles "were left alone with their own, now uncontested, memory of events" (Young, 1993: 116). Yet this is only partly true. Memoryscapes as models of the past contain accumulated signs that stubbornly resist destruction. Ruined synagogues and desecrated cemeteries remained in the landscape in spite of various administrative and spontaneous attempts to seize Jewish property and/or use

Jewish spaces for other purposes. Thanks to the active resistance of those few Jewish organizations—religious and secular—that were allowed to exist in Communist Poland, and thanks to the ambivalent attitudes of local and central authorities, Jewish memories maintained a material and spatial presence in Polish memoryscapes. The form of their presence, however, was often a matter of contest and argument, not only between "Jews" and "Communists" or "Jews" and "Poles," but also among different Jewish institutions (Urban, 2006).

The façade of a house in Goldhammer Street in Tarnów, a town in southern Poland, illustrates the persistence of Jewish memory in the face of oblivion. This photograph, taken at the very beginning of the 1990s, shows the original Yiddish words still visible on the wall alongside Polish-language signs advertising what was once a small Jewish business in a tiny Polish-Jewish street, despite the passage of more than 50 years since their last re-painting. (See Plate 10.1.)

The collapse of Communism in Poland meant, among other things, a democratization of access to public spaces. This included both a momentous reclaiming of the "national" past from distorting communist narratives, but also—and not insignificantly—an opportunity to put some fresh paint on old walls. Such an occasion can be seen in the photograph of the same façade, taken in 2000. (See Plate 10.2.) We can see that despite the best efforts of some individuals, the past is difficult to chase away; the old letters are still visible behind the layer of new paint, turning the façade into a palimpsestual message from a vanished world.

Being stubborn has its rewards. The message on the wall recently received a sort of posthumous revival due to a combination of postmodern nostalgia, an emergent local "multiculturally"-oriented tourist trade, and perhaps also a few good souls attempting to do justice to an embattled past. The photograph, taken in 2008, shows the result of a convergence of these strategies for preserving the Jewish past among the Polish dwellers of Goldhammer Street in Tarnów. (See Plate 10.3.)

Oblivion, erasure, and preservation, permanently accompanied by the persistence of the material traces of the past, are three modes of Jewish "presence" in Poland's memoryscape. These modes do not follow one another chronologically: we may find them all coexisting in any period of contemporary Polish history, and the status of each depends on the particular power relations and identity configurations dominant at a given moment. In addition, "preservation" of the Jewish past by Poles may take very different forms, from manipulative distortion to fair representation to alleged "restoration" that may result in pretentious imitation.

10.3 The Holocaust: erased and represented

The decade of the 1990s was marked by the "revival" of Jewish memory in Poland. One of the most important aspects of this development was the change in school curricula and special programs for teacher training in Holocaust education (Ambrosewicz-Jacobs and Hońdo, 2005). In addition, Polish-Jewish relations have received substantial media attention, and a number of commemorative ceremonies in which the authorities participated have helped focus public opinion on previously neglected Jewish aspects of Polish history. The process of change has also involved the Auschwitz-Birkenau concentration camp site where, with the participation of Jewish institutions, the Auschwitz-Birkenau Museum exhibition has been refurbished and updated. The Museum now emphasizes the function of the site as a symbol of the Holocaust, clearly indicating that it was foremost a site of mass extermination of men, women, and children, sent to their death because they were Jewish.

Poles have begun to interact more frequently with the increasing number of Jewish visitors to Poland, including organized meetings of Polish and Israeli high school students. At the same time a growing number of Poles have either discovered that they have Jewish roots or have decided to re-embrace previously repressed or rejected Jewish roots. This process has been assisted by various Jewish organizations that have become visible through their efforts to protect the material remnants of Jewish culture in Poland, and as supporters of religious, cultural, and educational initiatives. Correspondingly some Poles, acting out of intellectual interest, ethical sensibilities, or economic motives, have engaged in various initiatives: from opening a "Jewish" restaurant to assembling a band playing Jewish music, to organizing a festival of Jewish culture. This phenomenon has been described, alternatively, by Ruth Gruber (2002) as "virtual Jewishness"—a form of Jewish culture produced by and addressed to non-Jews—and by Erica Lehrer (2010) as a cultural politics of "conciliatory heritage."

Freed from the constraints of communist censorship, the debate about Polish-Jewish relations during the Shoah has continued, peaking in the wake of the publication of Jan T. Gross' book *Sąsiedzi* (*Neighbors*) in 2000. Due to the subsequent discussion of the murderous crimes committed by the Polish inhabitants of the town of Jedwabne against their Jewish neighbors, the "whole of Polish society was convulsed by an extraordinary self-examination" (Weinbaum, 2002: 132). While the discussion divided various sectors of Polish society, including the Church, it continued (although with less intensity) after the 2006 publication of Gross's subsequent book *Fear*, contributing greatly to the "return of memory" of the Jews and the Holocaust to Polish popular consciousness.

Despite the processes of "rediscovery" of heritage and the examination of Poland's past outlined above, the memory of the Jews in general and of the Holocaust in particular has not been integrated into Poland's "living memory." It exists—as a matter of dispute rather than consensus—among elites, and only occasionally appears in vernacular memories, usually in mass-mediated form. If in 1992 46 percent of Poles believed that Jews suffered more than Poles in the years of World War II, in 2002 only 38 percent held such an opinion. Similarly, the number of respondents who believed that Poles suffered more rose from 6 to 10 percent. However, the answer most frequently given in 2002 was that both Poles and Jews suffered equally: 47 percent were of that opinion, compared to 32 percent in 1992 (Krzemiński, 2004: 120).

It appears that while in the decade 1992–2002 the Polish population was exposed to a mass of new historical facts and narratives in new social frames of memory (free from communist control) the information received about the Holocaust and Jews was not easily integrated into pre-existing cognitive structures. Elsewhere I have explained this surprising gap with reference to discursive features of memory and the local circumstances of Polish debates about Jews (Kapralski, 2007). Here I am seeking a solution that considers instead the spatiality of memory, employing the notion of "memoryscapes" as the context in which memories are produced and reproduced.

I would claim that it is precisely the lack of material/spatial frames capable of embracing the new meanings of the past currently being elaborated in nationwide intellectual debate that prevents Jewish incorporation into Poland's living memory at the vernacular level. Deprived of a spatial dimension, the existing representations of the Holocaust (largely intellectual and "textual") may serve as "models of" but fail to present "models for" the Holocaust in popular memory, in the sense of allowing Poles to apprehend what happened to the Jews in the past, and the impact of this history in the present.[2]

The Jewish past has reappeared in Poland's memoryscapes as part of a nostalgic vision of a colorful, "multicultural" past, which glosses over both anti-Semitism (an everyday part and parcel of that multiculturalism) and the Holocaust. In constructing spaces of memory on the community level, local authorities and inhabitants who choose to commemorate the Jewish history of their area generally do so via renovation of a synagogue building or development of a Jewish section of a local museum rather than with a Holocaust memorial. Part of this bias is due to the fact that in many such localities modest Holocaust memorials were already in existence; they had been built by surviving Jews in the first years after the Holocaust. Typically on the terrain of Jewish cemeteries, these memory sites are relatively invisible to the non-Jewish population. Nevertheless, local authorities could argue that commemoration of the Holocaust "has been done" and choose to focus on representing other, less challenging aspects of their histories.

Such was the case with the synagogue building in Łańcut. Having served as a storehouse from its expropriation during World War II until 1956, it was subsequently renovated with financial assistance from the Polish government and local businesses (the first renovation took place in the 1960s, the second one from 1983–1990), and became a part of the local museum. Łańcut's Jewish cemetery (the newer one) contains a rather dilapidated Holocaust memorial from the early post-war years. Łańcut's memoryscape in the past decade, then, offered a musealized and aestheticized reference to the town's Jewish history without public commemoration of the Holocaust either with a new memorial or with an attempt to include this event in the existing one. The situation today may be poised to change: due to its restitution to the Jewish community the synagogue building is no longer part of the Museum, and thus the local authorities and museum curators, lacking control of a monumental site of Jewish memory, are faced with an open field for memorial strategies, if indeed they continue to pursue commemoration of Łańcut's Jews.[3]

Similar developments can be seen elsewhere, even in places where Jewish memory was continually present in the local memoryscape. In Tarnów, for example, a prominent Holocaust memorial, built by the community of Jewish survivors, has been present since 1946. Its key material elements consist of the remaining columns of the New Synagogue that was destroyed by the Nazis in 1939. The memorial, together with the section of the cemetery in which it is located, has been periodically renovated by the local museum and Society for Protection of Jewish Monuments, an organization set up by a group of Polish citizens of Tarnów interested in the Jewish past of their town. More recently, a memorial tablet was placed at the corner of Żydowska (Jewish) Street and the main square, on the site where thousands of Tarnów's Jews were murdered during the so-called "actions of liquidation" of the local ghetto in 1942.

The tablet, together with the few preserved cobblestones that "witnessed" the atrocities, indicates the penetration of Holocaust memory into the town's center. This new spatialization is amplified by the most recent commemorative gesture, a tablet designed and funded by an Italian entrepreneur who settled in Tarnów. As the Jewish population of Tarnów shortly before the war is estimated at 25,000, the figure of "40,000 Tarnowians" noted in the text on the tablet suggests an attempt to invoke a "unified community of memory" that embraces both the Jewish victims of the Holocaust and the Polish victims of World War II. Thus, the fate of Jewish and non-Jewish victims has been equated and incorporated within the "same God, City and Sacrifice." Controversial as this may be (as it negates the uniqueness of the Holocaust vis-à-vis Polish wartime suffering) it is an interesting intervention in the memoryscape with its clear intention to provide a "model for" a certain experience of the past. Given the long period during which Jews were completely excluded from the Polish community of memory, this kind of intervention may have an ameliorative effect on the way local people perceive Jews—perhaps slightly more as "one of us (Poles)." On the other hand, such attempts may also simply replicate the entrenched tendency—suggested by the survey results mentioned above—to treat Jewish and Polish wartime suffering as identical.

A similar attempt to represent the memory of the Holocaust in Polish public space can be found in Rzeszów. First, a memorial plaque was placed on the wall of one of the two surviving synagogue buildings, now housing an art gallery and local archives, along with a small research unit dedicated to the Jewish history of the region. The plaque was funded jointly by the community of Rzeszów's Jewish Holocaust survivors and the town authorities. Additionally, a memorial slab has been placed in the park area in front of the synagogue buildings, which was once the town's old Jewish cemetery. The text on the tombstone-like slab states, "In this place stood a sixteenth-century Jewish cemetery, destroyed during World War II by the Nazi occupiers. In the summer of 1942, Jews were gathered here before being taken to the death camps." In this way the older history of Jewish habitation in Rzeszów is connected with their fate during the Holocaust in a single commemorative act, reclaiming the whole area as an integrated Jewish memoryscape.[4]

10.4 Przeworsk: A brief history of a contested memoryscape

In Przeworsk, a small town east of Łańcut, Jews comprised half of the pre-war population and had developed a rich community life since the time of their settlement in the sixteenth century. The synagogue building in Przeworsk did not have as good fortune as the one in Łańcut; it was razed by the Nazis, who also pillaged gravestones from the town's Jewish cemetery to pave the yard of the local sugar refinery. During the Nazi occupation of Przeworsk the cemetery was occasionally used as an execution site: Jews, mostly those caught while trying to escape from transports to camps, were brought there and shot. After the war, the desecrated space of the cemetery became a stage for the performance of several "memorial" strategies—oblivion, erasure, and commemoration — thus forming a memoryscape of compounded difficulties.

Immediately after the war the terrain of the cemetery stood empty and untouched until a major road construction project to connect the larger cities of Kraków and Przemyśl damaged the cemetery's southern side. In 1969 a huge monument commemorating the 25th anniversary of the liberation of the town was erected. The expanse of the monument, known as *Pomnik Walki i Męczeństwa* (Monument to Battle and Martyrdom), encroached on the western side of the cemetery. Later, in the early 1980s, the municipal council decided to build a bus station on the remaining cemetery terrain.

Mr. Jan Sasak, a local stonecutter, and at the time a member of the council, voted against this decision. Although he was outvoted, he proposed at least placing some kind of sign indicating the former identity of the site. His proposal did not find support, and so he resolved to make a gesture of his own. In the northeast corner of the cemetery/bus station, he placed a modest stone with an inscription commemorating the Jews murdered during the war. A few years later the stone was moved—without Mr. Sasak's knowledge or consent—to the southeast corner of the former cemetery, behind a taxi stand, inconvenient for visitors. The former location of the stone had apparently been designated for commercial purposes.

This particular local history is rather exceptional, since the sites of Jewish cemeteries in the region, even if empty and unprotected, are generally not used for new construction projects. Nevertheless, the situation fits the overall pattern of removing—consciously or not—Jewish memory from the landscape. Building the road and bus station exemplify the "functional approach" to sites of Jewish memory: the Jews are no longer here, the gravestones were already removed by the Nazis, and life must go on—local people need roads and bus stations. This was the argument frequently used by the local authorities from the 1950s on when urban and industrial development inevitably bumped up against moral/religious claims to protect Jewish cemeteries, which were generally seen as a "problem" by local urban planning authorities (Urban, 2006: 445). The lack of sensitivity on the developers' side could certainly be interpreted in terms of open or latent anti-Semitism. But in the early years (the road construction) it could also be accounted for by low levels of sensitivity more generally, as a result of the brutality of the war period. And by the 1980s (the bus station), one could also refer to a process of forgetting, combined with an increased focus on national political events. All three factors likely played a role here.

Interpreting the motivations behind a monument erected in 1969 requires a slightly different approach. Here we confront a conscious attempt to present the Communist vision of history, staged expressly to aid in legitimizing state authority. It is worth noting that the date of the erection of the monument coincides with a well-known government-sponsored anti-Semitic campaign, a fact that may have influenced the decision about the monument's location, or at minimum quelled any hesitation about its appropriateness.

The monument itself is an interesting example of the Communist manipulation of history. It consists of two separate structures: the first, a vertical one, is made up of three columns symbolizing the three decades of Communist Poland that had been achieved. The columns are adorned with the Polish national emblem in its Communist incarnation: an eagle without a crown (the symbol of royalty was removed from the pre-war emblem). Below this eagle hangs another, this one the symbol of the first Polish dynasty—the Piasts—that ruled from the end of the tenth century to the middle of the fourteenth. This eagle also has no crown, since the title of royalty was granted to the dynasty only after the emblem had been established as its symbol.

We thus have a clear attempt to anchor Communist rule within Polish history, to present it as a logical and legitimate stage in the development of Polish statehood. Indeed, the Communists often referred positively to the Piast dynasty, juxtaposing it with the later period of the multinational Polish-Lithuanian Commonwealth. The reason for this could be strictly political: the borders of the Commonwealth reached far into areas that would later become the western territories of the Soviet Union (today the independent states of Lithuania, Belarus, and Ukraine). It could also be ideological: the Commonwealth, according to the official Communist interpretation of history, was a belligerent, expansionist state based on serfdom and egotistical exploitation of its resources by the aristocracy. Moreover, the "homogeneity" of Poland during the Piast dynasty was often presented in opposition to the "negative" multinational character of the Commonwealth and the Republic of Poland from the period 1918–39. In this way the Communists attempted to naturalize the forced homogenization of Poland after World War II—a result of war casualties and post-war borders changes—as a "return to the roots" of Polish statehood.

The second part of the monument, an upside-down pyramid, vaguely resembling a memorial candle, has on its front face the Polish Military Cross and the inscription: "To the heroes of the revolutionary struggles, trusty sons of Przeworsk soil, who fought against the oppression of the pre-war right wing Polish government, against the Nazi occupiers and against the forces of reaction, for national and social liberation, for socialist Poland." The vision of history expressed in the inscription identifies both the pre-war, "capitalist" Poland and the postwar anti-Communists with the Nazis. National liberation has been conflated with the Communist political program, thus excluding non-Communist members of the Polish resistance from the officially approved pantheon of "national martyrs." Together with the symbolism of the eagles, the inscription makes the Communist goal clear: the *telos* of Polish history is "socialist" Poland; those who did not participate in its establishment are not part of "us." Indeed, in Communism's Manichean vision of the world, they belong to "them," to the enemy.

Nor was there a place for Jews in this vision. Their difference was erased by the political need to define two main political camps. Although for quite different reasons, the Communists' homogeneous vision of Poland left no more place for Jews in Poland's memoryscape than the equally homogeneous vision produced by Polish nationalists. The history represented in Przeworsk's memoryscape has thus been falsified twofold: Jewish memory has been erased by the destruction of its material container, and also excised from the officially approved, concretely monumentalized vision of history. Indeed, a broad swath of Polish vernacular memory has been erased by official Communist symbolism and narrative. The only attempt to preserve Jewish memory took place at the initiative of a single individual, a form of "counter-memorialization" embodied in the modesty and authenticity of Mr. Sasak's memorial stone, so fundamentally at odds with the message of the Communist monument.

Since 1989 there has been much discussion about the "de-communization" of public space in Poland. Indeed, the process of destroying the monuments of the *ancien régime* and replacing its street names with those of newly resurrected national heroes it had previously erased is a phenomenon common in post-communist East/Central Europe. The process intensifies when right-wing nationalists win elections, and slows when the political pendulum swings to the other side of the spectrum. Przeworsk, however, has taken a quite unique approach to dealing with its Communist memorial. In the year 2000, inhabitants and visitors could still see the old monument standing, but in radically altered form. (See Figure 10.1)

On the columns symbolizing the three decades of Communism now hung a figure of the crucified Jesus, clearly proclaiming the role of Communism in repressing Poland's Catholic memory and identity. This addition also offers a "closure" of national history by replacing a Communist *telos* with a religious one: the anti-religious stance of the Communists is revealed as futile, and the true essence of Polish nationhood is now liberated. Once again, Poland's history of victimization is transformed into a victory of the oppressed, in a Romantic-religious vision of Poland as the "Christ of nations." The second meaning conveyed by the transformation of the monument relates simultaneously to the Catholic concept of redemption and to the idea of nationalism as a "secular transformation of fatality into continuity, contingency into meaning" (Anderson, 1991). The cross is the ultimate sign of redemption, prevailing over any kind of historical evil. Simultaneously, the nationalist discourse works toward a collective immortalization that helps survive national ruptures by evoking a "future imaginable throughout the past," and celebrating national identity as

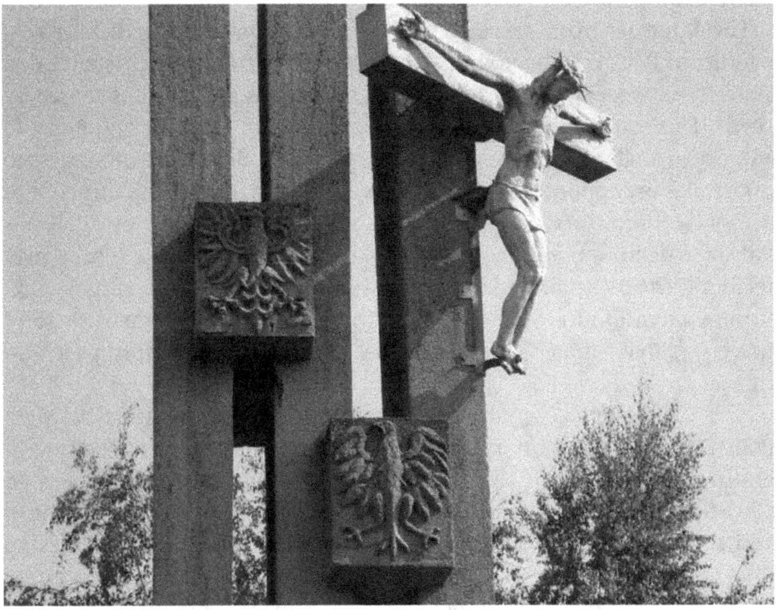

Figure 10.1 Communist memorial transformed. Przeworsk, Poland in 2000. (Photograph by Sławomir Kapralski.)

primordial, unified, and continuous (McCrone, 1998). While modern nationalisms employ secularized discourses, more traditional ones may martial religious discourse to similar ends.

The new inscription on the monument reads:

"Open the door for Christ"
(John Paul II)

To the victims of the struggle for freedom and human dignity.
In the Millennial Year
to honor
the pontificate of the Polish Pope
John Paul II.
From the Community of Przeworsk.

Here the values manifested in Polish history have been redefined (freedom and dignity), linked to Christianity (through a reference to Christ and the second millennium), and scaffolded by the authority of the Pope—perhaps the only Polish person, living or dead, who induces unity among Poles.

The figure of Christ "crucified on Communism" is thus a sign of internal conflict in Polish memory, and an attempt to confirm the persistence of a single "true essence of Polishness" that transcends the ruptures caused by "evil." This conflation of nationalist eschatology and theodicy provides an additional angle of interpretation of the local authorities' unwillingness to undertake any commemoration of Jews in the area: it has been turned into a mono-ethnic *Polish* memoryscape—a symbolic territory of "Polish–Polish" redemption and reconciliation. In terms of managing local power relations, the inclusion of Jews could only serve to complicate the picture, turning attention to evils worse than three decades of Communism, and to a group that suffered more than Poles in the course of history, to whom this piece of ground belonged in the first place.

As a consequence, what was originally a terrain of conflict between Polish and Jewish memory has been turned instead into a cleavage in Polish history between the "dark force" of Communism and a unified Christian Polishness. In this way, Przeworsk has been transformed into a site of Polish collective immortalization, enabling ethnic Poles to imagine themselves as a "community of history and destiny" and thus achieve the "measure of immortality" that gives individuals hope that their achievements will be saved from oblivion: "they will live on and bear fruit in the community"—their *own* community (Smith, 1986).

The control of memory through space is a powerful weapon in the fight for collective immortalization, and one that often results in the homogenizing of national narratives and the obscuring of ruptures in national histories. In the Polish case, religion only reinforces the contours of the national vessel, squeezing out potential "competitors" who might weaken its ability to contain the community of the present day.

With changes being instituted in the legal status of Jewish property, and new actors—including foreign Jews—entering the commemorative playing field, change may be afoot. It is the paradoxical nature of memoryscapes that while individuals do not generally have sufficient resources to control the landscape, they almost always find ways to mark their presence in it (Crumley, 2002). Their voices, however small, constantly trouble the official meaning of a memoryscape, both defying its closure and opening toward the future.

Notes

1. Following Bauman (1991: 1–17) and Giddens (1991: 27–32), I understand late modernity as a period in history characterized by the growing criticism of the classical modernity's narratives of order, which were based on the logics of capitalism, industrialism, science, and the nation-state system. Late modernity is characterized by a sense of contingency and de-centering of social institutions, globalization, risk, and uncertainty. All that contributes to modernity's self-reflexivity, which orients it back toward itself rather than to the traditional forms of social life that preceded modernity.
2. I am applying here a distinction that has been developed in a different context by Clifford Geertz (1973).
3. The future of the synagogue building is as yet undetermined. Other examples from Poland indicate that even synagogues taken over by Jewish religious organizations (mostly from abroad) and re-opened for religious purposes may under certain circumstances remain open to Polish visitors and thus continue to provide a source of "musealized" knowledge (as in Bobowa) or even become part of joint Jewish-Polish commemorative activities (as in Rymanów).
4. The reactions of the local inhabitants to the growing symbolic presence of Jewish memory vary from hostility (the commemorative tablet on Rzeszów's synagogue was covered with anti-Semitic graffiti shortly after it had been unveiled), to indifference (as is the case of Przeworsk, discussed below), to a sort of "local pride" and partial acceptance of the Jewish past as a part of the local history, as in the case of Tarnów.

Works cited

Ambrosewicz-Jacobs, Jolanta and Leszek Hońdo (eds) (2005). *Why Should We Teach About the Holocaust?* Kraków: The Jagiellonian University, Institute of European Studies.

Anderson, Benedict (1991). *Imagined Communities*. London: Verso.
Appadurai, Arjun (1996). *Modernity at Large. Cultural Dimensions of Globalization*. Minneapolis: University of Minnesota Press.
Bauman, Zygmunt (1991). *Modernity and Ambivalence*. Cambridge: Polity Press.
Crumley, Carole L. (2002). "Exploring Venues of Social Memory." In Jacob J. Climo and Maria G. Cattell (eds). *Social Memory and History. Anthropological Perspectives*. Walnut Creek: Altamira Press.
Delanty, Gerard (1999). *Social Theory in a Changing World: Conceptions of Modernity*. Cambridge: Polity Press.
Geertz, Clifford (1973). *The Interpretations of Cultures*. New York: Basic Books.
Giddens, Anthony (1991). *Modernity and Self-Identity: Self and Society in the Late Modern Age*. Stanford: Stanford University Press.
Gruber, Ruth Ellen (2002). *Virtually Jewish: Reinventing Jewish Culture in Europe*. Berkeley: University of California Press.
Irwin-Zarecka, Iwona (1994). *Frames of Remembrance. The Dynamics of Collective Memory*. New Brunswick: Transaction Publishers.
Kapralski, Sławomir (2007). "The Impact of Post-1989 Changes on Polish-Jewish Relations and Perceptions: Memories and Debates." In Lucia Faltin and Melanie Jane Wright (eds). *The Religious Roots of Contemporary European Identity*. London: Continuum.
Krzemiński, Ireneusz (2004). "Polacy i Ukraińcy o swoich narodach, o cierpieniu w czasie wojny i o Zagładzie Żydów." In Ireneusz Krzemiński (ed.). *Antysemityzm w Polsce i na Ukrainie. Raport z badań*. Warsaw: Wydawnictwo Naukowe Scholar.
Lehrer, Erica (2010). "Can there be a Conciliatory Heritage?" *International Journal of Heritage Studies* 16(4–5): 269–88.
McCrone, David (1998). *The Sociology of Nationalism: Tomorrow's Ancestors*. London: Routledge.
Muzaini, Hamzah and Brenda S. A. Yeoh (2005). "War Landscapes as 'Battlefields' of Collective Memories: Reading the Reflections at Bukit Chandu, Singapore." *Cultural Geographies* 12(3): 345–65.
Sewell, William H., Jr. (2005). *Logics of History. Social Theory and Social Transformation*. Chicago: The University of Chicago Press.
Smith, Anthony D. (1986). *The Ethnic Origins of Nations*. Oxford: Blackwell.
Urban, K. (2006). *Cmentarze żydowskie, synagogi i domy modlitwy w Polsce w latach 1944–1966 (wybór materiałów)*. Kraków: Nomos.
Weinbaum, Lawrence (2002). "Penitence and Prejudice: The Roman Catholic Church and Jedwabne." *Jewish Political Studies Review* 14: 3–4.
Young, James E. (1993). *The Texture of Memory. Holocaust Memorials and Meaning*. New Haven: Yale University Press.

Afterword: The Turn to Pedagogy: A Needed Conversation on the Practice of Curating Difficult Knowledge

Roger I. Simon

As we begin the second decade of the twenty-first century, the media through which public history is enacted has become substantially complicated. Museums and galleries are situated in relation to cinema, television, radio, newspapers, books, and Internet websites as institutions of social memory with a potential public role in constituting what members of any given society understand as their cultural heritage. Beyond presenting what has been institutionally designated as revered heritage, many of these institutions have begun to acknowledge that taking one's historical inheritance seriously requires a commitment to critically engage a past that is both inspiring *and* despairing. Thus it is no surprise that over the last 30 years, many institutions of social memory have attempted to move away from a singular emphasis on affirming presentations of patriotism, triumph, and great deeds toward a greater appreciation of the complexities, competing motivations, and potential for aggression inherent in human relationships.

As evident throughout the previous chapters of this book, cultural institutions are increasingly willing to initiate practices of remembrance related to conflict, violence, loss, and death, topics often characterized as "difficult knowledge." Reading through the myriad of examples provided in these chapters, it is clear that the practice of curating difficult knowledge encompasses a set of complex issues that are only beginning to be adequately named and discussed. No doubt, any advance in the future study and practice of such curation will greatly benefit from the insights drawn from discussions such as those presented in this volume, particularly as these bear on the framing of the various problems requiring curatorial judgment and the clarification of the terms on which one might most usefully think through these concerns. Preliminary but quite necessary in this regard is the need, at least provisionally, to come to grips with what the term "curating" references. While the terms "curating" and "curation" are now commonplace in discussions of the decisions and tasks required to constitute a discursive/material event for public engagement, there remains considerable argument as to what is entailed within the responsibilities of curatorial practice. These arguments of course will always require some degree of contextual specificity. Hence the need for the recognition of the particular issues encompassed when working in forums as various as museums and galleries, cinema, radio, and digital new media. In addition, curatorial issues surely differ depending on whether one is working in the domains of history, anthropology, and sociology on the one hand, or in the expressive arts on the other. Taking the need for specificity into account, no single metaphorical frame or abstract definition of curating will likely settle the discussion of what we might understand as its parameters. Yet setting the terms for any given discussion of curatorial practice is necessary in order to constitute the framework of a coherent discussion. In this respect, my intention in this epilogue is to provide a heuristic perspective on some of the responsibilities of curatorial judgment that might help in coming to grips with a few of the central problems that must be addressed when presenting "difficult knowledge" for public engagement. Basic to this development is clarifying what mean by knowledge that is "difficult."

One way an exhibition may be said to offer difficult knowledge is when it confronts visitors with significant challenges to their expectations and interpretive abilities. This may occur when an exhibition offers multiple, conflicting perspectives on historical events resulting in narratives whose conclusions remain complex and uncertain. As a consequence, such an exhibition might require some visitors to re-think their expectations, demanding they complicate their desire for relatively straightforward and conclusive ways of telling a story. In the face of such a demand, a specific exhibition may be contested or refused while provoking degrees of anxiety, anger, and disappointment. Somewhat differently, an exhibition might also be encountered as difficult if it is experienced as eliciting the burden of "negative emotions," those vexing and troublesome feelings of revulsion, grief, anger, and/or shame that histories can produce, particularly if they raise the possibility of the complicity of one's country, culture, or family in systemic violence such as the seizure of aboriginal land, the slave trade, or the perpetration of genocide. Finally, exhibitions may be judged as consisting of difficult knowledge if they evoke the heightened anxiety (and the potential for secondary traumatization) that accompanies feelings of identification with either the victims of violence, the perpetrators of such violence, or those identified as bystanders passively acquiescent in regard to scenes of brutalization.

Evident in the above examples is the thought that what might be experienced as "difficult knowledge" does not lie inherently within particular artifacts, images and discourses; that is, "difficulty" is not to be taken as a property or a character of the substance of any given knowledge in and of itself (see Pitt and Britzman, 2003). Rather, the locus of difficulty within "difficult knowledge" resides in the indeterminate yet potentially problematic relation between the affective force provoked within the experience of an exhibition and the possible sense one might make of one's experience of this force and its relation to one's understanding of an exhibition's images, artifacts, text, and sounds. The term "affective force" references a non-specific, immediate sensation that is not pre-coded by a representational system that settles its substance within a set of specific linguistic markers that offer an understanding of just what it is that one is feeling (e.g., the emotions of sadness, anger, etc.) (Massumi, 2002). Rather, the affective force integral to the experience of difficult knowledge incites and compels thought in at least two respects. It compels thought that attempts to name and clarify the range of emotions that one is feeling and it compels thought as to what within an exhibition (and within oneself) has provoked these feelings. Taken together such reflection constitutes a consideration of the ways any given exhibition might become significant for either confirming or altering one's framework for acting in the world (Bennett, 2005). In other words, at the heart of the matter regarding questions of difficult knowledge is the provocation of affect and affect's dynamic relation to the possibilities and limits of thought.

What is at stake here for any museum or gallery offering visitors encounters with images and artifacts tracing the realities of suffering and death is suitably illustrated by Mieke Bal (2007) in her discussion of the photography exhibition *Beautiful Suffering* presented at the Williams College Museum of Art in 2006. This exhibition displayed a wide range of contemporary photography of various instances of human suffering in an attempt to explore photography's "traffic in pain." At the beginning of her commentary on this exhibition, Bal ruminates on her visceral response to Nicholas Nixon's *Tom Moran, October 1987*, a photograph of a young man looking at his mirror image, showing his body devastated by disease. Reading the man's face as "beautiful but skeletal" and his chest as "emaciated," and noting the date of the photograph, Bal associates the image with the ravages of AIDS. This visual encounter provokes a sense of anxiety. Standing before the photograph she feels something that she interprets as "grief, compassion, and anger" (2007: 93). But she is also aware that simply rendering her feelings on these terms leaves her with "nowhere to go." As she put it, "Alone, I am not witnessing anyone's suffering. In all likelihood, the man is long dead, and he will never know that, in 2006, someone unknown to him felt an emotion for him that might approximate grief" (2007: 93). It is this diffuse quality of sensation, reflexively coded as grief but without direction, that Bal labels the "number one problem of the 'traffic in pain' that the exhibition *Beautiful Suffering* analyzes and questions and, to an extent, inevitably and boldly performs" (2007: 93–4). Bal understands quite clearly that this difficulty in traversing the relation between affect and thought is not simply a consequence of particular photographs being viscerally difficult to look at. Rather the problem of undirected emotions (and possibly an indifference that might act as a shield to bear their weight) is apprehended as an underlying curatorial problem of the exhibition itself. That is, Bal directs us to the question of the possible ways an exhibition's *mise-en-scène* might help frame, forge, and support a mode of looking within which the affective force of images could be directed toward thought as to one's responsibilities as a viewer who might yet become an ethical witness to the scenes of suffering they have just encountered. As we shall see below, what constitutes such a witness is very much an open question. However, as Bal's comments above suggest, and as I will make clear by the end of this Afterword, to bear witness to an encounter with scenes of suffering at the very least opens the question of the possible forms within which a movement between affect and thought may happen, a movement (it is worth repeating) whose precise content can never be specified in advance, nor assumed to be unitary, singular, or shared.

What this means for the practice of curating difficult knowledge is that curatorial decisions are inevitably implicated in the way the scene of an exhibition operates both as a provocation of affect *and* as a way of structuring affect's relation to the possibilities of thought and judgment. It is for this reason that when discussing the curation of difficult knowledge it is inadequate to suggest that it is only possible to consider the intentional denotations of an exhibition's display and the connotative rhetoric of its form, since individuated, affective responses to an exhibition are largely unconscious and uncontrollable, and hence beyond the influence of curatorial judgment. The significance made of the various exhibitions discussed in this book does not just rest on what historical narratives they convey, but also on the consequences of the affects their presentation provokes among those who engage them. That the substance of an exhibition might be described as either "shocking," "disturbing," or "appalling" is an inadequate but still telling indication that the public re-presentation of these "difficult" images and artifacts casts forward a force felt as an indeterminate instigation of affect. While clearly curatorial practice can never (and in my view *should* never attempt to) over-determine responses to any given set of presented images and artifacts, the comparative study of how different exhibitions are variously designed and developed so as to exert influence upon the movement between affect and thought does suggest that curatorial judgment matters in this regard. In my view, how it is that curatorial judgment might shape the relation between affect and thought is precisely what productive discussions of curating difficult knowledge must engage.

At stake here is how we might rethink the notion of a *pedagogy* of an exhibition in ways that recognize the indeterminacy of response. I realize that for some people the terms "curation" and "pedagogy" do not sit together easily. This is particularly so for those who associate the term pedagogy with either a didactic communication of a pre-established message or narrated "truth," or that which is represented in an exhibition: a message often framed within a hegemonic framework fostered by the interests of ruling elites.[1] In conversations among participants at the conference that gave rise to this volume, there was considerable unease about evoking the notion of pedagogy as central to curatorial work. Often expressed was the thought that, given the idiosyncrasies of individual visitors, what constitutes a response to difficult knowledge is inevitably, inescapably indeterminate. For this reason it was argued that one must maintain a deep skepticism of curatorial pedagogy since a visitor's knowledge, interests, and obsessions will over-determine any educational intentions associated with the mounting of an exhibition. Such skepticism is unfortunately at the root of the failure to imagine a practice of education that is anything other than a restrictive disciplinary regime whose legitimacy is underwritten by institutional authorities. It is a failure to imagine what Irit Rogoff (2007) has characterized as "pedagogy at peace with its partiality, a pedagogy not preoccupied with succeeding but with trying." The indeterminacy of visitor feeling and thought should not cancel questions of pedagogy as inherent to the practice of curation; on the contrary, it demands a further clarification of what might be meant by a curatorial pedagogy of difficult knowledge. To consider this issue more concretely, I will discuss three aspects of curatorial practice and how these may be informed by embracing pedagogy as a problem central to developing exhibitions of difficult knowledge. These aspects of curatorial practice are: (1) the justifications given for the re-presentation of images and artifacts that trace past violence; (2) the design characteristics of a *mise-en-scène* for engaging materials to be exhibited; and (3) the attention needed in regard to the inter-relation between an exhibition and what is to be understood as its accompanying circumstances.

The problem of justification

One might reasonably ask what may be gained by re-siting and re-signing images and artifacts to bring them together in a display which makes evident the horrific realities of past systemic violence and human suffering. Curatorial judgment in this regard begins with the recognition that the images and artifacts deployed within practices of public history are not sovereign objects unaffected by their travels through space and time. The force and meaning of any given set of artifacts on display are never produced in isolation but are always situated within a broader discursive economy of other images, objects, and text. This is by no means to suggest that such a discursive economy always over determines the significance of any given image. However, it is extremely rare that any museum or gallery would present an exhibition of "difficult knowledge" without any accompanying text that provides a justification of its display (even if the legitimating and supervisory authority of such text is rendered all but mute at the moment of encounter between a viewer and an exhibition).

No doubt there are dangers inherent in public exhibitions of violence and suffering. These dangers range from the re-activation of past conflicts and lingering animosities, to a (re)traumatization that leaves viewers feeling helpless in the face of overwhelming suffering, to the commodification of pain within a framing which offers a voyeuristic spectacle of suffering. Yet the fundamental premise of most exhibitions of "difficult knowledge" is that, properly re-contextualized, the recovery and subsequent display of images and artifacts that reference past brutality and suffering, particularly when supplemented by print and audio, would have something to offer the community in which such an exhibition appears. When their public display is carefully conceived, the traces of past violence can be placed within a redemptive, reparative narrative and consequently pain and death can be partially redeemed as memories that might function to secure more progressive, less violent futures. On such terms, public memory is taken as having the potential to make a difference in how we live our lives. Exhibitions of difficult knowledge are seen as informing a citizenry about historically significant events and serving as a stimulus to actions that would guard against the re-occurrence of such violence.

Curatorial practice on these terms is very much invested in enacting a form of public history that defines a "useable past" via the institutional acknowledgment of past injustice and the hope that a societal awareness of such injustice will prevent its repetition. As desirable as this often sounds, it requires a framing of curatorial judgment that constitutes historical memory as a political instrument aligned with specific social commitments and interests. As several authors in this volume note, political instrumentalization of curatorial judgment may at times lead to the simplification of history. For example, certain items may be left off an artifact list in order to keep an exhibition's main purpose clear and coherent. Similarly, given that exhibitions might be understood as discursive interventions within a particular societal space, while there may be a number of different narratives through which an historical event might be presented, just one might be judged as the most important to present in a particular conjuncture, given the social context in which the exhibition would appear. Such a decision to focus on a limited number of narratives necessarily reduces the level of complexity. As several chapters in this volume have amply illustrated, such attempts to instrumentalize historical narratives risk impoverishing the challenges that a critical historical consciousness must confront. But the curatorial problems at hand run deeper than this. Clearly curating difficult knowledge cannot be a neutral enterprise. The work of curation inevitably must address questions as to what sets of relationships and social policies constitute a desirable society as well as what sort of pedagogy might be mobilized to support the attainment of such a society. At stake here is not only the relevance and responsibilities of curatorial judgment in regard to cultural practices that stir a collective toward desirable ways of living, but also how such judgment enacts a pedagogy that enables the possibility of accomplishing this project. A premise common to curating difficult knowledge is that it should structure a pedagogy in which viewers engage with documents that expose them to the painful realities experienced by those subjected to violence. In this respect, one might suggest that in its most fundamental sense, curating difficult knowledge constitutes a "pedagogy of witness." But such a phrase too easily functions as a simplified gloss. More precisely, how might such a pedagogy be understood and employed? At the very least, such a pedagogy is concerned both to establish the factual occurrence of violence and its lived consequences, *and* to mobilize a productive affective response to the representation of this violence. Thus one is not only to be informed about past events of which one might not have been aware, but also, it is hoped through this process, one might be moved to both rethink one's understanding of a particular history and convey this understanding into the present in ways that impact on one's current thoughts and actions. This said, there still remain very different ways of conceiving how this might take place. Central to these differences is the question of how the affect provoked in an encounter with difficult knowledge is to function pedagogically and how this may be influenced by curatorial judgments. In a chapter that considers various recent monuments and other practices of cultural memory in Kosovo, Croatia, and Bosnia-Herzegovina, Andrew Herscher (this volume) makes clear what such differences might look like. It is evident from his discussion of these practices that there is a dominant pedagogy of witness that is typically employed by state authorities, though not exclusively so. This pedagogy takes the form of practices of remembrance and memorialization that are intended to suture the affect elicited by such practices to pre-emptive "authoritative" judgments as to the significance of particular historical events referenced through specific memory practices, including the admonitions and exhortations that accrue from such judgments. Alternatively, rather than deciding in advance what the lessons of history should be, Herscher argues that a pedagogy of witness might be designed so that the affect mobilized by cultural practices provokes a form of memory work which opens on to the problem of historicity (Hirsch and Stewart, 2005).[2] In such an instance, the justification of curating difficult knowledge might lie in a conception of pedagogy intended to reflexively explore the circumstances through which people make possible relations between the past, present, and future (Simon, 2005). In such a pedagogy, affect is understood as mobilizing thought about the substance and limitations of any given historical narrative and it significance, without attempting to guarantee in advance what this thought might be.

The design of a *mise-en-scène* for engaging difficult knowledge

If the fundamental question inherent in the curation of difficult knowledge is what might be the desired and possible relation between affect and thought, then the pedagogical concerns of exhibition design take on particular significance. In this context, exhibition design constitutes a generative *mise-en-scène*, a dynamic space that embodies a pedagogy of emplacement with the potential not only to mobilize the dialectical movement between affect and thought, but also to effect some degree of influence in regard to the direction and substance of this movement. On such terms, curating an exhibition of difficult knowledge clearly involves much more than devising an iconic display of images and artifacts whose significance is rendered through emotionally underwritten moral injunctions and admonitions. Much more is required than devising and displaying compelling, transparent narratives with the hope that, correctly comprehended, they would be received as stories that could serve as much needed personal and social counsel. Quite differently, what is required is a form of curatorial judgment that devises a space wherein the testamentary face of history is effectively lived as an inhabiting force that challenges people to work out what they might be feeling in relation not only to information they have acquired, but also to the questions, thoughts, and commitments provoked by the exhibition experience. Another way of putting this is that the *mise-en-scène* of an exhibition constitutes what Tamar Katriel (this volume) has called "a social area in which activities are organized that invite the performative act of witnessing." While such a formulation is helpful in beginning to think through what might constitute an exhibition as a generative *mise-en-scène*, clarification is still needed as to what it is that might comprise an act of witness and how this implicates a particular relation between affect and thought.

Assuming that an act of witness is composed in the movement between affect and thought, we can now consider why judgments as to the substance of an exhibition's *mise-en-scène* are of central importance to the problem of working out a desirable curatorial pedagogy. In this respect, it is useful to turn again to Mieke Bal. In the context of her commentary on the aforementioned exhibition *Beautiful Suffering*, Bal addressed the issue succinctly: "Let me phrase it bluntly . . . put about one hundred such photographs [of violence and suffering] together [in an exhibition], and the hardship vanishes" (2007: 97). The hardship Bal is referring to is the difficulty of making and sustaining a relation with the affective force of an image. As she put it, "one cannot sustain the difficulty offered by any given photograph through the confrontation with so many photographs." Commenting on the proliferation of various images of pain and death presented in *Beautiful Suffering*—an image of the impact of famine here, a corpse lying about there, and a wounded figure drenched in blood just over there, "soon the turbulent emotions vanish." Under such circumstances the movement between affect and thought stops. In the place of an unresolved, but productive force to thought, a customary ease develops as one grasps the thematic conceptual frame that allows one to settle the meaning that resides in the presentation of each and all these images. Given this, Bal adds one qualification: perhaps an unease remains resulting from the recognition that one's gaze serves no purpose other than to provide a self-affirming reading of the particulars of images on the terms of the moral certainties that we hold dear. This observation presents an important challenge to the curation of difficult knowledge since such exhibitions are clearly intended to offer more than social rituals wherein those possessing a consciousness of historical injustice would gain some satisfaction by experiencing the grief and indignation provoked by viewing irrefutable evidence of other people's suffering. The pedagogical worry here is that a particular *mise-en-scène* entices the viewer to see the previously unseen—a solicitation that holds the possibility that one might slip from critical remembering into a fetishistic, self-gratifying gaze that narcissistically appropriates the pain of others. Indeed, this gaze might be considered exploitative since it can leave one feeling good about oneself, enjoying the fact that one is able "to feel oneself feeling."

Some of the complexity of what is at issue in the example above becomes apparent when we juxtapose Bal's remarks with those of photographer Ed Burtynsky. In commentary incorporated as one of the special features on the DVD version of the film *Manufactured Landscapes* (Baichwal, 2007), Burtynsky offered the view that the exhibition of a single image means nothing since, alone, it is unable to "create a language." While not specifically commenting on the exhibition of difficult knowledge, Burtynsky is making the point that an exhibition's *mise-en-scène* needs to contain multiple images if it is to articulate a view of the world that opens up different ways of seeing and different forms of thought. Yet in the context of exhibitions of human suffering, Bal is concerned with precisely the opposite possibility, that the multiplication of images (and the danger of their thematic over-determination by always present contextualizing discourses) actually reduces the possibility of any such photographic language adequate to its subject.

Clearly it is not a matter of choosing between different positions articulated by Bal and Burtynsky but rather attending to how, for any given exhibition, one might balance traces of a non-comparable, *singular* life that has been subject to violence and pain with a framing "language" that makes clear the particular historical significance of such subjection. What is especially important in this balance is the possibility that the degree of affective force of an exhibition may be dependent on the preservation of a sense of singularity in any given encounter experienced in the context of an exhibition, particularly in the face of the desire to translate this singularity into an exemplary instance of a problematic practice of violence (De Duve, 2008). The problems here are in fact compounded when the images, artifacts, and texts of an exhibition are primarily taken as offering historical evidence of past oppression. Thematically understood on such terms, the various components of an exhibition are all too easily appropriated within forms of vicarious identification or are alternatively viewed as tracing a spectacle of suffering.

When viewed as spectacle, exhibitions of difficult knowledge risk offering an apprehension of horrific suffering and/or death while attenuating the thinking through of one's relation to an image of the situated, particular death of another. In her discussion of what constitutes "the social contract of photography," Ariella Azoulay (2008) emphasizes that while a photograph bears the seal of the "photographic event," to avoid an apprehension of a photograph of suffering as a form of visual spectacle that short-circuits thought and action, the *mise-en-scène* of one's engagement with an image must do more than help identify what is shown and appreciate its significance as a component of an evidentiary record. She argues for the importance of not just looking at a photographic image but "watching" it as one would a film. Thus, Azoulay is asserting that a photograph itself entails a dimension of time and movement that needs to be re-animated in the context of one's response to an image. The significance of this position is clarified when we consider the remarks of W. G. Sebald regarding photographs. He noted two functions of photographic images: verification and the arrest of time (Wachtel, 2007). Sebald recognizes the same problem articulated by Azoulay, though on different terms. In the context of a conversation about the function of photographs in his novels, Sebald argued that looking at a photograph released one from the passage of time, slowing down the comprehension of narrative. When applied to the viewing of traces of suffering and death, the danger of such an arrest of time is that it situates one as entrapped in the spectacle of death, complicit in the subjection of those violated to an enduring public abasement constituted by the fascinated gaze of those who cannot help but stand before the scene as onlookers. Indeed, on such terms we must acknowledge the possibility that an image of suffering might compound or add to suffering. Such concerns require that we keep in mind Darren Newbury's evocation (this volume) of Aimé Césaire's admonition that "life is not a spectacle, a sea of miseries is not a proscenium, a man screaming is not a dancing bear."

What is to be understood as the accompanying circumstances of an exhibition

As most of the chapters in this book have made clear, curatorial judgment always needs to be context sensitive. Yet to say this simply begs the question of what such judgment should take into account in the practice of curation. In other words, it is not adequate to consider an exhibition's "context" as the entirety of the surrounding circumstances that bear on how it will be understood. Rather, we need to think through how various conceptions of an exhibition inherent in practices of curatorial judgment are always already tuned to particular aspects of the circumstances in which an exhibition will take place by understanding curating difficult knowledge as a fundamentally pedagogical problem that concerns the movement between affect and thought. For example, as all the authors of the previous chapters have argued, when curating difficult knowledge it is crucial to be mindful of the various contextually specific expectations, emotional needs, epistemological assumptions, and degrees of knowledge of exhibition visitors. In most instances where exhibitions of difficult knowledge have been presented, institutional staff are clearly aware of the virtual impossibility of viewing particular images and artifacts without experiencing their imbrication within one's psychic network of knowledge, identifications, and desires. They know full well that the witness provoked by such exhibitions inevitably raises questions as to the pedagogical implications of museum visitors' affective responses, questions rooted in the realization that those who see their exhibitions would likely be personally moved toward various but indeterminate states of feeling and related frames of thought. Obviously, in circumstances where there are both visitors who directly experienced the events portrayed as well as those more peripheral to what happened, one could reasonably anticipate that the movement of the affect provoked by any given exhibition would have multiple and different lines of direction. Of course those responsible for an exhibition must care for and respect those who have been subject to oppression and violence (as well as members of their families) while being conscious of the dignity and safety of all visitors. Yet the question remains as to how the affect differently mobilized in an exhibition might serve the purpose of publicly presenting difficult material, particularly if this purpose is to move through and beyond the acknowledgment of previously marginalized or occluded suffering to an active consideration of how such past injustices inform one's current perspectives and commitments. The implication of this concern is the need for a conversation as to how any given *mise-en-scène* and its associated programming might support multiple trajectories for addressing such considerations.

This said, the circumstances of particular relevance to a curatorial pedagogy of witness are not just those related to the subject positions through which individual visitors to an exhibition might be addressed. To the degree that curating difficult knowledge will involve the public display of degradation and death, the pedagogy of an exhibition also needs to be mindful of its possible complicity with the perpetuation of historically entrenched, taken-for-granted social hierarchies often enmeshed in justifications of violence. Given that historically some "types" of dead/wounded bodies have been more readily made available for public display than others, curators must consider the cultural politics of exhibition or risk reproducing not only the differential distribution and display of these bodies but also the intensely violent distinctions regarding the value of life and its grievability (Butler, 2009). Dora Apel addresses some of these concerns in her analysis of a series of museum- and gallery-based exhibitions of photographs taken at lynchings in the United States mainly during the first half of the twentieth century. While defending the necessity of public exhibition of these photographs, Apel acknowledged that displaying the vulnerable black body risked "reproducing the prurient interest and humiliating effect of racist violence" (2004: 2). Nevertheless, she concluded that this was a risk worth taking, given that the US could not afford innocently to ignore the history of violent racism traced by these images. Curatorial judgment must grapple with how a given *mise-en-scène* might be shaped to minimize such a risk through judgments that attend to the questions of what materials to display and what to hold back from view, and (as previously mentioned) how a *mise-en-scène* might constrain the display of death and suffering from becoming a stupefying spectacle. Such exhibitions do not just represent anguish and suffering, but are, for a variety of reasons, potentially productive of a grief provoked by the act of witnessing this anguish and suffering. If the affect associated with deep feelings of grief are, as Mieke Bal expressed, feelings that leave one with "nowhere to go," any exhibition of suffering and death may merely serve to extend the moment of violation of the humanity of those shown, those who are dead or dying.

So far, my illustrations of circumstantial relevance have pertained to elements related to risks associated with the likely affective force experienced when engaging difficult knowledge. However, there is much more to curating difficult knowledge. Exhibitions of difficult knowledge face the persistent pedagogical question of how to represent the death and suffering of others so as to provoke sustained attention, concern, and corrective action rather than a few days' sensation that is soon forgotten. As we have seen, all exhibitions of difficult knowledge embody the hope that they and the history they are attempting to make present will matter in regard to both contemporary existence and future forms of social life. For this reason, understanding how the pedagogy of an exhibition might be impacted by the context within which it takes place is of considerable importance. Particularly when curating difficult knowledge, it is impossible to maintain the distinction between curatorial practice and other forms of cultural and political activity that are supposedly peripheral to it. This means that in considering curation as a practice of pedagogy, one also has to come to terms with how such a pedagogy is understood to function as a situated practice that is always in an articulated relation to other practices of cultural pedagogy operating within a particular conjuncture. How and why might an exhibition function as an extension, supplementation, and linkage with and to other practices? It is only through such thought that one might begin to grasp a sense of how and why any given exhibition might be an important pedagogical intervention in a public sphere. Katriel evokes such concerns when she writes of the *Breaking the Silence* exhibition that "It was only in performing an act of speaking out, in breaking the societal silence in which they [the organizers and curators] and the exhibition's viewers had been enmeshed, that they were able to regain their sense of agency and begin to generate an audience for their protest that they hoped would lead to actual political change." Curatorial judgment must consider how an exhibition's pedagogy might work in conjunction with—or in some cases explicitly against—cultural workers in other locations attempting to influence the view of the past events on which a contemporary community is founded.

Conclusion

It is often taken for granted that exhibitions of difficult knowledge are invaluable because by revealing what happened at a particular time and place they bear witness. Such revelations are seen as essential to re-thinking our present and opening new possibilities for a future beyond the repetition of the forms of violence depicted. Understood on these terms, our main requirement is simply to look at such images and artifacts, or more charitably to work through and overcome our resistance to looking and thus no longer look away. However, as I have been arguing, neither consuming information about past events nor simply registering this information through one's acquisitive gaze can satisfy what is required by a "pedagogy of witness." If witnessing simply devolves into the act of refusing to turn away, of looking straight-on at events that are difficult to face, what constitutes an act of witness might remain relatively impoverished. This certainly would be the case if any given exhibition of difficult knowledge was to be grasped as a "sad past," but one that has no currency in the present. Curating difficult knowledge calls for a cultural pedagogy capable of bridging past and present without reducing one to the other or dictating the terms on which this is to be accomplished. In this respect, curatorial judgments do not and cannot prescribe what viewers see and comprehend, but they can be understood as implicated in modes of apprehension and thought that might be occluded through a too quick settling of what is felt and understood in regard to one's encounter with an exhibition.

It should be evident by now that my conception of curatorial practice is quite expansive and not tied to conventional forms of division of labor in large museums and galleries. In my view, curatorial practice encompasses a very broad set of judgments that set the framing for the presentation of combinations of images, objects, text, and sound within a particular *mise-en-scène*. Curatorial judgments include decisions as to what is to be shown, the placement of these artifacts in space, the creation of the textual environment that will inscribe that space (including object or image labels, brochures, and press releases), and the programming intended to stimulate visitors to engage with both the exhibition's *mise-en-scène* and one another. On such terms, curatorial practice is inherently pedagogical with much of the substance of the pedagogy at work in any given exhibition determined by the exercise of curatorial judgment.

Unfortunately, there is ample evidence that an awareness and moral assessment of previous unjust violence and brutality does not automatically constitute a bridge for linking the past and present so as to diminish the recurrence of injustice. This leaves us with the (still quite salient) project of envisioning a curatorial practice as an ethical force, opening the way to a political discourse with contemporary currency. To accomplish this we will need a curatorial pedagogy of difficult knowledge committed to retaining that which does not expend itself as information. Certainly, this pedagogy must be cognizant that the transmission and condensation of past events through thematically mediated concepts structure the readability and effective circulation of the primary narratives that underwrite the significance of an exhibition.

However, as the exhibitions previously discussed in this book have made clear, curating difficult knowledge involves not only judgments as to the presentation of images and artifacts to be interrogated, but also consideration of their status as evidence supporting the truth value of particular narratives. Curating difficult knowledge also requires judgments that establish a *mise-en-scène* within which images and artifacts act as perlocutionary signs of entreaty, embodying an affective force provoking thought and action. In other words, curating difficult knowledge must ultimately be concerned with the question of how exhibitions might be presented so as to serve a *transitive* function that could open up an indeterminate reconsideration of the force of history in social life so that exhibitions that trace the lives of those who have lived and died in times and places other than our own may yet have some force that enjoins our capacities and felt responsibilities.

Notes

1. For a different perspective that re-thinks the relation between curation and pedagogy see O'Neil and Wilson, 2009.
2. See also Herscher's discussion of the provocation to memory installed at the entrance ways to the reconstructed Old Bridge in Mostar (this volume).

Works cited

Apel, Dora (2004). *Imagery of Lynching: Black Men, White Women, and the Mob.* New Brunswick: Rutgers University Press.

Azoulay, Ariella (2008). *The Civil Contract of Photography.* New York: Zone Books.

Baichwal, Jennifer (2007). *Manufacturing Landscapes.* Zeitgeist Films (DVD).

Bal, Mieke (2007). "The Pain of Images." In Mark Reinhardt, Holly Edwards, and Erina Duganne (eds). *Beautiful Suffering: Photography and the Traffic in Pain.* Chicago: University of Chicago Press, 93–115.

Bennett, Jill (2005). *Emphatic Vision: Affect, Trauma, and Contemporary Art.* Stanford: Stanford University Press.

Butler, Judith (2009). *Frames of War: When is Life Grievable?* New York: Verso.

De Duve, Thierry (2008). "Art in the Face of Radical Evil." *October* (125): 3–23.

Hirsch, Eric and Charles Stewart (2005). "Introduction: Ethnographies of Historicity." *History and Anthropology* 16(3): 261–74.

Pitt, Alice and Deborah Britzman (2003). "Speculations on Qualities of Difficult Knowledge in Teaching and Learning: An Experiment in Psychoanalytic Research." *International Journal of Qualitative Studies in Education* 16(6): 755–76.

Massumi, Brian (2002). "Introduction: Like a Thought." In Brian Massumi (ed.). *A Shock to Thought: Expression After Deleuze and Guattari.* New York: Routledge.

O'Neil, Paul and Mick Wilson (eds) (2009). *Curating and the Educational Turn.* Amsterdam: Open Editions/De Appel Arts Centre.

Rogoff, Irit (2007). "Academy as Potentiality." Available at http://summit.kein.org/node/191. [Accessed October 26, 2010].

Simon, Roger I. (2005). *The Touch of the Past: Remembrance, Learning and Ethics*. New York: Palgrave Macmillan.

Wachtel, Eleanor (2007). "Ghost Hunter." In Lynne Sharon Schwartz (ed.). *The Emergence of Memory: Conversations with W. G. Sebald*. New York: Seven Stories Press, 37–62.

Index